W9-APO-535

Birnbaum's

Disneyland® RESORT

Expert Advice from the Inside Source

Wendy Lefkon EDITORIAL DIRECTOR

Jill Safro EDITOR

Michael Farmer DESIGN DIRECTOR

Pisaza Design Studio, Ltd. DESIGNER

Jody Revenson CONSULTING EDITOR

Alexandra Mayes Birnbaum CONSULTING EDITOR

Stephen Birnbaum FOUNDING EDITOR

DISNEY EDITIONS

For Steve, who merely made this all possible

Copyright © 2004 Disney Enterprises, Inc.

All Disney artwork and photographs (unless otherwise credited)
copyright © 2004 Disney Enterprises, Inc.

Cover photograph by Michael Carroll.

Indiana Jones photograph © Disney/Lucasfilm Ltd.

Indiana Jones™ Adventure

Roger Rabbit character © Touchstone Pictures and Amblin Entertainment, Inc.

Tarzan® Owned by Edgar Rice Burroughs, Inc. and Used by Permission. All Tarzan
materials copyright © 2004 Edgar Rice Burroughs, Inc., and Disney Enterprises, Inc. All Rights Reserved.

All rights reserved. No part of this work may be reproduced or transmitted
in any form or by any means, electronic or mechanical, including photocopying,
recording, or by any information storage and retrieval system, without
written permission from the publisher.

For information address Disney Editions, 114 Fifth Avenue, New York, New York 10011-5690.

Visit www.disneyeditions.com

ISBN 0-7868-5430-8

Printed in the United States of America

Other 2005 Birnbaum's Official Disney Guides

Disney Cruise Line
Walt Disney World
Walt Disney World Dining
Walt Disney World For Kids, By Kids
Walt Disney World Without Kids

Contents

99 Disney's California Adventure

From the glittering lights of Hollywood to the swells of the Pacific to the thrill rides of an amusement pier, Disney pays tribute to the glories of the Golden State in this compact theme park. Our exclusive coverage reveals all there is to see and do—follow our advice and Hot Tips on how to tour the area like a pro and be sure to catch all of the park's greatest hits.

115 Good Meals, Great Times

Whether it's a simple snack or a multicourse meal, the Disneyland Resort offers something for every palate and pocketbook. For a change of scenery, venture a bit farther afield into Orange County to Anaheim, other inland communities, or nearby beach towns. Our entertainment section reflects the area's wide range of possibilities, from the nightclubs in Downtown Disney to the dinner shows, concert halls, and lounges of Orange County.

135 Sports

Perhaps you dream of catching the perfect wave, hiking along cliffs above the Pacific coast, polishing your serve, or simply taking in a spectator sport. It's a cinch to fulfill your fondest athletic fantasies in the land of sun and surf.

141 Orange County & Beyond

Besides the Disneyland Resort and other family-oriented attractions, Orange County is home to impressive art museums, a presidential library, two seaside resort towns, a famous mission, a mammoth glass cathedral, and state-of-the-art performance venues. After you have thoroughly explored Disney's environs, why not plan a trip to see other parts of Southern California? The options are as diverse as the landscape itself.

A Word from the Editor

PHOTO BY CAROLYN BRUNETTO

Walt Disney, the man who pioneered the realm of family entertainment, was at once an artist, entrepreneur, and creative visionary. He was also a dad. And, like many of the folks who visit Disneyland each year, Walt treasured the time he spent with his children. In fact, while his two daughters were growing up, Walt accompanied them to carnivals, zoos, and local amusement parks. It was something of a Saturday tradition for the Disney family. During these outings he would often make the same observation: the youngsters were happily entertained, but the adults didn't have much to do. It didn't seem right that he'd be stuck sitting on a bench while the kids had all the fun. To his way of thinking, a park should appeal to the sense of wonder and exploration in guests of *all* ages. His vision became a reality on July 17, 1955, when Disneyland opened in Anaheim, California.

This year, Disneyland celebrates its golden anniversary in spectaculr style, with special new parades, shows, and attractions. In fact, the occasion is being marked with such fanfare that we've added a special bonus section of this book to describe the highlights. While Disneyland Park is wonderfully familiar to us—practically a second home—Disney's California Adventure is a newer playing ground, and finding the best ways to take it in has been an adventure in itself. (Even now, it remains a work in progress, as with new attractions, such as the Twilight Zone Tower of Terror, being added to further guest satisfaction.)

When Steve Birnbaum launched this guide, he made it clear what was expected of anyone who worked on it. The book would be meticulously revised each year, leaving no attraction untested, no meal untasted, no hotel untried. First-hand experiences like these, accumulated over the years, make this book the most authoritative guide to the Disneyland Resort. Our expertise, however, was not achieved by being escorted through back doors of attractions. Instead, we've waited in lines with everyone else, always hoping to have a Disney experience like any other guest.

Of course, there's more to the Disneyland Resort than the theme parks. There's also a dining, shopping, and entertainment district known as Downtown Disney, and three Disney hotels. It all adds up to a total that is truly greater than the sum of its parts. And, though it has a half century of history under its belt, this is just the beginning—as per its founder's wishes, "Disneyland will never be completed. It will continue to grow as long as there is imagination left in the world."

Take Our Advice

In creating this book, we have considered every possible aspect of your trip, from planning it to plotting day-to-day activities. We realize that even the most meticulous vacation planner needs detailed, accurate, and objective information to prepare a successful itinerary. To achieve that goal, we encourage the submission of factual information and insight from Disneyland staffers—but the decision to use or lose such information is entirely up to the discretion of the editor.

We have also packaged handy bits of advice in the form of "hot tips" throughout the book. This advice comes directly from the copious notes we've taken during our countless trips to the Disneyland Resort and the surrounding Anaheim area. We've also used our "Birnbaum's Best" stamp of approval wherever we deemed it appropriate, highlighting our favorite attractions and restaurants—the crowd pleasers we feel stand head, shoulders, and ears above the rest.

You, the reader, benefit from the combination of years of experience—coupled with access to up-to-date inside information from the Disneyland staff—that makes this guide unique. We like to think it's indispensable, but you be the judge of that 150 pages from now.

Credit Where Credit Is Due

Both in the parks and behind the scenes, Disneyland staffers have been a critical source of factual data. We hope we are not omitting any names in thanking Duncan Wardle, Ryan Burriss, Joe Aguirre, Dan Hough, Bill Rowland, Greg Glover, Duane Dike, Adrian Fischer, Michelle Harker, Valerie Poulos, Jodie Frandsen, and Kelley Haggert. Special thanks to Jeannine O'Malley, who does so much to ensure the factual accuracy of *Birnbaum's Official Guide to Disneyland*.

Kudos to Michelle Magenheim for her outstanding fact-checking, and to copy editors extraordinaire Diane Hodges and Robert Rohr. We would also like to tip our hats to Dave Linker, Monica Mayper, Sue Cole, Janet Castiglione, Jennifer Mullin, Guy Cunningham, and Michael Farmer for their editorial support and production panache.

Of course, no list of acknowledgments would be complete without mentioning our founding editor, Steve Birnbaum, whose spirit, wisdom, and humor still infuse these pages, as well as Alexandra Mayes Birnbaum, who continues to be a guiding light—to say nothing of a careful reader of every word.

The Last Word

Finally, it's important to remember that every worthwhile travel guide is a living enterprise; the book you hold in your hands is our best effort at explaining how to enjoy the Disneyland Resort at the moment, but its text is no way etched in stone. Disneyland is always changing and growing, and in each annual edition we refine and expand our material to serve your needs better. Just before the grand opening of Disneyland, Walt Disney remarked that the main attraction was still missing—people. That's where you come in.

Have a wonderful time!

DON'T FORGET TO WRITE!

No contribution is of greater value to us in preparing the next edition of this book than your comments on its usefulness and your own experiences at the Disneyland Resort. Drop us a postcard or send a letter to the address on the right.

Official Disney Guides
Birnbaum's Disneyland 2005
Disney Editions
114 Fifth Avenue, 12th Floor
New York, NY 10011

Getting Ready to Go

Anyone who visited the Anaheim area over the last few years was sure to see evidence of the Disney Imagineers at work. Behind closed gates, construction went on day and night, and finally, the results were unveiled— a 430-acre Disneyland Resort, with Walt Disney's original theme park, Disneyland (although true Disney-o-philes may still refer to it fondly as the "Magic Kingdom"), at its heart. Besides this "Happiest Place on Earth," guests will find Disney's California Adventure theme park, the Downtown Disney entertainment district, and Disney's Grand Californian Hotel—which completes the trio of Disney's on-property hotels. Of course, you'll want to do and see it all, but where should you start? When should you go? And then there are the all-important questions of how to get there and where to stay. Maybe you want to extend your vacation—perhaps you'll include a visit to (or a stay at) the beach or one of the other nearby attractions. . . .

   That's a lot to think about. But don't worry. By the time you've read through this chapter, you'll have all the information you need to make smart decisions. So read on, and remember: A little advance planning goes a long way.

When to Go

When you weigh the best times to visit the Disneyland Resort, the most obvious possibilities seem to be Christmas, Easter, and summer vacation—particularly if there are children in the family. But there are a few good reasons to avoid these periods—the major one being that almost everybody else wants to go then, too. Keep in mind, however, that the pedestrian traffic at Disney's California Adventure is always lighter than it is at Disneyland park.

If you can only visit during one of these busy times and worry that the crowds might spoil your fun, there are some tactics for making optimum use of every minute and avoiding the lines—notably, go to the park early to get a jump on the day (and on the crowds), take advantage of the time-saving Fastpass system whenever possible, and remember that Disney keeps the parks open later during busy seasons, so pace yourself and stay until the park closes. Note that early entry is no longer offered to guests staying at Disneyland Resort hotels.

On the other hand, choosing to visit when the parks are least crowded may mean that you miss some of the most entertaining parades and special events. For instance, Disneyland Park's Fantasmic! show and the fireworks might not be on the entertainment schedule, and certain attractions may be closed for annual refurbishment.

A wonderful time to visit Disneyland—when it's not too crowded but everything is still open—is the period between Thanksgiving and Christmas, when the parks are decorated to the hilt, the Christmas parade takes place, and carolers add festive music to the mix. Other good times to visit are the period after summer vacation—September through early October—and after New Year's Day.

When Not to Go: If crowds make you queasy, keep in mind that Saturday is usually the busiest day year-round. In summer, Monday and Friday are the next busiest. If you decide to visit Disneyland park during a weekend, opt for Sunday. And remember that the weeks before Christmas through New Year's Day, Easter week, and the period from early July through Labor Day are packed.

Crowd Patterns

Average Attendance

- End of Presidents' week to week before Easter

- Sundays in spring, autumn, and winter, except holiday weekends

- Memorial Day week to beginning of summer vacation

- Labor Day week

- Columbus Day to Thanksgiving weekend

Most Crowded

- Any Saturday

- Sundays during summer and holiday weekends

- Presidents' week

- Weeks before and weeks after Easter Sunday

- Beginning of summer through Labor Day weekend

- Thanksgiving weekend (Thursday through Sunday)

- Week before Christmas through New Year's Day

Least Crowded

- First week in January to Presidents' week

- Two weeks after Easter Sunday to Memorial Day week

- End of Labor Day week to Columbus Day

- End of Thanksgiving weekend to week before Christmas

Keeping Disney Hours

The Disneyland Resort has many more important hours to keep track of than ever before. Operating hours fluctuate according to the season, so call 714-781-4565 or 714-781-7290, or visit *www.disneyland.com* for current schedules.

DISNEYLAND PARK: This park is typically open from about 9 A.M. to 8 P.M. weekdays, 9 A.M. to 11 P.M. on Saturdays, and 9 A.M. to 9 P.M. on Sundays. Hours are often extended in the summer and during holiday seasons.

DISNEY'S CALIFORNIA ADVENTURE: Hours are subject to change and may extend if the park ever hits capacity during the day. The park generally opens at 10 A.M. and closes at about 6 P.M. on weekdays, and later on weekends. Call 714-781-4565 for specifics.

DOWNTOWN DISNEY: Many shops and restaurants in this shopping and entertainment district open as early as the theme parks do (around 9 or 10 A.M.). Shops keep their doors open until about 9 P.M. on weekdays, 10 P.M. on weekends. Most restaurants stay open until

about midnight. Expect this area to start hopping around dinnertime and stay active until the early hours of the morning.

TRANSPORTATION: The monorail generally begins making its 2½-mile loop a half hour before Disneyland opens, and continues running until about 30 minutes after the park closes. Trams transporting guests between the main parking structure or the Timon parking lot and the theme parks begin picking up guests about 30 minutes before the first park opens, and continues transporting guests back to parking areas until the last group is dropped off, about an hour or so after the last park closes.

Disneyland Weather

If dry, sunny weather is your ideal, Anaheim may seem like a dream come true. Rainy days are few and far between, and generally occur between the months of November and April, which is also the coolest time of year. During this season, Santa Ana winds sometimes produce short periods of dry, crisp, warm desert weather and sparkling-clear skies that unveil distant mountains usually hidden by smog. In summer, thin, low morning clouds make it prudent to plan expeditions to the beach for the afternoon, when the haze burns off and the mercury rises. Mornings and nights are generally cool. The average daytime year-round temperature is 73 degrees.

	TEMPERATURE AVERAGE		RAINFALL AVERAGE
	HIGH	LOW	(INCHES)
January	65	47	3.12
February	67	49	3.11
March	68	50	2.66
April	70	53	1.09
May	72	56	0.31
June	77	60	0.06
July	82	64	0.01
August	83	65	0.06
September	81	63	0.24
October	77	59	0.49
November	73	52	1.39
December	67	48	2.58

Holidays & Special Events

GETTING READY TO GO

The Disneyland Resort sponsors several special events during the year. Here are a few highlights. For more details, call Disney Guest Relations (714-781-7290) about four to six weeks before the event. In addition, you can find out about specific events at Disneyland Resort hotels by calling 714-956-6413 or visiting *www.disneyland.com*.

JANUARY–FEBRUARY

Valentine's Day: Sweethearts will swoon over the romantic backdrop that Disneyland Park provides on this love-struck holiday.

Mardi Gras: With its Creole and Cajun cuisine, and boutiques brimming with beaded necklaces, holiday hats, and parade masks, Disneyland's New Orleans Square offers the most traditional Mardi Gras setting. Meanwhile, the clubs at Downtown Disney keep the party going late into the night. Expect Ralph Brennan's Jazz Kitchen to be hopping.

MARCH–MAY

Easter: The parks remain open late the week before and the week after Easter, making this a popular time to visit. At the Disneyland Hotel, "Alice in Wonderland's Easter Basket Buffet" takes place on Easter Sunday in the Wonderland-themed Grand Ballroom, where Alice, the White Rabbit, the Mad Hatter, and friends frolic. Reserve at least one month in advance (714-781-3463).

Mother's Day: Cinderella and other famous Disney princesses and their friends honor Mom during "Disney's Royal Buffet for Mother's Day" in the Disneyland Hotel's Grand Ballroom. The room is transformed with castles and other magical backdrops, creating a fairy-tale atmosphere. Reserve at least one month in advance (714-781-3463).

JUNE–AUGUST

Summer Flag Retreat: Disney's All-American College Band performs for nine weeks during the summer (usually beginning in mid-June), Tuesday through Saturday, at about 6:30 P.M.

The performance takes place in front of the flagpole in Town Square; it includes patriotic Sousa marches and concludes with "The Star-Spangled Banner," which brings any guests, not already standing, to their feet.

Fourth of July: This is one of the busiest days of the year—and one to avoid if you're overwhelmed by crowds. The more-patriotic-than-usual day features an exceptionally festive fireworks display at Disneyland park.

NOVEMBER–DECEMBER

Thanksgiving Weekend: The four days of this holiday weekend are filled with musical entertainment and the first installments of Disneyland's Christmas Fantasy Parade and It's a Small World Holiday, both of which kick off on Thanksgiving Day. The parks observe extended hours. At the Disneyland Hotel, the characters host "A Disney Family Thanksgiving" buffet in the Grand Ballroom. Reserve at least one month in advance (714-781-3463).

Christmas Festivities: This may be the Disneyland Resort's most beautiful season. Main Street in Disneyland Park is festooned with greenery and hundreds of poinsettias, while a 60-foot Christmas tree decorated with about 5,000 colorful lights and ornaments further embellishes the scene. Carolers lead sing-alongs in front of the tree, and during two nights early in the season, there's a candlelight ceremony involving a procession, music sung by a choir, and a reading of a Christmas story by a well-known entertainer.

In Fantasyland, It's a Small World is transformed into a world of holiday magic and music. The lively Christmas Fantasy Parade also takes place.

> ## Hot Tip!
> The holiday season kicks off early around these parts. Expect the parks to be completely decked out in festive regalia by mid- to late November.

The Haunted Mansion, in New Orleans Square, also goes all out for the holidays. Expect this spooky spot to sport a wonderfully elaborate *Nightmare Before Christmas* motif—inside and out.

The weeks before the holiday rank among the best times of year to visit the Disneyland Resort. The week afterward, however, is one of the busiest, so plan accordingly.

MAGICAL MILESTONES

When the Disneyland Resort underwent its dramatic expansion, adding a theme park (Disney's California Adventure) and a shopping, dining, and entertainment district (Downtown Disney), it exemplified the kind of bold achievement for which the Disney Company is famous. Here's a sampling of major milestones and important dates in Disney history.

1901
Walter Ellas Disney is born on December 5 in Chicago, Illinois. He spends his boyhood in Marceline, Missouri.

1922
Walt and collaborator Ub Iwerks start Laugh-O-Gram Films, an animation studio located in Kansas City, Missouri. (The business lasts one year.)

1923
Walt and his brother Roy open the Disney Bros. Studio in Hollywood, California.

1928

Disney's studio introduces the world to the immortal Mickey Mouse with *Steamboat Willie,* the world's first cartoon with a synchronized sound track. (Walt Disney himself provides the voice for Mickey.)

1934
The Three Little Pigs wins the Disney Studios its first Academy Award, for cartoon short subject.

1937

Disney releases *Snow White and the Seven Dwarfs,* the world's first feature-length animated film.

1940
Great works of classical music meet Disney animation with the release of *Fantasia.*

1955
Disneyland opens its doors in Anaheim, while television's original *Mickey Mouse Club* begins a four-year run.

1971
Walt Disney World opens in Orlando, Florida.

1989

Disney animation experiences a renaissance of sorts with the release of the Studios' 28th animated film, *The Little Mermaid.*

1992
The Disney magic travels overseas with the opening of Disneyland Paris.

1994
Disney makes its Broadway debut, as *Beauty and the Beast* opens in New York to sold-out houses. (*The Lion King* would follow in 1997, and *Aida* in 2000.)

1996
Disney's kid-oriented radio station, Radio Disney, hits the airwaves.

2001
For the first time since its opening, the Disneyland Resort gets a new theme park: Disney's California Adventure.

2003
The Many Adventures of Winnie the Pooh makes its debut in Disneyland park's Critter Country.

2004
The Twilight Zone Tower of Terror starts shaking up guests at Disney's California Adventure.

2005
Disneyland marks its 50th anniversary. Though the official date is July 17, 2005, an 18-month golden celebration begins in May, 2005.

Weddings & Honeymoons

The Disneyland Resort's customized Fairy Tale Weddings program lets brides and grooms create an affair to remember at the Castle Garden inside Disneyland, or at one of the three Disney hotels—either indoors or out. Couples may go the traditional route or plan a themed event with invitations, decorations, souvenirs, napkins, and thank-you notes emblazoned with their favorite Disney character couples, including Cinderella and her Prince and Mickey and Minnie Mouse.

One special spot for tying the knot is the gazebo at the Disneyland Hotel, in a picturesque garden setting where the bride or couple may arrive in a horse-drawn glass coach. Or they can take their vows at the poolside gazebo at Disney's Paradise

Pier Hotel. Perhaps the most romantic choice is the courtyard area in the garden at Disney's Grand Californian. A Cinderella Fantasy reception may follow (at any of the three hotels), at which the newlyweds are greeted by a fanfare of trumpets provided by musicians clad in medieval attire as the couple steps onto a red carpet and through a re-creation of Cinderella's Castle. Here, they are serenaded by a string ensemble and greeted by some extra-special guests—assorted Disney characters dressed in their party finery.

A special-event coordinator will help make all the necessary arrangements for the wedding and reception—everything, that is, except providing Prince (or Princess) Charming.

The bridal salon at Disney's Grand Californian resort helps guests through the planning and preparation stages, and even through those pre-ceremony jitters.

For more information about creating a happy occasion in a happy location, contact the Disneyland Fairy Tale Weddings department, which coordinates events at all three hotels and in Disneyland; 714-956-6527.

Planning Ahead

Collect as much information as you can about the attractions you're interested in from the sources listed below. Then consider all the possibilities before making any definite travel plans.

Information

For current information about special events and performance times, the latest ticket prices, operating hours, rides under refurbishment, and other Disneyland Resort specifics, contact:

Disneyland Resort Guest Relations:
Box 3232; Anaheim, CA 92803; 714-781-4565 (for recorded information), or 714-781-7290 (to speak directly with a Disney employee); *www.disneyland.com*.

If you are staying at one of the Disneyland Resort hotels (see the *Accommodations* chapter), contact Guest Services at the hotel for help in planning your visit to both the parks and the surrounding area.

Inside the Disneyland Resort: Cast members (the friendly folks who work at Disneyland) can answer questions on just about anything.

www.disneyland.com

For up-to-date online information, head to *www.disneyland.com*, the official Disneyland Resort website. Using the handy Trip Wizard, you can actually plan your vacation, find out about the three Disneyland Resort hotels, book travel packages, and order park tickets, plus check park hours and show schedules. You can also book your Disneyland vacation online through *www.disneytravel.com*.

Specific information stations in Disneyland Park include City Hall, on the west side of Town Square; and the Information Board on the west side of Central Plaza, at the far end of Main Street. In Disney's California Adventure theme park, Guest Relations Lobby is located on the east side of the Entry Plaza before the Golden Gate Bridge, and Information Boards can be found by the sun icon at the far end of the Gateway Plaza and on the bridge leading to Paradise Pier. At any Disneyland Resort hotel, visit the Guest Services desk in the lobby for assistance.

For other area information, contact these bureaus of tourism:

Anaheim/Orange County Visitor & Convention Bureau; Box 4270; Anaheim, CA 92803; 714-765-8899 (ask about their Adventure Cards). You can visit them at 800 West Katella Avenue. To order some free informative publications, call 888-598-3200; for a recorded message detailing current goings-on in the area, call 714-765-8899, ext. 9888; *www.anaheimoc.org*.

California Tourism; *www.visitcalifornia.com*.

Huntington Beach Conference & Visitors Bureau; 301 Main St., Suite 208; Huntington Beach, CA 92648; 714-969-3492 or 800-729-6232; *www.hbvisit.com*.

Laguna Beach Visitors Bureau; 252 Broadway; Box 221; Laguna Beach, CA 92651; 949-497-9229 or 800-877-1115; *www.lagunabeachinfo.org*.

Long Beach Convention & Visitors Bureau; One World Trade Center, Third Floor; Long Beach, CA 90831; 562-436-3645 or 800-452-7829; *www.visitlongbeach.org*.

Los Angeles Convention & Visitors Bureau; 685 S. Figueroa St.; Los Angeles, CA 90017; 213-624-7300 or 800-228-2452; *www.visitlanow.com*.

Newport Beach Conference & Visitors Bureau; 110 Newport Center Dr., Suite 120; Newport Beach, CA 92660; 949-719-6100 or 800-942-6278; *www.newportbeach-cvb.com*.

Orange Chamber of Commerce & Visitor Bureau; 439 E. Chapman Ave.; Orange, CA 92866; 714-538-3581; *www.orangechamber.com*.

San Diego Convention & Visitors Bureau; 401 B St., Suite 1400; San Diego, CA 92101; 619-236-1212; *www.sandiego.org*.

Reservations

With the Disneyland Resort's recent expansion, advance planning has become essential. To get your choice of accommodations, especially for visits during the busy spring and summer seasons, make lodging reservations as far in advance as possible—at least six months ahead, if you can, since area hotels fill up rather quickly during these months. For visits at other times of the year, check with the Anaheim/Orange County Visitor & Convention Bureau (714-765-8899) to see if any conventions are scheduled when you want to travel. Some of these events can crowd facilities enough to warrant altering your plans.

Travel Packages

The biggest advantage to purchasing a travel package is that it almost always saves you money over what you'd pay separately for the individual elements of your vacation, or it offers special options not available if you simply buy a ticket at the ticket booth. This is especially true the longer you stay. And there is the convenience of having all the details arranged in advance by someone else.

Finding the best package for yourself means deciding what sort of vacation you want and studying what's available. Don't choose a package that includes elements that don't interest you—remember, you're paying for them. And if it's Disney theming and extras you want, you should consider a Walt Disney Travel Company package.

The Walt Disney Travel Company offers packages that include a stay at a Disney hotel, a Resort Park Hopper Ticket, and choice of an extra, such as breakfast in the park or a guided tour of Disneyland, as well as admission to another Anaheim-area attraction, such as Sea World or Universal Studios Hollywood.

Besides booking guests into an official Disneyland Resort hotel, the Walt Disney Travel Company also works closely with more than 30 Good Neighbor hotels and motels (see page 46 for details), and they are included in its packages as well. To book a vacation package at the Disneyland Resort, go to their website: *www.disneyland.com*, contact a travel agent, or call the Walt Disney Travel Company at 877-700-DISNEY(*www.disneytravel.com*).

The Disneyland Resort is also featured in a wide variety of non-Disney-run package tours, including those sponsored by individual hotels, Amtrak, airlines (United Vacations and Delta Vacations both offer fly-drive packages, for instance), and organizations. AAA Vacations packages are available to members and nonmembers alike, while AAA Disney Magic Moments packages represent savings and benefits for members only.

This book's selective guide to Anaheim-area hotels and motels can help you decide initially which property best suits your travel style, needs, and budget (refer to the *Accommodations* chapter). Pick one, then contact a travel agent or the desired hotel directly to make a reservation, or book a Disneyland Resort package. Happy hunting!

What to Pack

Southern California isn't so laid-back that you only need to pack a few pairs of shorts and a T-shirt. Nor is it a place that demands formal attire. Casual wear will suffice in all but the fanciest restaurants, and even there, men can usually wear sports jackets without ties. Bathing suits are an obvious must if you plan to take advantage of your hotel's swimming pool or go for a walk on a long, surf-pounded Pacific beach. It's also a good idea to bring along a bathing suit cover-up and sunglasses (and don't forget the sunscreen). Tennis togs or golf gear may be necessary if you plan to hit the courts or the course. The weather in summer can be hot, but because Southern California air-conditioning is often over-efficient, take a lightweight sweater or jacket to wear indoors.

In winter, warm clothing is a must for evening; during nighttime visits to the parks, a heavy jacket may be a godsend. Whatever the time of year, come prepared for the unexpected: Pack an umbrella, a T-shirt, and a jacket—just in case the weather suddenly turns wet or unseasonably warm or cool.

Making a Budget

Vacation expenses tend to fall into five major categories: (1) transportation (which may include costs for airfare, airport transfers, train tickets, car rental, gas, parking, and taxi service); (2) lodging; (3) theme park tickets; (4) meals; and (5) miscellaneous (recreational activities, souvenirs, postcards, film, toiletries, and expenses such as pet boarding, etc.).

When budgeting, first consider what level of service suits your needs. Some prefer to spend fewer days at the Resort, but stay at a deluxe hotel like the Grand Californian or dine at pricier restaurants. Others want a longer vacation with a value-priced Good Neighbor hotel and less expensive meals. The choice is up to you. (Having said that, we do feel that a great deal of the Disney experience comes from staying on property, and recommend at least making room in your budget for accommodations at the more moderately priced Disneyland or Paradise Pier hotel.)

Once you've established your spending priorities, determine your price limit. Then make sure you don't exceed it when approximating your expenses—without a ballpark figure to work around, it's easy to get carried away.

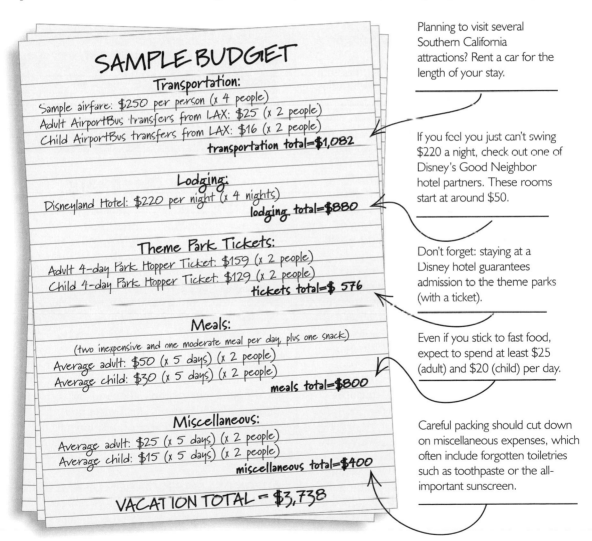

SAMPLE BUDGET

Transportation:
Sample airfare: $250 per person (x 4 people)
Adult AirportBus transfers from LAX: $25 (x 2 people)
Child AirportBus transfers from LAX: $16 (x 2 people)
transportation total=$1,082

Lodging:
Disneyland Hotel: $220 per night (x 4 nights)
lodging total=$880

Theme Park Tickets:
Adult 4-day Park Hopper Ticket: $159 (x 2 people)
Child 4-day Park Hopper Ticket: $129 (x 2 people)
tickets total=$576

Meals:
(two inexpensive and one moderate meal per day, plus one snack)
Average adult: $50 (x 5 days) (x 2 people)
Average child: $30 (x 5 days) (x 2 people)
meals total=$800

Miscellaneous:
Average adult: $25 (x 5 days) (x 2 people)
Average child: $15 (x 5 days) (x 2 people)
miscellaneous total=$400

VACATION TOTAL = $3,738

Planning to visit several Southern California attractions? Rent a car for the length of your stay.

If you feel you just can't swing $220 a night, check out one of Disney's Good Neighbor hotel partners. These rooms start at around $50.

Don't forget: staying at a Disney hotel guarantees admission to the theme parks (with a ticket).

Even if you stick to fast food, expect to spend at least $25 (adult) and $20 (child) per day.

Careful packing should cut down on miscellaneous expenses, which often include forgotten toiletries such as toothpaste or the all-important sunscreen.

This is an example of a moderately priced budget for a family of four (two adults and two kids staying at the Disneyland Resort for four nights and five days). Totals include tax; theme park ticket prices are likely to increase in 2005.

Money-Saving Strategies

Cost-Cutting Tips

LODGING: The most important rule is not to pay for more than you need. Budget chains don't offer many frills, but they are usually clean and provide the essentials; many even have a swimming pool, albeit a small one.

You can also save by checking the cutoff age at which children can no longer share their parents' room for free. Many of the hotels and motels in the Anaheim area allow children under 18 to stay free. Some places have a cutoff age of 12 or 16, so it's good to find out before making a reservation. And ask about special rates or discounts, especially if you are a California resident, a member of AAA or AARP, or are in the military.

Bed-and-breakfasts sometimes represent an excellent buy, though not so much for families, since they generally charge extra for more than two people in a room, regardless of age. While there are no B&Bs in Anaheim proper, there are some charming ones on the coast, within an hour of the Disneyland Resort.

Hostels and campgrounds also offer lower-priced lodging alternatives. Contact the Anaheim/Orange County Visitor & Convention Bureau at 714-765-8899 for a listing of those areas closest to the Disneyland Resort.

FOOD: The budget-minded (and who isn't?) should plan to have meals in coffee shops or fast-food restaurants, or save your splurges for the buffets, to get your fill and your money's worth. If you want to try an upscale place, go for lunch; the entrées are often the same as those at dinnertime, but usually cost less.

Pack a picnic and enjoy lunches outside. At the Disneyland Resort, there's a picnic area just outside the main gates of the two theme parks. Vending machines dispense soft drinks.

You can also save significantly on meals by choosing lodging with kitchen facilities and opting to eat in some of the time. The savings on food may more than cover the additional cost of accommodations. Don't forget to pack snack items, too—especially if you are traveling with small children.

In the Anaheim area, a number of places offer refrigerators or full kitchen facilities (look for suite hotels); some also provide complimentary breakfast.

TRANSPORTATION: When calculating the cost of driving to the Disneyland Resort, consider your car's gas mileage, the price of gasoline, and the expense of the accommodations and food en route. If you are thinking of traveling by plane, don't forget about the cost of getting from your home to the airport and later to your hotel. Also factor in the cost of renting a car at your destination, if that's part of your plan. Remember to ask if your hotel charges for parking (the Disneyland Resort hotels charge a daily fee) or shuttle transportation to the Disneyland Resort—these daily charges can tack a substantial amount onto a family's room bill.

Hot Tip!

For a book of coupons to many of Anaheim's hotels, restaurants, and attractions, call 714-765-8899.

Disney Discounts

ANNUAL PASSPORT: Bearers are granted special (sometimes substantial) savings on Disneyland Resort hotel accommodations (pending availability); Disneyland Resort restaurants; select merchandise throughout the theme parks and Downtown Disney, in the Disney Stores, and from the Disney Catalog; and select guided tours; as well as free parking at the theme parks.

DISNEY VISA: Members who pay for purchases with the Disney Bank One Visa card earn points that can be redeemed for various discounts and Disney items throughout the year. Note that purchases do not have to be made at Disneyland and all purchases count. Details are subject to change.

AUTOMOBILE ASSOCIATION OF AMERICA (AAA): Auto Club members can purchase discounted park tickets as well as special vacation packages through local AAA offices. Contact your local AAA office for details.

DISCOUNT FOR SENIORS: Senior citizens receive a $2 discount on one-day park tickets.

Theme Park Tickets

Along with the many changes to the Disneyland Resort comes a restructuring of the theme park ticketing system. Most admission media (with the exception of annual passes) are now called "tickets" rather than "passports." One-day tickets let you visit one park. Multi-day tickets allow you unlimited park hopping between Disneyland and Disney's California Adventure. All admission tickets to the theme parks include unlimited use of all attractions (except arcades) once inside. Note that ticket prices are subject to change.

Ticket Options

One-Day Tickets feature admission to one Disneyland Resort theme park, while Two-, Three-, and Four-Day Resort Park Hopper Tickets (which expire 14 days after first use) allow you to "hop" between Disneyland and Disney's California Adventure.

The two main types of annual passports are known as the Deluxe and Premium versions. Each affords the bearer shopping and dining discounts, as well as the privilege of "park-hopping"—that is, visiting both theme parks on the same day.

The Premium Annual Passport is valid year-round and includes parking (it has no block-out periods). The Deluxe Annual Passport is valid many days of the year but has block-out periods, such as each Saturday from March through June (passholders may enter the park on a blocked-out day by paying $25). An optional one-time parking fee, currently $40, is available to Deluxe Annual Passholders.

Annual passes are sold at the ticket booth near the turnstiles and processed at the Plaza Pavilion on Main Street.

There are usually special passes available for purchase by Southern California residents. Offers change from time to time, so be sure to inquire before you visit. Call 714-781-4565 or visit *www.disneyland.com* for details.

Purchasing Tickets

Long lines have been known to form at the Disney ticket booths–especially in the morning, as the parks open for business. Avoid the wait by buying your tickets ahead of time. If that's not incentive enough, consider the possibility of saving a little money by purchasing tickets prior to your arrival.

Where to Buy Tickets: One-, Three-, Four- and Five-Day Tickets are sold at park ticket booths, the Downtown Disney monorail station, and West Coast Disney Stores. Special Resort Park Hopper Tickets are sold to guests at the Disney hotels, via the Walt Disney Travel Company, or through a travel agent.

Tickets by Mail: Send a personal check or a money order and ticket request (plus a $10 handling fee for orders over $200), to Disneyland Ticket Mail Order Services; Box 61061; Anaheim, CA 92803. Allow five to ten business days for processing.

Tickets Online: Select tickets are available at *www.disneyland.com*. Allow plenty of time for delivery. There are often online special offers, such as five days for the price of three.

Tickets by Phone: Call 714-781-4043 and have a credit card handy. Allow five days for delivery; ten during busy times of the year.

How to Pay for Tickets: Cash, traveler's checks, personal checks, American Express, Visa, MasterCard, JCB Card, and the Discover Card are accepted. Personal checks must be imprinted with name and address, and accompanied by a government-issued photo ID.

Note that ticket structures and pricing are apt to change. For the latest information, visit *www.disneyland.com*.

Ticket Prices

Although prices are always subject to change, the following will give you an idea of what you can expect to pay. Note that prices and ticketing structure are likely to increase in 2005. For current prices, visit *www.disneyland.com,* or call 714-781-4565.

	Adults	Children*
One-Day Ticket	$49.75	$39.75
Two-Day Ticket**	$99	$79
Three-Day Ticket	$129	$99
Four-Day Ticket	$159	$129
Five-Day Ticket	$184	$149

Two-Park Deluxe Annual Passport	$179
Two-Park Premium Annual Passport	$279

*3 through 9 years of age; children under 3 free
**Available to Disneyland Resort hotel guests only

Customized Travel Tips

Traveling with Children

When you tell your kids that a Disney vacation is in the works, the challenge is keeping them relatively calm until you actually arrive at the resort.

PLANNING: Get youngsters involved in plotting the trip from the outset, putting each child in charge of a small part of the vacation preparation—such as writing for travel brochures, choosing which attractions to see and in what order to see them, and deciding which other activities to include in your Southern California visit.

EN ROUTE: Certain resources can stave off the "Are we there yet?" chorus, such as travel games, books and magazines, and snacks to quiet rumbling stomachs. If you drive, take plenty of breaks along the way. If you fly, try to time your departure and return flights for off-peak hours and during the off-season, when chances are better that an empty seat or two will be available. During takeoffs and landings, encourage toddlers to suck on bottles and pacifiers to keep ears clear, and supply older children with chewing gum or a drink of water.

IN THE HOTELS: During the summer, several hotels offer special kids' programs at no (or low) charge. Some offer baby-sitting services or baby-sitting referrals year-round. Pinocchio's Workshop at the Grand Californian is available to take requests for "day-of"child-care services for hotel guests.

IN THE THEME PARKS: The smiles that light up your kids' faces as they enter a Disney theme park will repay you a thousandfold for any fuss en route. No place in the world is more aware of the needs of children—or their parents—than this one.

Favorite Attractions: Fantasyland and Mickey's Toontown in Disneyland Park are great places to start with small kids, who delight in the bright colors and familiar characters. In Disney's California Adventure, A Bug's Land, The Playhouse Disney show, and the Redwood Creek Challenge Trail have the biggest kid appeal. If you have children of different ages in your party, you may have to do some juggling or split the group up for a few hours, so that older kids won't have to spend their whole vacation waiting in line for Dumbo. Some rides, like Snow White's Scary Adventures, may be too frightening for some youngsters. If they're afraid of the witch, skip the attraction.

Strollers: They can be rented for $7 ($12 for two) at the Stroller Shop, located to the right as you enter the main gate in Disneyland park and on the right side as you enter Disney's California Adventure. If yours disappears while you're at an attraction, go to a replacement center (a Disney cast member can point the way), show your claim ticket, and get another. If you plan to park-hop, you'll have to return the stroller before doing so. Keep the receipt and get another stroller at the next park at no additional charge (provided that it's the same day).

Baby Care: Baby Care Centers feature toddler-size flush toilets that are quite cute—and functional. In addition, there are changing tables, a limited selection of formulas, strained baby foods, and diapers for sale, plus facilities for warming baby food and bottles (you can wash out your bottles here, too). A special room with comfortable chairs is available for nursing mothers.

The decor is soothing, and a stop here for diaper changing or feeding is a tranquil break for parent and child alike. The Baby Care Centers are located on the east side of the Central Plaza, at the Castle end of Main Street in Disneyland, and near Cocina Cucamonga in the Golden State at Disney's California Adventure.

Changing tables and diaper machines are also available in many of the women's and men's restrooms found throughout the Disneyland Resort.

Note: We recommend that parents of toddlers pack a few pairs of waterproof diapers. They'll come in handy for children who want to spend time splashing in the interactive water fountains at each of the parks.

Where to Buy Baby Care Items: Besides being at the Baby Care Centers, disposable diapers and baby bottles are sold at select shops throughout the parks.

Lost Children: When a child suddenly disappears or fails to show up on time, it's reassuring to know that Disney's security force and all cast members are carefully trained to follow specific procedures when they encounter a lost child.

Up to age 10, a youngster may be taken to Child Services, adjacent to First Aid, where Disney movies and books provide temporary amusement. The child's name is registered in the lost children's logbook there. Kids 12 and

older may leave messages and check in often at City Hall in Disneyland park, or Guest Relations in the entrance area of Disney's California Adventure.

The telephone number for Lost Children is 714-781-4210; if you're calling from inside a park, dial extension 4210.

Traveling without Children

The Disneyland Resort is as enjoyable for solo travelers and couples as it is for families for several reasons: its ambience encourages interaction, if you're in the mood; cast members (Disney employees) are outgoing and helpful; and the attractions are naturally shared events.

PLANNING: Read Disney literature carefully before you arrive to familiarize yourself with the resort's layout and activities. Also request tourist information from other places in Southern California that you intend to visit.

IN THE THEME PARKS: Disney brings out the child in most adults, who suddenly find themselves donning Mouse ears and beaming after getting a hug from Minnie.

Park Tour: A good way to learn the lay of the lands in Disneyland is to take the "Red Carpet Tour." It costs $25 per person and includes a 2½-hour tour experience in which guests are shown the "lay of the Land"—including Disneyland, Disney's California Adventure, and Downtown Disney. It includes a starter pin lanyard with trading pins, snacks, a ride on the Monorail, fastpass entrance to Pirates of the Caribbean, and VIP viewing for Aladdin—A Musical Adventure. Another tour option is called "A Walk in Walt's Footsteps." Led by a knowledgeable guide, the tour covers the whole park. If you already have a park ticket, you pay an extra $49 (all ages) for the 3-hour tour. It includes lunch, a collectible pin, a sneak peek at the exclusive Club 33, and a visit to the Enchanted Tiki Room.

Walking tours depart every morning from City Hall in Disneyland. For details or to book a tour, call 714-781-4400. Tours may be booked up to 30 days in advance.

Food for Thought: Sightseeing takes energy, and only healthy meals can provide it at a consistent level. Don't try to save money by scrimping on food. Prices for meals at the parks (particularly at Disneyland) are relatively reasonable, and there are many healthy options, even in the fast-food restaurants.

Height Ho!

At attractions with age and/or height restrictions, a parent who waits with a child too young or too small to ride while the other parent goes on the attraction may stay at the front of the line and take a turn as soon as the first parent comes off. This is called the "rider switch" policy, and if lines are long, it can save a lot of time. Be sure to ask the attendant, and he or she will explain what to do.

Health Matters: If you visit in summer, avoid getting overheated; August in particular can be sweltering. Protect yourself from the sun with a hat and plenty of sunscreen, rest in the shade often, and beat the mid-afternoon heat with a cold drink or a snack in an air-conditioned spot.

If you feel ill, speak to a Disney cast member or go to First Aid and lie down for a while. Above all, don't take unnecessary risks. If you have a back problem, heart condition, or other physical ailment, suffer from motion sickness, or are pregnant, you should steer clear of rough rides. Any restrictions are noted at the entrance to each ride in the park, as well as at the end of the individual listings in theme park chapters of this book.

Lost Companions: Traveling companions do occasionally get separated. If someone in your party wanders off or fails to show up at an appointed meeting spot, head for City Hall in Disneyland or Guest Relations in California Adventure. Here you will find a book in which guests can leave and receive messages for one another during the day.

Making Your Exit: If you are part of a bus tour, allow plenty of time to return to the coach at the end of the day. One tactic is to save the entrance area sights for last. If you arrive at the main gate too far in advance of the group's meeting time, you can spend the extra minutes at those attractions. Expect the tram ride from the entrance of the park to the tour bus pickup point to take at least 10 minutes, and plan accordingly.

MEETING OTHER ADULTS: Downtown Disney, with its mix of restaurants and nightclubs, is the best spot to mingle. While each of Disney's three hotels has lounges worth visiting, those at the Grand Californian are

---

Park Resource

The *Guidebook for Guests with Disabilities* describes accessibility to each theme park's shops, restaurants, and attractions, and tells where to find the wheelchair entrances. It is available at Guest Relations in Disneyland and Disney's California Adventure. It can also be obtained by writing to Disneyland Resort Guest Relations, Box 3232, Anaheim, CA 92803 (allow two to three weeks for delivery).

---

among the most sophisticated on-property. As far as the parks go, Disney's California Adventure tends to attract more grown-ups than Disneyland park does.

Travelers with Disabilities

The Disneyland Resort is extremely accessible to guests with disabilities, and as a result, it makes an excellent choice as a vacation destination. But advance planning is still essential, and nothing is more useful than the free *Guidebook for Guests with Disabilities*. Allow enough time to order a copy and study the information in it before your trip. It's also available at *www.disneyland.com*.

Getting to Anaheim

Probably the most effective means of ensuring a smooth trip is to make as many advance contacts as possible at every phase of your journey. It's important to make any necessary phone calls regarding transportation well before your departure date to arrange for any special facilities or services you may need en route.

The Society for Accessible Travel & Hospitality (347 Fifth Ave., Suite 610, New York, NY 10016; 212-447-7284; *www.sath.org*) has member travel agents who book trips for travelers with disabilities, keeping their special needs in mind. Membership in the organization costs $45, or $30 for seniors 65 and older and for students.

The following travel agencies specialize in booking trips for travelers with physical disabilities: Accessible Journeys, Ridley Park, PA (*www.accessiblejourneys.com*, 610-521-0339, or 800-846-4537), and Flying Wheels Travel, Owatonna, MN (call 507-451-5005 or e-mail *www.flyingwheelstravel.com*).

Hertz (800-654-3131) and National (888-273-5262) have a few hand-control cars available for rent in Southern California, most of which are available at Los Angeles International Airport and in Anaheim.

Though less convenient, it is also possible to access the area by public transportation. All buses operated by the Orange County Transportation Authority (714-636-7433), the public bus company that serves Orange County, are outfitted with lifts so that travelers using wheelchairs can board them easily. Many routes pass the Disneyland Resort.

Sightseeing tour buses are another option. Though only a few of them are wheelchair accessible, all have storage facilities for collapsible chairs, making this a possibility for travelers who have a companion to help them on and off the bus. Coach USA is wheelchair accessible. It offers tours to many Disneyland Resort–area attractions. Make reservations (at least 48 hours in advance) by calling 714-978-8855 or 800-828-6699.

ScootAround rents standard and electric wheelchairs, as well as scooters. Pick-up and delivery is available to all hotels in the Disneyland Resort area. Call 888-441-7575. Wheelchair Getaways, in La Brea, rents wheelchair accessible vans and has pick up and delivery options for most hotels in the area. Call 800-638-1912 or 650-589-5554.

Lodging

Most hotels and motels in Orange County have rooms equipped for guests with disabilities, with extra-wide doorways, grab bars in the bathroom for shower or bath and toilet, and sinks at wheelchair height, along with ramps at curbs and steps to allow wheelchair access. Unless otherwise indicated, all the lodging described in the *Accommodations* chapter provide rooms for travelers with disabilities.

Inside the Disneyland Resort

Cars displaying a "disability" placard will be directed to a section of each Disney parking lot, next to the tram pickup and drop-off area.

Wheelchairs and Electric Convenience Vehicles (ECVs) can be rented at the Stroller Shop just inside the main gate in Disneyland and across from Guest Relations in the Entry Plaza of California Adventure. The rental price ($7 per park per day for wheelchairs, $30 for ECVs) includes a refundable deposit of $20. A small number of wheelchairs are also available free of charge (the guest is charged if the wheelchair isn't returned) from Disney's three hotels; inquire at the front desk.

Most waiting areas are accessible, though some attractions have auxiliary entrances for guests using wheelchairs or other mobility devices, who may be accompanied by up to five other party members using the special entry point. The Main Street Train Station is a registered historical landmark building, and as such is not wheelchair accessible. Guests using wheelchairs may access the train in New Orleans Square, Toontown, or Tomorrowland.

Accessibility information is provided in the *Guidebook for Guests with Disabilities* (see "Park Resource" on page 20). In all cases, guests with mobility disabilities should be escorted by someone in their party who can assist as needed.

In some attractions, guests may remain in their wheelchair or ECV; in others, they must be able to transfer in and out of their wheelchair or ECV. In a few attractions, they must be able to leave their wheelchair or ECV and remain ambulatory during the majority of the attraction experience.

All the shops and food locations in the theme parks are completely accessible to guests in wheelchairs, with one exception: At Disneyland's River Belle Terrace, the stanchions designating the cafeteria line are spaced too closely together to permit wheelchair passage (otherwise, it is accessible).

For guests with visual disabilities: A tape recorder and cassette describing the park, along with the *Braille Guidebook*, are available upon request at City Hall in Disneyland and at Guest Relations in California Adventure.

Service animals are permitted almost everywhere, except on attractions that involve a great deal of motion. In such instances, the service animal waits with a Disney cast member while the guest goes on the ride.

For guests with hearing disabilities: Several dozen attractions provide a written story line for guests to follow while they experience the attraction. Check at City Hall in Disneyland and Guest Relations in California Adventure for additional information.

Closed captioning is available in the pre-show areas of select attractions; contact Guest Relations for the use of a remote. Reflective captioning is available at several shows as well; inquire at each attraction.

Text typewriters (TTY) are located in Disneyland near the Guest Relations window at the main entrance (next to the kennel), and at the pay phones near the exit to Space Mountain. In Disney's California Adventure, TTYs can be found in the Bay Area by Golden Dreams, beside King Triton's Carrousel, and inside the Guest Relations Lobby.

Sign language interpretation is available for select shows and attractions. Reservations must be made at least seven days in advance. To make this arrangement, contact Resort Tour Services at 714-817-2229.

Volume-control telephones are located throughout the theme parks. Audio tours and closed captioning devices are available to borrow at City Hall and the Guest Relations Lobby for a $20 refundable deposit.

How to Get There

Most visitors to the Disneyland Resort arrive by car. Many of those who live nearby own an annual pass and drive down frequently to spend a day or weekend at the resort. But for those traveling any significant distance, it tends to cost less to fly than to drive, and certainly saves time. During your days at the Disneyland Resort, you can rely on Disney transportation (in the form of monorails, trams, and double-decker buses) to take you anywhere you want to go on-property. Plan to rent a car for the days you'll venture off-property, or rely on local tours to see the area sights. If you prefer to leave the driving to someone else altogether, traveling by bus or train are other alternatives.

By Car

SOUTHERN CALIFORNIA FREEWAYS:
Driving almost anywhere in Orange County, or farther afield, requires negotiating a combination of freeways and surface streets. But once you familiarize yourself with a few names and numbers, navigating becomes much more manageable.

The freeways are well marked and fast, barring (common) traffic snags. And locals are good drivers: slow to lose patience, but quick to apply their brakes when necessary. They tend to leave more than a full car-length space in front of them, knowing that abrupt lane switching is commonplace here.

Proper names of most roads change, depending on where you are. I-5, for instance, is called the Santa Ana Freeway in Orange County, but in the Los Angeles area it becomes the Golden State Freeway; to the south it's the San Diego Freeway. It's a good idea to learn both the name and the route number of any freeway on which you plan to travel. The exit signs will most likely indicate one or the other but not both.

It's also useful to have an idea of the overall layout of the freeways. Several run parallel to the Pacific coast and are intersected by others running east and west. While this scheme is fairly straightforward, it is complicated by a couple of freeways that squiggle diagonally across the map.

CALIFORNIA DRIVING LAWS: Under California law, seat belts are required for all front- and backseat passengers; right turns at red lights are legal unless otherwise posted, as are U-turns at intersections; and pedestrians have the right-of-way at crosswalks.

AUTOMOBILE CLUBS: Any one of the nation's leading automobile clubs will come to your aid in the event of a breakdown en route (be sure to bring your membership card with you), as well as provide insurance covering accidents, arrest, bail bond, lawyers' fees for defense of contested traffic cases, and personal injury. They also offer useful trip-planning services—not merely advice, but also free maps and route-mapping assistance. AAA and the Auto Club of Southern California provide select free services to all Disneyland Resort guests (see page 33).

MAPS: Many car rental agencies provide helpful maps, but it's still wise to buy one before your trip. Or drop by a visitor information office; it can usually provide a map showing tourist attractions, major roads, and some minor streets. Local gas stations and bookstores often sell maps, as do some hotel gift shops. Routes can also be plotted ahead of time through *www.mapquest.com*.

By Air

Anaheim lies about 45 minutes southeast of Los Angeles by car. Most Disneyland Resort guests who arrive by plane disembark at Los Angeles International Airport (LAX), one of

Hot Tip!

Freeway traffic updates can help you avoid a jam. Tune in to 980 AM (Anaheim) or 1070 AM (Los Angeles).

the busiest in the world. It handles approximately 1,900 departures and arrivals daily of more than 100 commercial airlines. Major carriers serving Los Angeles include American, Continental, Delta, and United.

Much closer to Anaheim, Orange County's John Wayne Airport, in Santa Ana, is less than a half hour away from Disney and is served by 12 commercial airlines and more than 240 flights a day. It is sometimes possible to find the same fare to John Wayne/Orange County Airport as to LAX, and if it's a nonstop flight, so much the better. There aren't as many direct flights available, but given the airport's proximity to Disneyland, it's worth considering. Another airport vying for attention is the Long Beach Airport. It is also near Anaheim, but few airlines serve it on a nonstop basis. At press time, JetBlue offered service from several major U.S. cities. Visit *www.jetblue.com* for information.

HOW TO GET THE BEST AIRFARE: These days, airfares are constantly in flux, changing from day to day, seemingly hour to hour. That makes it important to shop around—or have your travel agent do so. It pays (literally) to keep these suggestions in mind:

• Find out the names of all the airlines serving your destination and then call them all. Tell the airline's reservationist how many people are in your party, and emphasize that you're interested in economy. Ask if you can get a lower fare by slightly altering the dates of your trip, the hour of departure, or the duration of your stay—or, if you live halfway between two airports, by leaving from one rather than the other or by flying into a different area airport.

• Fly weekends on routes heavily used by business travelers, and midweek on routes more commonly patronized by vacationers.

• Purchase your tickets online. Airlines often offer lower fares or bonus frequent flier miles for tickets purchased through their website.

• Keep an eye on your local newspapers for advertisements announcing new or special promotional fares.

• Plan and pay as far ahead as possible. Most carriers guarantee their fares, which means you won't have to pay more if fares have gone up since you purchased your ticket. On the other hand, if you have not paid for your ticket, you will be required to pay the higher charge. Similarly, if you change dates of travel or flight times and your ticket has to be reissued, you'll have to pay the new fare, plus any penalties that may apply. If fares have come down in price since you paid for your ticket, the difference will be refunded to you by the airline, even if you've already paid the higher fare in full. Be sure to watch the newspaper ads and to call the airline to check for new, lower fares, since you have to request the refund to get it.

AIRPORT TRANSPORTATION: Frequent scheduled bus service is provided by AirportBus (*www.airportbus.com*; or call 714-938-8937 or 800-938-8933). It not only goes to the Disneyland Resort hotels and the properties in Anaheim, but also Buena Park (seven miles away and the home of Knott's Berry Farm). The bus stops at each LAX airline terminal, outside the baggage claim area; look for the green bus stop signs on the center island and for the words DISNEYLAND or ANAHEIM above the bus windshield.

To Anaheim from the Airports

	Airport Bus	SuperShuttle
Los Angeles Int'l Airport	$16 ($25 round-trip) per adult $ 9 ($16 round-trip) per child 3–11	$15 per person
John Wayne Airport	$11 ($18 round-trip) per adult $ 8 ($13 round-trip) per child 3–11	$10 per person
Long Beach Airport	Not Available	$33 for the first guest in the party, $9 for each additional guest.

Children under 3 ride free. Prices were accurate at press time, but are subject to change.

Those who fly into John Wayne Airport (named after one of Orange County's most famous residents), 16 miles from the Disneyland Resort, have an easier time of it. The ride into town takes half the time. From the baggage claim area, proceed to the AirportBus ticket booth across the street at the Ground Transportation Center and the designated AirportBus stop. Look for the AirportBus that has the words DISNEYLAND or ANAHEIM displayed above the windshield.

Hot Tip!

The SuperShuttle often carries a smaller group than the AirportBus. Expect it to make fewer stops before reaching your destination.

SuperShuttle (call 310-782-6600 or visit *www.supershuttle.com*) also serves area airports. At Los Angeles International Airport, go to the curb outside baggage claim to request pickup. A van should arrive within 15 minutes.

For passengers arriving at John Wayne or Long Beach Airport, in Orange County, SuperShuttle recommends 24-hour advance reservations; call 310-782-6600. Upon arrival, use a courtesy phone to request a pickup; the van should arrive outside the terminal within 15 minutes.

To return to any airport, check with your hotel front desk the day before the departure for bus schedules and reservation information.

CAR RENTALS: Several major car rental agencies have locations at the airport, at many hotels, and elsewhere in Anaheim. Expect to pay between $150 and $230 a week for a mid-size car, and $60 to $100 for a four-day weekend, with unlimited mileage included. Some rental companies to choose from are Avis (800-331-1212), Budget (800-527-0700), Dollar (800-800-4000), Hertz (800-654-3131), and National (800-227-7368).

It pays to call all the agencies to get the best available deal. Be sure to ask about any special promotions or discounts. Collision damage waiver (CDW) insurance is essential for your protection in case of an accident, but it can add a hefty chunk to your bill (usually at least $9 a day). Most vacation packages that include a rental car do not include the CDW. If you have your own car

insurance, check with your carrier to see what they cover.

An increasing number of credit-card companies offer free collision damage coverage for charging the rental to their card, and some may provide primary coverage. That means your credit-card company may deal with the rental company directly in the event of an accident, rather than compensate you after your insurance has kicked in. It's worth a phone call to find out.

If you're renting a car at Los Angeles International Airport, the drive to the Disneyland Resort is only 31 miles, but it will take about 45 minutes with no traffic, or up to two hours if the roads are congested.

From John Wayne Airport, take I-405 north to Highway 55 north to I-5 north, exit at Katella, proceed straight to Disney Way, then follow signs to the theme park parking entrance. The drive takes about 25 minutes (without traffic).

By Train

Amtrak (800-872-7245) and Metrolink commuter service (800-371-5465) to and from Los Angeles; trains stop at Anaheim's Edison Stadium, only a mile from the Disneyland Resort. Taxis are available from the station.

Union Station in Los Angeles is served by a number of trains from the rest of the state, as well as the Northwest, the South, and the Midwest. To get to Anaheim from L.A., you can take Amtrak's Pacific Surfliner or rent a car. The major car rental agencies have phones at Union Station by which to arrange rental.

Amtrak also offers vacation packages to Disneyland (800-321-8684). They feature transportation to Anaheim via the Pacific Surfliner and a one-day or multi-day Disney ticket.

By Bus

Buses make sense if you're traveling a fairly short distance, if you have plenty of time to spend in transit, if there are only two or three people in your party, or if cost-control is key.

Buses make the trip from Los Angeles and San Diego, though they usually make a few stops along the way. Travel from most other destinations usually requires a change of vehicles in Los Angeles. The Greyhound bus terminal is located at 100 West Winston Road in Anaheim, about one mile north of the Disneyland Resort; 714-232-1256 or 800-231-2222. Taxis can take you to Disneyland.

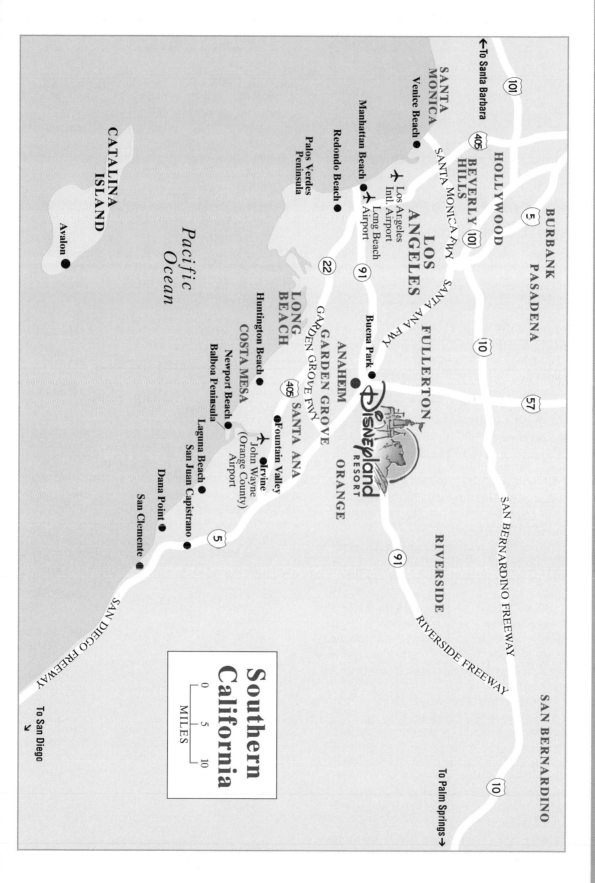

Southern
California

0   5   10
MILES

←To Santa Barbara

101

SANTA
MONICA
Venice Beach ●

405

BEVERLY
HILLS

HOLLYWOOD

SANTA MONICA FWY

5

BURBANK

PASADENA

101

Manhattan Beach ●

Palos Verdes
Peninsula

Redondo Beach ●

CATALINA
ISLAND

Avalon ●

Pacific
Ocean

Los Angeles
Intl. Airport

LOS
ANGELES

Long Beach
Airport

22

91

SANTA ANA FWY

10

57

SAN BERNARDINO

Buena Park ●

LONG
BEACH

Huntington Beach ●

COSTA MESA

Newport Beach ●

Balboa Peninsula

GARDEN GROVE FWY

GARDEN GROVE

405

ANAHEIM

FULLERTON

Disneyland RESORT

RIVERSIDE

SAN BERNARDINO FREEWAY

Laguna Beach ●

San Juan Capistrano ●

Dana Point ●

San Clemente ●

SANTA ANA

Fountain Valley
Irvine
John Wayne
(Orange County)
Airport

ORANGE

5

91

RIVERSIDE FREEWAY

To Palm Springs →

10

SAN DIEGO FREEWAY

To San Diego
↘

25

Getting Oriented

Southern California's patchwork of small communities has undeniably blurred borders. The Disneyland Resort is in Anaheim, but you might not know if you were in that city or one of its immediate neighbors except for the signs. Buena Park lies to the northwest, Garden Grove to the southwest, Santa Ana to the southeast, and Orange to the east.

Farther south—in Huntington Beach, Newport Beach, Laguna Beach, and San Juan Capistrano—there's a bit more breathing room between communities. Heading northwest from Anaheim, you'll come to Los Angeles International Airport.

Proceeding north through Los Angeles, you'll pass Beverly Hills, Hollywood and West Hollywood (an independent municipality), Santa Monica (its own municipality as well), Malibu, Glendale, and Burbank, home of Walt Disney Studios. The San Fernando Valley lies farther north and a bit inland from L.A., while Santa Barbara, Southern California's northern boundary, is on the coast, about two hours to the north.

North–South Freeways: There are two. I-5 (the Santa Ana Freeway) runs from Vancouver, Canada, to San Diego, and is the principal inland route in Southern California, linking Los Angeles and San Diego. I-405 (the San Diego Freeway) sprouts from I-5 near Hollywood, veers toward the coast, then rejoins I-5 at Irvine, south of Anaheim.

East–West Freeways: Of the roads that intersect the two principal north–south arteries, one of the closest to the Disneyland Resort is Route 22, also known as the Garden Grove Freeway; it begins near the ocean in Long Beach and runs across the southern border of Anaheim. Route 91, called the Artesia Freeway on the west side of I-5 and the Riverside Freeway on the east, lies about eight miles north of Route 22.

The next east–west route as you travel north is I-10, called the Santa Monica Freeway from its beginning near the Pacific shore in Santa Monica to just east of downtown Los Angeles. At this point, it jogs north and then turns east again, becoming the San Bernardino Freeway. I-10 is located about 12 miles north of Route 91.

North of I-10 (anywhere from two to eight miles, depending on your location) is U.S. 101, which heads south from Ventura and then due east across I-405. West of I-405, it is known as the Ventura Freeway; at a point a few miles beyond the intersection with I-405, it angles south, becomes the Hollywood Freeway, and eventually crosses I-5.

Travel Times

To/from the Resort	Approx. Distance	Drive Time
Balboa	30 miles	40 min.
Buena Park	7 miles	12 min.
Carlsbad	50 miles	60 min.
Costa Mesa	20 miles	30 min.
Dana Point	30 miles	40 min.
Garden Grove	5 miles	10 min.
Huntington Beach	15 miles	25 min.
John Wayne Airport	16 miles	25 min.
Laguna Beach	30 miles	45 min.
Las Vegas	280 miles	4–5 hrs.
Long Beach	20 miles	30 min.
Los Angeles (downtown and airport)	31 miles	45–90 min.
Newport Beach	20 miles	30 min.
Palm Springs	180 miles	2–3 hrs.
San Diego	87 miles	90 min.
San Juan Capistrano	32 miles	45 min.
San Simeon	270 miles	5-6 hrs.
Santa Ana	5 miles	10 min.
Santa Barbara	110 miles	2 hrs.

Drive times are under optimal conditions; rain or rush-hour traffic could increase or even double the time.

HOW TO GET THERE: The Disneyland Resort is on Harbor Boulevard between Katella Avenue, Disneyland Drive, and Ball Road, 31 miles south of downtown Los Angeles and 87 miles north of San Diego. Many visitors drive to the resort from elsewhere in Southern California, while those who come from farther away fly into one of the area airports, rent a car, and drive from there. Once at their hotel, guests may prefer to use the hotel's shuttle for transportation to and from Disney.

Southbound I-5 Exit: To get to Disneyland, southbound I-5 (the Santa Ana Freeway) travelers should exit at Disneyland Drive, turn left, pass through Ball Road, and proceed to the theme park parking entrance.

Northbound I-5 Exit: Northbound travelers should exit I-5 at Katella Avenue, proceed straight to Disney Way, and then follow signs to the most convenient parking area.

From John Wayne/Orange County Airport: Take I-405 north to CA-55 north to north I-5 north. Exit at Katella Ave. exit, head straight to Disney Way, then follow signs to the the most convenient parking area.

From Los Angeles International Airport: Take I-105 east to I-605 north to I-5 south. Take Disneyland Drive exit twoard Ball Road. Merge onto Disneyland Drive and proceed to the theme park parking entrance.

Exit off Orange Freeway: Travelers on the 57 freeway should exit on Katella Avenue and proceed west to Harbor Boulevard. Turn right on Harbor and follow signs to the most convenient parking area.

Note: When traffic is heavy, Harbor Boulevard and Ball Road and the freeways leading to them often get backed up. In this case, if you're coming from the north, take the Katella Avenue exit off I-5 and proceed straight to Disney Way. If you are coming from I-5 south, you should exit onto Katella and proceed to West Street, which will eventually turn into Disneyland Drive.

ANAHEIM-AREA SURFACE STREETS: The Disneyland Resort is in the center of the Anaheim resort, a 1,100-acre garden district which also includes the Anaheim Convention Center. Disneyland is bounded by Harbor Boulevard on the east, Disneyland Drive (a segment of West Street) on the west, Ball Road on the north, and Katella Avenue on the south. Many of the city's hotels and motels are located on these streets.

Harbor Boulevard, near Ball Road, is the most convenient place to pick up I-5 (Santa Ana Freeway) going north to Los Angeles. Katella Avenue past Anaheim Boulevard is the most convenient entrance to southbound I-5 going to Newport Beach and points south.

Note: Be sure to park in a designated parking lot or feed the parking meter as often as possible. Parking fines can run as high as $40 in Orange County.

Hot Tip!

Guests getting picked up or dropped off by car should arrange to meet their ride in the Disneyland Resort's short-term parking area. It's by the main entrance on Harbor Boulevard.

LOCAL TRANSPORTATION: The Orange County Transportation Authority (OCTA; 714-636-7433) provides daily bus service throughout the area, with limited weekend service. Several lines stop at Disneyland, but know that public transportation can involve considerable waiting and transferring. Fares are $1 for a one-way fare or $2.50 for a one-day unlimited pass. Seniors 65 and older and people with disabilities pay 25 cents one-way or 50 cents for a one-day pass. Exact change is required.

If you have wanderlust but lack wheels, your best bet is to sign up for a bus tour, such as one of those offered by Pacific Coast Sightseeing/Gray Line of Anaheim (714-978-8855). Hotel and motel desks can provide information on tour schedules and prices, sell you the tickets, and even arrange to have the sightseeing company come and pick you up at the hotel. (If you're going to Disneyland, you do not need prior arrangements—a bus will come to your area.)

The Metropolitan Transportation Authority (MTA) serves Los Angeles County and the major attractions of Orange County (213-626-4455). Exact change is required.

TAXIS: The only licensed taxi company approved to serve the Disneyland Resort is Yellow Cab of North Orange County (714-535-2211). Cab fare to John Wayne Airport from the Disneyland Hotel runs about $36; if you're going to LAX, figure about $85; Long Beach Airport runs $38. Gratuity is extra. Prices for town cars are slightly higher. Taxis can be called to pick you up at train and bus stations.

Planning Your Itinerary

For those lucky enough to live in the Los Angeles/Orange County area, the Disneyland Resort offers the opportunity to return frequently. And over the past few years, Disney has given locals more incentive to do just that. With a second theme park and a shopping, dining, and dancing district, the "things to do" list at Disney has tripled in length since the turn of the millennium. Seasoned visitors and first-timers alike will do well to plan each step of their visit far in advance—make the travel arrangements as soon as vacation dates are set (refer to the "Trip Planning Time Line" below to make sure you don't miss any crucial steps), and then study the following chapters of this book to decide how you'd like to spend each day of the trip.

How many days should you spend with the Mouse? Well, that's up to you, but to experience the Disneyland Resort at its best, we recommend a stay of about four full days—you'll have enough time to see every attraction, parade, and show (plus revisit all of your favorites), lounge by your hotel's pool, enjoy a character meal, shop for souvenirs, and dance the night away. If you'd like to visit other area attractions, like Sea World, Universal Studios, or Hollywood, add on one day for each excursion. But don't try to cram too much into one visit; this is a vacation, after all.

Once you've decided how many days you're going to dedicate to Disney, it's time to decide how you'll split up your time on-property. We suggest that you begin with a day at Disneyland Park (for the original and quintessential Disney experience), followed by a visit to Disney's California Adventure (to sample the rides and shows). On the third day return to Disneyland and hit the park's highlights, plus any attractions you missed on the first day, and save time for souvenir shopping. Day four should be dedicated to your preferred park and some downtime by the pool or in Downtown Disney's shopping plaza. Evenings can be spent in the park, if it's open late, or in Downtown Disney's clubs, lounges, and movie theaters. The options are plentiful.

On the next four pages, we've provided full-day schedules to guide you through four days in the theme parks (with special tips for families with young children and priorities for days when the lines are at their longest). The schedules are meant to be flexible and fun (not Disney boot camp), so take them at your own pace and plan breaks to relax: have a Mickey Mouse Ice Cream Bar, browse through the shops, feed the ducks, or just pick a bench and watch the crowds rush by.

Trip Planning Time Line

First Things First

- Make hotel and transportation reservations as far ahead as possible. Call 714-956-6425 to book a room at a Disney hotel (see page 42 for details); remember that a deposit must be paid within 21 days of the reservation. Log all confirmation numbers in the Trip Planner at the beginning of this book.

- Decide where you will be on each day of your vacation, and create a simple day-by-day schedule.

6 Months

- Unless you opted for a vacation package that includes theme park admission, it's time to purchase Disney park tickets (see page 17 for ticket options and ordering methods). Your tickets should arrive in about a week.

3 Months

- Find out park hours, the attraction refurbishment schedule, and details on any special events by calling 714-781-4565 or by visiting *www.disneyland.com*; add this information to your day-by-day schedule.

1 Month

- Make dining reservations (they're only necessary at certain Disney restaurants), and add the information to your day-by-day schedule. Refer to the *Good Meals, Great Times* chapter for details on Disneyland Resort and Orange County dining options.

2 Weeks

- Airline tickets and travel vouchers should have arrived in the mail by now. Contact your travel agent or the travel company if they haven't come yet.

1 Week

- Reconfirm all reservations and finalize your day-by-day schedule.

- Add all your important telephone numbers (doctor, family members, house sitter) to the Trip Planner, and be sure to bring the Trip Planner and your day-by-day schedule with you!

1 Day

- Be sure to bring any park tickets you may have purchased, as well as photo ID.

Disneyland Park One-Day Schedule

*Also known as the Magic Kingdom

• Disneyland's breakfast options are limited, so grab a bite to eat before entering the park.
• Take in the sights as you walk down Main Street, but don't stop to shop or snack now (you'll have time for that later). Instead, head straight to Adventureland's Indiana Jones†, Jungle Cruise, Tarzan's Treehouse, and Enchanted Tiki Room before making your way to Splash Mountain† and The Many Adventures of Winnie the Pooh†, in Critter Country. (If you plan to dine at the Blue Bayou, be sure to make a reservation in advance by calling 714-781-3463.)
• Backtrack to New Orleans Square and visit the Haunted Mansion† and Pirates of the Caribbean† before breaking for an early lunch.
• Next, see the show at the Golden Horseshoe, take a relaxing river cruise on the Mark Twain or raft over to Tom Sawyer Island before tackling Big Thunder Mountain† in Frontierland.
• Walk through the Castle into Fantasyland and visit Snow White, Pinocchio, Peter Pan, and Mr. Toad. Then see Alice, the Mad Tea Party, the Matterhorn, and It's a Small World.

IF YOU HAVE YOUNG CHILDREN

First, enjoy The Many Adventures of Winnie the Pooh. Then head to Fantasyland and visit each area attraction (note that some are scary for small children) before heading to Mickey's Toontown.

Scope out a spot on a Main Street curb at least 30 minutes before the parade.

Take tykes for a ride on the Disneyland Railroad and a drive at Autopia. If you need cooling off, backtrack to Toontown and splash at Donald's Boat.

Ride the Jungle Cruise, then see the Tiki Birds in Adventureland and Tarzan's Treehouse before returning to your favorite rides.

LINE BUSTERS

When the park is packed, head to the Disneyland Railroad, Enchanted Tiki Room, Pirates of the Caribbean, Haunted Mansion, and Great Moments with Mr. Lincoln.

†Fastpass is available for this ride. Retrieve your time-saving Fastpass before visiting the land's remaining attractions. To learn how the system works, see page 64.

Continued on page 30

GETTING READY TO GO

Hot Tip!

If you enter the park via monorail, you'll begin your tour in Tomorrowland. Hit the land's major attractions if you wish, and then ride the railroad to Main Street and follow this schedule from there.

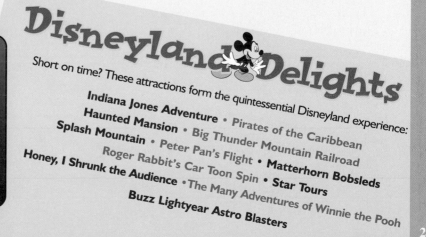

Disneyland Delights

Short on time? These attractions form the quintessential Disneyland experience:

Indiana Jones Adventure • Pirates of the Caribbean
Haunted Mansion • Big Thunder Mountain Railroad
Splash Mountain • Peter Pan's Flight • Matterhorn Bobsleds
Roger Rabbit's Car Toon Spin • Star Tours
Honey, I Shrunk the Audience • The Many Adventures of Winnie the Pooh
Buzz Lightyear Astro Blasters

Disneyland Park One-Day Schedule

• Keep an eye on the time and try to fit the afternoon parade into your schedule.

• Make your way to Mickey's Toontown and see as many of this land's attractions as you can, making Roger Rabbit's Car Toon Spin† a priority.

• Hop on the Disneyland Railroad and disembark in Tomorrowland. Visit Buzz Lightyear Astro Blasters and Space Mountain (if it's open) before heading for dinner.

Note: If the park is open late, board the monorail in Tomorrowland and dine in Downtown Disney before returning to the park.

• After dinner, catch a screening of Honey, I Shrunk the Audience before riding Autopia†, Star Tours†, or Astro Orbitor.

• Take little ones to Mickey's Toontown before it closes for the day—it closes earlier than the rest of the park when there is a fireworks presentation.

• On nights when Fantasmic! is presented, make a point of getting to Frontierland in plenty of time to see it. (Check park guidemap for the schedule, or inquire at City Hall.) If there is more than one performance scheduled, the later one is usually less crowded.

• Stroll back to Main Street. Shop, stop for dessert, see the Walt Disney Story, and watch the fireworks burst over the castle.

• If there's time, take a second spin on your favorite attractions.

MEET THE CHARACTERS!

There are lots of places to mix and mingle with Disney characters in this park. Some of the best spots include Toontown (Mickey, Minnie, Donald, Goofy, and more), Critter Country (Pooh and pals), and near Sleeping Beauty Castle (Disney princesses). Check a park map for specific times and locations. And don't forget the camera!

†Fastpass is available for this ride. Retrieve your Fastpass before visiting the land's remaining attractions.

Top Shops

Whether you're browsing or buying, Disneyland is a shopper's paradise. Here are a few of the spots where wallets get a workout:

Candy Palace Emporium • Main Street Magic Shop
Market House • Heraldry Shop
Jewel of New Orleans • Pieces of Eight
Pioneer Mercantile • The Star Trader
South Seas Traders • Villains Lair

Hot Tip!

If you'd like to meet Mickey Mouse, make a beeline for his Toontown house—the big cheese greets guests in the movie barn out back. For the shortest wait, get there as soon as Toontown opens. And don't forget your camera!

GETTING READY TO GO

Disney's California Adventure One-Day Schedule

- Begin your California adventure by snagging a Fastpass for The Twilight Zone Tower of Terror†. Check a park times guide to see when Aladdin—A Musical Spectacular is playing. Then enjoy a high-flying ride on Soarin' Over California†. Catch your breath and continue the lesson in aviation by navigating your way through the airfield's exhibits on history-making pilots and planes.
- Depart from Condor Flats and head into the Hollywood Pictures Backlot, via the Gateway Plaza. Refer to a park guidemap for the Hyperion Theater's† next showtime, and plan to arrive at the theater at least 30 minutes before the show. In the meantime, enjoy the in-your-face fun of Muppet*Vision 3-D† and Disney Animation. Take toddlers to the show at Playhouse Disney.
- Head to A Bug's Land and don your insect eyes for a creepy-crawly screening of It's Tough to be a Bug!†
- Now it's time for a little mountain climbing: Make your way over to Grizzly Peak, and get set to get wet on the drenching Grizzly River Run† white-water raft ride. If you're up for it (and properly shoed), next take the Redwood Creek Challenge Trail before viewing Golden Dreams.
- Keep an eye on the time and find a curbside spot in the San Francisco district about 20 minutes before the parade starts.
- Pick up some wine-pairing tips or sample California's finest at the Wine Country Trattoria, and settle in for an early dinner.
- Tour the micro-factories of the Pacific Wharf before proceeding on to Paradise Pier's daredevil rides.
- Work your way around the Paradise Pier Lagoon, stopping for each attraction, but making sure California Screamin'† and the Sun Wheel† are top priorities.
- Stroll along the boardwalk and try some Midway games, or enjoy a sweet treat. If there's a parade scheduled, be sure and catch it.

IF YOU HAVE YOUNG CHILDREN

Compared to its sister park next door, California Adventure has considerably fewer attractions geared toward the 5-and-under set.

Head straight to the Muppets. Next, pay a visit to Playhouse Disney. Then maneuver young water lovers through the sprinkler maze and gardens of A Bug's Land. Note that It's Tough to be a Bug! features a few familiar characters from the film *A Bug's Life*, but often frightens young children.

Try the kid-friendly obstacle course on the Redwood Creek Challenge Trail (save time for some campside storytelling).

Take a spin on the carrousel and visit the SS *Rustworthy*, a water-spouting boat and play area before spending some time at the Paradise Pier Midway.

LINE BUSTERS

When lines abound at Disney's California Adventure, we suggest the following: the Golden State's micro-factories, Bountiful Valley Farm, Redwood Creek Challenge Trail, King Triton's Carousel, the SS *Rustworthy*, and Paradise Pier's Midway.

†Fastpass is available for this ride. Retrieve your Fastpass before visiting the land's remaining attractions.

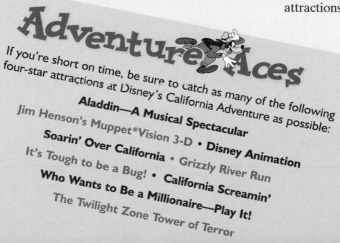

Adventure Aces

If you're short on time, be sure to catch as many of the following four-star attractions at Disney's California Adventure as possible:

Aladdin—A Musical Spectacular
Jim Henson's Muppet*Vision 3-D • Disney Animation
Soarin' Over California • Grizzly River Run
It's Tough to be a Bug! • California Screamin'
Who Wants to Be a Millionaire—Play It!
The Twilight Zone Tower of Terror

A Second Day in Disneyland Park

Returning for a second or third day in each of the theme parks means more time to savor the atmosphere, try any attractions you missed the first day, and revisit all the old and new favorites. Knowing that there will be a second day also makes for a much less harried pace on day one. Longer stays also allow time for full-day excursions to attractions like Universal Studios or Knott's Berry Farm (see *Orange County & Beyond* for day-trip options).

• Start the morning with a character breakfast at the Plaza Inn (you can also share a morning meal with the characters outside the park at Goofy's Kitchen in the Disneyland Hotel, the Grand Californian's Storyteller's Cafe, or PCH Grill in Disney's Paradise Pier Hotel).

• Head to Tomorrowland and ride Space Mountain (if it is operating), Star Tours, Buzz Lightyear Astro Blasters and other favorite attractions.

• Hop on the train to Mickey's Toontown. See the sights and spend some time mingling with resident Disney characters.

• Visit It's a Small World and the nearby character greeting area, and then tour Fantasyland.

• Stroll, shop, and stop for lunch in Main Street, U.S.A.

• Watch the afternoon parade from the Main Street Railroad depot, or secure a curbside spot.

• Ride a Main Street Vehicle up to Town Square and then continue on foot toward Adventureland.

• Stop at Indiana Jones and the Jungle Cruise before heading on to New Orleans Square. Here the priorities are the Haunted Mansion and Pirates of the Caribbean. Visit them and move on to Splash Mountain, in Critter Country.

• Meander through the shops of New Orleans Square and then stop for a leisurely dinner at a nearby eatery. Riverbelle Terrace, the French Market, Cafe Orleans, and the full-service Blue Bayou are all excellent options.

• Select a spot lagoonside about 45 minutes ahead for the evening's performance of Fantasmic! (if it is scheduled).

• Wait for the crowds to disperse at show's end, and make your way to Big Thunder Mountain for one last ride before the park closes.

A Second Day in Disney's California Adventure

• Grab a quick breakfast before arriving at the park, so that your stomach will have time to settle before the big rides.

• Cut through the Golden State and head straight for Twilight Zone Tower of Terror. Then move over to Paradise Pier.

• Thrill seekers will flip for California Screamin' and the Sun Wheel, while King Triton's Carousel and Jumpin' Jellyfish offer less dizzying alternatives.

• Take a lunch break at Burger Invasion or Pacific Wharf Cafe; or, if the park is open late, head back to your hotel to relax or splash in the pool (remember to get your hand stamped before exiting, so that you can return to California Adventure later in the day). Another option is to spend the afternoon in Downtown Disney—the restaurants and shops will all be open by noon.

• Your California Adventure picks up again with a tour of the Golden State, including Golden Dreams, It's Tough to be a Bug!, Grizzly River Run, and Soarin' Over California.

• Stop for the parade if you haven't seen it already, and then make your way toward Hollywood Pictures Backlot.

• Wander through the Backlot, enjoying the impromptu entertainment, and catch the next showing of Muppet*Vision 3-D. Consider taking Aladdin fans to see his musical spectacular a second time.

• Line up at least 30 minutes early for the evening's performance at the Hyperion Theater.

• If time permits after the show, revisit some of your favorite attractions or search for last-minute souvenirs at the large shops in the park's Entry Plaza.

Fingertip Reference Guide

BARBERS AND SALONS

Hair may be cut or coiffed at the Coral Tree, in the Anaheim Marriott (700 W. Convention Way; 714-750-6573). Besides haircutting and styling, the salon offers manicures and pedicures, and welcomes both men and women.

CAR CARE

AAA and the Automobile Club of Southern California (ACSC) offer the following services free to all Disneyland Resort guests (not just to Auto Club members): assistance with stalled cars and flat tires, and towing up to three miles. Jump starts and lock-out services are provided by Disneyland. For assistance, contact any cast member. The Anaheim office of the ACSC is located at 420 Euclid Avenue; 714-774-2392. For ACSC emergency roadside service, call 800-400-4222.

There is a Touring & Travel Services Center (operated by ACSC) located inside Disneyland Park. Adjacent to City Hall on Main Street, U.S.A., the center provides a variety of services to park guests.

DRINKING POLICIES

While there's a strict no-alcohol policy at Disneyland Park, drinking is an option at many of the dining spots in its sister park, Disney's California Adventure, as well as at Downtown Disney. Alcohol may also be purchased at the lounges and restaurants of the three Disney hotels. The legal drinking age in California is 21.

LOCKERS

Lockers of various sizes are available just outside the main entrance of the parks; inside Disneyland on Main Street (behind the Market House) and inside Disney's California Adventure (D.C.A.) across from Guest Relations. Prices are $4, $5, or $6 per day, depending on the locker's size. These storage facilities make it convenient to intersperse frolicking on the attractions with shopping; just make your purchases, stash them in a locker. Availability is limited, and during busy periods all

Hot Tip!

To avoid the sometimes maddening congestion at the Main Street locker location, consider stowing your stuff at the lockers near the picnic area, just outside Disneyland Park's turnstiles.

the space can be taken well before noon. Disney's California Adventure guests may stash items in lockers for free while they ride Grizzly River Run. They are off to the side of the attraction's entrance.

LOST AND FOUND

At any given time, a survey of the shelves of Lost and Found might turn up cameras, umbrellas, strollers, handbags, lens caps, sunglasses, radios, jewelry, and even a few crutches, false teeth, and hubcaps. Once, a wallet containing $1,700 in cash was turned in. The Disneyland Resort will return lost items to guests who fill out a report, at no cost.

If you find a lost item, you'll be asked to fill out a card with your name and address; if the object isn't claimed within 60 days, you have the option of keeping it. This system encourages honesty, so if you lose something, check at the Lost and Found office. You'll find it outside the turnstiles (on the left) at Disney's California Adventure main gate. If you lose something at a resort, contact the front desk.

MAIL

Postcards are sold in gift shops all over Anaheim, in many shops and souvenir stands on Disney property, and at the three Disney hotels. Stamps are sold in both theme parks and at all three Disney hotels.

Cards and letters that are deposited in the small mailboxes positioned throughout the theme parks are picked up and delivered to the U.S. Post Office once a day, early in the morning. All items are postmarked Anaheim, not Disneyland. (By the way, don't forget to arrange for your own mail to be held by the post office or picked up by a neighbor while you're on vacation.)

Due to the heavy volume, expect delivery to take a bit longer than usual. (There's a lot to write home about in these parts!)

Post Office: The U.S. Post Office closest to the Disneyland Resort is Holiday Station, about a half mile from the parks (1180 W. Ball Rd.; Anaheim; 714-533-8182). It's open from 8:30 A.M. to 5 P.M. weekdays only.

MEDICAL MATTERS

Blisters are the most common complaint received by Disney's First Aid departments, located at the north end of Main Street adjacent to Lost Children in Disneyland, and by Mission Tortilla Factory in the Pacific Wharf area of Disney's California Adventure. So be forewarned and wear comfortable, broken-in shoes (bring a back-up pair, too)—and pack Band-Aids, just in case.

If you have a serious medical problem while on-property, contact any Disney cast member. He or she will get in touch with First Aid to make further arrangements. First Aid, staffed by registered nurses, will store breathing machines and crutches for guests. It will not dispense medication to anyone under 18 without the consent of a parent or chaperone.

It's a good idea to carry an insurance card and any other pertinent medical information. Those with chronic health problems should carry copies of all their prescriptions, along with their doctor's telephone number.

Prescriptions: The pharmacy at Sav-on Drugs, about a mile from Disney, is open 9 A.M. to 7 P.M. Monday through Saturday, and Sundays 9 A.M. to 6 P.M. (1660 W. Katella Ave., at Euclid; Anaheim; 714-530-0500). Another Sav-on, three miles away, is open 24 hours daily (12031 Brookhurst St., at Chapman, Garden Grove; 714-530-5280).

Refrigerator Facilities: In the parks, insulin and antibiotics that must be refrigerated can be stored for the day at First Aid. (It does not store breast milk for nursing mothers, however.) Outside the parks, there are refrigerators in many of the area's hotels and motels. If your room doesn't have one, a fridge can usually be supplied at a nominal charge. Or the hotel or motel can store insulin in its own refrigerator. Inquire in advance.

MONEY

Cash, traveler's checks, personal checks, Disney Dollars, American Express, Visa, MasterCard, the Disney Credit Card, and the Discover Card are accepted as payment for admission to the theme parks, for merchandise purchased in shops, and for meals (except at souvenir and food carts, where it's strictly cash only). Checks must be imprinted with the guest's name and address, drawn on a U.S. bank, and accompanied by proper ID—that is, a valid driver's license and a major credit card. Department store charge cards are not acceptable identification for check-writing purposes. Disney hotel guests who have left a credit card number at check-in can charge most expenses in the parks to their hotel bill.

Disney Dollars: Accepted as cash throughout the parks, Disney Dollars are the equivalent in value of U.S. dollars. They are sold at the main entrances of the parks, as well as at City Hall in Disneyland, at select shops on-property, and at most Disney Stores nationwide. Kids love to use them; they also make good inexpensive gifts and souvenirs, and may be accepted as cash at Disney Store locations

Financial Services: ATMs are located at each park's main entrance; in Disneyland at the Bank of Main Street, by the Fantasyland Theatre, in the Frontierland Stockade, and in the Starcade; in California Adventure at the Entry Plaza, by the Bay Area near Golden Dreams, beside Cocina Cucamonga, near Burger Invasion, and by Malibu-Ritos; in Downtown Disney by Häagen-Dazs; and in all three Disneyland Resort hotels.

It's possible to cash a personal check made out to Disneyland for up to $100 at the main entrance to each park and at the Bank of Main Street or City Hall; proper identification is required. The ATMs at the main entrance accept credit cards for cash advances.

AAA Services: The Touring & Travel Services Center, beside City Hall on Main Street, U.S.A., in Disneyland, provides many services to guests, including the sales of AAA memberships and traveler's checks, and help with booking rooms at Disneyland Resort hotels or Good Neighbor hotels (about thirty area hotels with which the Walt Disney Travel Company works closely).

American Express Cardmember Services: American Express cardholders can cash personal checks up to $1,000 per week ($200 in cash and the rest in traveler's checks) with a personal American Express card, or up to $2,500 per week ($500 in cash and the rest in traveler's checks) with a Gold Card. They can also get a cash advance of $500 on their Optima Card (with a valid PIN number). All services are offered at the American Express Travel Agency, located at 763 S. Main St., Suite 190, Orange; 714-541-3318.

This office can also exchange foreign currency (for a $5 fee, regardless of the amount) and replce lost cards or traveler's checks within 24 hours (for cards, 800-528-4800; for checks, 800-221-7282). Hours are usually 9 A.M. to 6 P.M. Monday through Friday and 9 A.M. to 4 P.M. Saturday.

Many banks in the Anaheim area also sell American Express traveler's checks, usually for a 1 percent fee.

Other Major Credit Cards and Traveler's Checks: Cash advances on Visa credit cards can be arranged through the Western Union office, open from 8 A.M. to 8 P.M. Monday through Saturday (616 N. Anaheim Blvd.; Anaheim; 714-991-3300). To report lost Visa or MasterCard credit cards, guests in the Anaheim area should call 800-556-5678.

Most foreign currencies can be exchanged (for a fee) at the Travelex office in Downtown Disney; 714-502-0811.

PETS

Except for service animals, pets are not allowed in Disneyland or Disney's California Adventure. However, any nonpoisonous creatures can be boarded in the air-conditioned Disneyland Pet Care Kennel, which is located by the entrance to the Disneyland park. Reservations are not necessary (the kennel rarely reaches capacity). Pets may be boarded for the day or for overnight stays. At press time, it cost $10 per day, per pet. To inquire about kennel rates during your visit, call 714-781-7290.

Disney personnel do not handle the animals, so the pet owners themselves must put their animals into the cages and take them out again. Guests are encouraged to drop by to visit with and walk their pets several times a day. Kennel attendants are not responsible for walking any animals in their care.

Note: During busy seasons there may be a morning rush, starting about 30 minutes before the parks open, so you may encounter some delay in arranging your pet's stay.

Outside the Disneyland Resort: If you plan to stay at a Disneyland Resort hotel and want to board your pet nearby, contact Animal Inns of America, 10852 Garden Grove Blvd.; Garden Grove; 714-636-4455; *www.thepetproject.com/animalinns*.

Some hotels and motels in the Disneyland area accept well-behaved (preferably small) pets, but most do not allow guests to leave their pets in the room unattended. The pet-friendly Anaheim Marriott (714-750-8000), within walking distance of the Disneyland Resort, is an exception.

To find out about other possibilities for pets, contact the Anaheim/Orange County Visitor & Convention Bureau; 714-765-8888.

PHOTOGRAPHIC NEEDS

The Main Street Photo Supply Co. inside Disneyland can answer questions and recharge most batteries (or you can bring your own charger and plug it in there). Disney's California Adventure offers similar services. For anything more serious, rent a camera and have a factory-authorized shop do the work on your camera when you return home. If you've lost your lens cover, it's worth checking at Lost and Found (see page 33); they may not have your cap, but they often have extras. Chances are one will fit your camera.

Same-day film processing is available through Spectrum Photo Film Processing at select shops on Disney property. Allow at least three hours before picking up the prints.

For a bigger selection of film and camera equipment, go to Main Photo, 6916 Katella Ave.; 714-894-2526.

Try not to take your camera on rough or bumpy rides. Stash it in a locker or with a non-riding member of your party.

RELIGIOUS SERVICES

A number of religious services are held in the area surrounding the Disneyland Resort.

Catholic: St. Justin Martyr; 2050 W. Ball Rd.; 714-774-2595; about two miles from the Disneyland Resort. Weekday masses are held at 6:30 A.M. and 8:30 A.M.; Saturday at 8:30 A.M. and 5:30 P.M. (English) and 7 P.M. (Spanish); and Sunday at 6:45 A.M., 8 A.M., 11 A.M., 12:30 P.M. and 5:30 P.M. (English) and 9:30 A.M. and 7 P.M. (Spanish). Holy day masses are at 6:30 A.M., 8:30 A.M., and 7 P.M.; holy day eve, 5:30 P.M. (English) and 7 P.M. (Spanish).

Episcopal: St. Michael's Episcopal Church; 311 W. South St.; 714-535-4654; about seven blocks from the Disneyland Resort. Sunday services are at 8 A.M. and 10:15 A.M. (English) and at 8:15 A.M. and 12:30 P.M. (Spanish). Bible study is at 8:30 A.M.; Sunday school, at 10 A.M.

Jewish: Temple Beth Emet; 1770 W. Cerritos Ave.; 714-772-4720; less than a mile from the Disneyland Resort. Services are held on Fridays at 6:30 P.M., and the last Friday of each month at 8 P.M., and 9 A.M. Saturdays.

Lutheran: Prince of Peace Church; 1421 W. Ball Rd.; 714-774-0993; about one mile from the Disneyland Resort. Sunday services are at 8 A.M. and 10:45 A.M. (traditional) and 9:15 A.M. (contemporary).

Non-denominational: The Kindred Community Church; 8712 E. Santa Ana Canyon Rd.; 714-282-9941. Services are held on Sunday at 8:45 A.M.

United Methodist: West Anaheim United Methodist Church; 2045 W. Ball Rd.; 714-772-6030; approximately two miles from Disneyland. Sunday services are at 10:30 A.M.

SHOPPING FOR NECESSITIES

It's a rare vacationer who doesn't leave some essential at home or run out of it midtrip. Gift shops in almost all the hotels stock items no traveler should be without, but they usually cost more than in conventional retail shops. One good source is Sav-on Drugs, about a mile from the Disneyland Resort; 1660 W. Katella Ave.; 714-530-0500.

Inside the theme parks, aspirin, bandages, antacids, suntan lotions, and other sundries are sold at a variety of shops; just ask a cast member to direct you to the closest one. Some items are also available at each park's First Aid location and Baby Care Center. A shop at each Disneyland Resort hotel also offers a wide selection of sundries.

SMOKING POLICIES

State law bans smoking anywhere inside restaurants, bars, and cocktail lounges, but most establishments provide patios for puffing and often heat them on chilly evenings. At the Disney theme parks, smoking is permitted in designated smoking areas. Check a park guidemap for exact locations.

TELEPHONES

Local calls from most pay phones in Southern California cost 35 cents. Most hotels in the same area charge an average of 75 cents or more for local, toll-free, and credit-card calls made from your room. So try to use a public pay phone whenever possible (it's worth making a trip to the lobby to do so).

If you plan to tap into the Internet via personal computer, be sure bring local access numbers with you.

For long-distance calls, policies vary from hotel to hotel, but charges are always higher than they would be for direct-dial calls made from a pay phone. It makes the most sense to use a calling card when dialing long distance.

Phone Cards: Disney offers AT&T prepaid phone cards in values of $10 and $20. They can be purchased from machines in Disneyland and Disney's California Adventure, and at the Disneyland and Grand Californian hotels.

Weather Hotlines: Storm clouds have you worried? For Orange County weather, call 714-550-4636. The National Weather Service, which has an office in Los Angeles, can provide current Southern California forecasts; *www.nws.noaa.gov*.

Wireless Phones: To ensure a dose of uninterrupted magic for you and those around you, turn the power off your cell phone, or switch it to vibrate mode. You'll be glad you did.

TIPPING

The standard gratuities around Anaheim are about the same as in any other city of its size. Expect to tip bellhops about $1 per bag. Generally tip cabdrivers 15 percent; outstanding shuttle or tour bus drivers, $1. Valets usually get $1—when you pick up the car, not when you drop it off. In restaurants, a 15 to 20 percent gratuity is the norm. If you are pleased with the condition of your hotel room, it is customary to leave a gratuity of $1–$2 per day for the housekeeper (leave a note with the tip to avoid confusion). Note that room-service bills often include a gratuity.

Disneyland's Happiest Celebration on Earth

In the early 1950s, Walt Disney imagined a place where kids and grown-ups could have fun together. After an extensive search, he settled on a place where he'd make the dream a reality. And on July 17, 1955, a 160-acre site in Anaheim, California, was officially dedicated as Disneyland. And with that, a revolutionary new form of family entertainment was born. It was an instant success, drawing more than a million guests within its opening months. In the five decades since, more than 400 million guests have passed through the turnstiles of "the happiest place on Earth."

This year, Disneyland is marking its fiftieth anniversary in grand style, with an 18-month-long party being kicked off on May 5. In keeping with Walt's belief that the park should always be growing and changing, attractions, including some created specifically for the Happiest Celebration on Earth, will be opening throughout 2005. Some old favorites will be spruced up for the occasion, too — not the least of which is Space Mountain, which will be making its triumphant return in July. All in all, it promises to be a unique and exciting celebration (as all golden anniversaries should be). For more information on specific attractions and activities planned for the big bash, turn to page 38.

Celebrate Disneyland's

DISNEYLAND—THE FIRST 50 YEARS

Take a stroll down magical memory lane at this specially designed exhibit devoted to Disneyland history. The multi-media tribute to the happiest place on earth is housed in the Main Street Opera House. Here you'll find a stirring film featuring newly discovered archival footage that has not been seen in half a century. It covers major events in the park's history and shows how Disneyland has evolved over the years. Authentic attraction models and concept artwork are also on display, shedding light on the park's innovative design and construction. There's even artwork depicting rides and attractions that were never actually built–giving guests a chance to envision a Disneyland that might have been.

WALT DISNEY'S PARADE OF DREAMS

What celebration would be complete without a parade? Certainly not the "Happiest Celebration on Earth." May 5, 2005 marks the premiere of Walt Disney's Parade of Dreams, an all-new processional that includes a diverse array of floats and other happy hoopla.

Each colorful float serves as a kind of mini-stage, with puppeteers, dancers, and other entertainers. Highlights include Tinker Bell's Gateway to Dreams float, where Tinker Bell, Cinderella's Fairy Godmother, and Merlin the Wizard douse the crowd in pixie dust. Other floats include characters from *The Lion King*, *The Little Mermaid*, *Beauty and the Beast*, and other Disney films. The parade culminates with a special "Dreams Come True" float, featuring Snow White and the other Disney Princesses, not to mention Mickey and Minnie Mouse. For more information, see page 95.

SLEEPING BEAUTY CASTLE

Perhaps nothing (besides the Mouse himself, of course) defines Disneyland to people like the storybook castle at the far end of Main Street. The revered landmark first lowered its drawbridge the day the park opened in 1955, and has since become one of the most-photographed and best-remembered sights in the entire park.

In 2005, the Disneyland icon will don its finery in an edifice's equivalent to "black tie." This is, after all, a party! The castle's glitzy new look will include five regal turret "crowns" which sit atop its towers: one for each decade the park has been open. Other touches include richly colored royal banners and glimmering gem stones. A high powered projection system will create different "looks" for the castle at night, by changing its color, or even by adding animated characters (like our four-footed friends from *101 Dalmatians*) to the castle walls. So get your camera ready. . . the castle is ready for its close-up!

Golden Anniversary

BUZZ LIGHTYEAR ASTRO BLASTERS

In keeping with Walt Disney's declaration that "Disneyland will never be completed," the park is set to unveil a high-flying new attraction amid this year's anniversary festivities. Buzz Lightyear Astro Blasters is a 4-minute, interactive spin through outer space, in a universe populated entirely with toys. After a quick orientation from Buzz himself, players assume their roles as Junior Rangers. The mission? To battle the forces of the evil Emperor Zurg (with a special laser cannon and a rider-controlled "spacecraft"—and to rack up points for yourself along the way. The more points you tally, the closer you'll be to earning the title of Galactic Hero. For more information on this stellar attraction, turn to page 41.

REMEMBER . . . DREAMS COME TRUE

Not unlike its predecessor, Believe: There's Magic in the Stars, this new fireworks extravaganza is as colorful and explosive as can be. The action starts with a dramatic flight by Tinker Bell and soon more than 200 pyrotechnic shells light up the night sky.

This is the most elaborate fireworks display ever put on at Disneyland, with special lighting effects on hand to augment the performance. The colorful exhibition is accompanied by a rousing, synchronized musical score. For more information, turn to page 96.

SPACE MOUNTAIN

For some people, the fiftieth-anniversary celebration is only the second-most exciting thing to hit Disneyland in 2005. That's because after enduring two years of a Space Mountain–free Disneyland, the wait is finally over. This year marks the "relaunch" of what is easily one of the most popular attractions in theme park history.

The ride's concept originated with Walt himself in the early 1960s and finally came to fruition in 1977. It immediately rocketed to the top of Disneyland thrill seekers must-do list. Since its doors were shuttered in 2003, Space Mountain has undergone a splendid transformation, having been renovated and updated for the 21st century.

While the Disney Imagineers kept the classic Space Mountain facade intact (it's white again!), the ride now boasts new elements, including a high-tech launch port that appears to orbit the Earth. After boarding all-new "spaceships," riders are whipped through a tunnel, narrowly missing a stray meteor and other "hazards" along the way. The action includes a whirlwind tour of the cosmos, passing by brilliant stars and galaxies. Each car is equipped with a synchronized instrumental sound track, which dramatically accentuates every twist and turn. In the evening, a psychedelic light show adds to the experience. For more on the new Space Mountain, turn to page 86.

BLOCK PARTY BASH

The anniversary fun isn't confined to Disneyland itself. The park's next-door neighbor, Disney's California Adventure, is marking the occasion by presenting the Block Party Bash. Billed as a spontaneous street party, it's a series of random shindigs which are sprung upon park-goers without warning. (So if, out of the blue, you find yourself in the middle of a rollicking crowd of people, don't say we didn't warn you.)

There are actually five different bashes erupting around park-goers. Each one has its own atmosphere, theme, and style of music (for example, Lilo's Luau is "crashed" by an enthusiastic Elvis Presley impersonator). The impromptu parties feature Disney characters such as Lilo and Stitch, Flik and Atta, Mickey Mouse, and other furry favorites.

MAGICAL MEMORIES

By Alexandra Mayes Birnbaum

No need for 20/20 hindsight: July 17, 1955 is crystal clear. Dressed as an almost fourteen-year-old of the '50s from New York City in a full-skirted, cinch-waist dress, Capezio flats on my feet, and my hair tied up in what I smugly recall was a perfect ponytail, I was standing at the gates of the about-to-be opened Disneyland.

Yikes! 50 years ago. Eisenhower was in the White House; the Cold War was icy, there were two Berlins, the first McDonalds had recently opened, the Dodgers were still firmly in Brooklyn, there were still only 48 states, baby boomers were in nursery school, Mickey Mouse was in his twenties, and Orlando was still a steamy Central Florida swamp.

Now, I confess to being a devout Disneyphile almost from birth. Walt himself was a family acquaintance; my first toy was a plush velvet Pluto; *Pinocchio* was the first movie I ever saw; and *Wonderful World of Disney* was my idea of not-to-be-missed TV. Though none of the foregoing passion for things Disney entitled me to be front and center in Anaheim on that long ago summer's day, somehow an invitation to attend the very opening of this new "land" entitled my parents, sister, and me to be among the first folks to enter the gates of the Magic Kingdom and stroll down Main Street.

My first glimpse of Sleeping Beauty Castle conjured up pure romance—hey, we all believed in Prince Charming back then—and I was dazzled by that first ride on Peter Pan's flight over Never Land. I was genuinely shook up as I spun around in the Mad Hatter's teacups as my staid 1950s parents watched from the sidelines, and I screeched with delight on Toad's wild ride. Tomorrowland's Space Station X-1, with its scenic panning of earth, was about as far into the future as anything I'd ever seen, to say nothing of the cinematic swoop of Circarama-360. I remember feigning teenage indifference aboard the Mark Twain Riverboat, then losing my cool completely and demanding an autograph from Mickey himself—much to the embarrasment of my older sisiter.

To be sure, the original "Land" now encompasses Disneyland Park and Disney's California Adventure and new attractions continue to open, but today's Disneyland still possesses the unique charm, intimacy, and hospitality defined in the 1950s. So grab a spot to watch the brand new Parade of Dreams, take a ride on Buzz Lightyear's just-opened Astro Blasters and the re-opened Space Mountain, and head to Sleeping Beauty Castle for a glorious celebration of 50 fabulous years! Okay, that long ago teenager now confesses to being a "Senior," but she still finds this one of the "Happiest Places on Earth."

"I only hope that we never lose sight of one thing—that it was all started by a mouse."
—Walt Disney

Accommodations

ACCOMMODATIONS

The welcome sign is always out at the Disneyland Resort hotels, where themed meals, amenities, and decor are definitely in character and add to the fun of a Disneyland vacation. And the resort's newest hotel, the Grand Californian, takes staying at Disneyland to a new level of luxury.

In addition to the three hotels within the Disneyland Resort, there are about three dozen properties in Orange County, known as Disneyland Good Neighbor hotels, that the Walt Disney Travel Company has handpicked to round out their Disney lodging options. We've selected a bunch of these recommended hotels, based on services and proximity to Disneyland, to highlight in this chapter.

If the sole purpose of your trip is to visit Disney, plan to stay in Anaheim, either on Disneyland property or at one of the surrounding hotels. Once you arrive and check in, you won't need your car again until you leave. Free transportation to and from the parks is provided by monorails and trams serving the Disneyland Resort, and by buses serving neighboring hotels, motels, and inns. If struck with a bit of wanderlust, know that Anaheim is within range of a host of Southern California destinations, including movie studios, museums, beaches, and more.

We've provided a variety of options in Anaheim, from old-fashioned to contemporary, simple to sublime. We've also included a selection of Orange County's seaside escapes and charming bed-and-breakfast inns, for those interested in venturing beyond the Disney region.

Disneyland Resort Hotels

With the addition of Disney's Grand Californian to the hotel scene, fans of the Disneyland Resort are faced with a difficult decision. It isn't whether or not to stay on-property (that's recommended if it's within the budget), but which of the three hotels to choose. Some factors to consider:

The whimsical pool area, arcade, musical fountain show, and popular character meals continue to make the Disneyland Hotel, the first hotel built on Disneyland property, appeal to the kids in the family (and the kid in us all).

Meanwhile, Disney's Paradise Pier Hotel boasts a sunny facade to complement Disney's California Adventure. The splashy look is a warm welcome to all guests. Inside, the Disney decor is still subtle, and the dining options are divine.

But the Disney design team has outdone itself with the Grand Californian. Located inside Disney's California Adventure, this hotel's theming and style touch every detail, right down to the floorboards.

Whichever hotel you choose for your visit, one thing is certain—a stay on-property is sure to complete the overall Disney experience. From a resort information TV channel to wake-up calls from Mickey Mouse himself, every detail reminds you that you're in Disney's land.

Exclusive benefits: Several perks are reserved exclusively for those guests staying on-property. Perhaps the most significant of these is preferred admission (with a ticket) to a theme park if it reaches capacity, while others, even if they have a ticket, will be asked to return later.

One of the most convenient perks is the ability to charge almost any expense incurred at a Disney theme park back to the hotel room, if a credit card imprint was taken at check-in. Purchases can be charged to the room from the time of check-in until 11 A.M. on the day of departure. (**Note:** This does not apply to most Downtown Disney purchases.)

Shoppers may also enjoy the benefit of having purchases delivered directly to their hotel's Bell Desk, where they can pick up their packages at the end of the day—rather than having to carry them through the parks all day. Note that this service may not be available during your stay.

Other on-property Disneyland perks include complimentary transportation to Disneyland and Disney's California Adventure (the former is via the ever-popular monorail system, at the Downtown Disney Station), not to mention continuous in-lobby screenings of Disney's animated classics, and wake-up calls from Mickey. Courtesy pick-up is available for guests with disabilities to and from Paradise Pier in Disney's California Adventure park.

Hot Tip!

Nonsmoking rooms and rooms equipped for guests with disabilities are available at all three Disney hotels.

Check-in and Check-out: Check-in begins at 3 P.M., but guests who arrive early can check in, store their luggage at the Bell Desk, and go have fun. A photo ID is required at check-in. Check-out is at 11 A.M., and, again, bags can be stored until guests are ready to depart. Express check-out is available by leaving a credit card imprint at check-in.

Prices: Rates start at about $200. They vary according to hotel, view, and season. Expect "regular" rates to apply April 14–April 29, June 2–August 26, and December 22–December 31. Slightly discounted "value" rates are in effect from January 1–April 13, April 30–June 1, and August 27–December 21. Disneyland Resort room tax is 15 percent.

Deposit requirements: A deposit equal to one night's lodging is required within 21 days from the time the reservation is made. Reservations are automatically canceled if a deposit is not received in that time period. Reservations booked fewer than 21 days prior to arrival are held for about a week without deposit. Deposit payment can be mailed in the form of check or money order, or can be guaranteed by a credit card over the phone (in which case the card is not actually billed until check-in).

Cancellation policy: The deposit will be refunded if the reservation is canceled at least 72 hours before the scheduled arrival.

Additional costs: Room rates at all three hotels are based on double occupancy. While there is no charge for kids under 18 sharing their parents' room, extra adults will each cost

$15 extra per night. Note that there is no fee for rollaway beds, sleeping bags, or cribs.

A $5 per day resort service fee includes overnight parking, use of the fitness centers, and local telephone calls. Valet parking is available for $15 per day.

Discounts: Special savings are available to Disney Club members (see *Getting Ready to Go* for details). Annual Passport bearers are also rewarded with special rates.

Packages: The Walt Disney Travel Company offers several packages that feature a stay at one of the Disneyland Resort hotels. See "Travel Packages" in *Getting Ready to Go*, or contact the Walt Disney Travel Company at 714-520-5050.

DISNEYLAND HOTEL: This laid-back resort adjacent to Downtown Disney was the first hotel erected at the Disneyland Resort. The family-friendly property features a Never Land-themed outdoor area with a 5,000-square-foot swimming pool that incorporates a 100-foot water slide, a pirate ship, and (waiting beside the ship) a comical sculpture of Tick Tock, the hungry crocodile from Disney's classic movie *Peter Pan*. A winding shoreline, lush flower gardens, rock formations, and a wedding gazebo add to the property's picturesque terrain.

The hotel has 990 rooms, including 62 suites, located in three separate towers. Most tower rooms have two double beds, and many can easily accommodate up to five people (one of them on a daybed). All the interior tower rooms have small balconies that are ideal for cooling off or catching a glimpse of the twice-nightly Fantasy Waters fountain show, which features music from favorite Disney films. The 11-story East Tower looks toward Downtown Disney and Disney's California Adventure on one side and the main pool on the other. The 14-story South Tower's rooms provide city views as well as windows overlooking the waterfall and koi fish pond. The 11-story North Tower offers rooms with pool views, but only on one side; guests on the other side look out over city rooftops.

A monorail stop is a short walk away, in neighboring Downtown Disney, which means extremely easy access to Disneyland (it drops guests off in Tomorrowland), an enormous convenience for guests who relish a break in their park-going with a quick trip to one of the hotel's pools; to the small beach, perfect for sandcastle-building and volleyball; or to Team Mickey's Workout, a gym that features weight machines and aerobic exercise equipment. The workout room is featured in a $5-per-day package that also includes guest parking, local telephone calls, and daily newspaper delivery.

Guests also enjoy Horseshoe Falls, a 165-foot-wide cascade that visitors can walk under. Nearby, a tranquil pool is filled with Japanese koi fish. The large arcade, a big draw for younger guests, is located in the shopping area that fronts the South Tower. The hotel's pools, beach, and Fantasy Waters show (a modest, though beloved fountain show) set were all upgraded a few years back.

In the lobby of the North Tower, a large shop called Fantasia sells Disney souvenirs. Goofy's Kitchen, hosted by Chef Goofy and his Disney pals, is an extremely popular buffet open for breakfast, lunch, and dinner; and Hook's Pointe & Wine Cellar features a mesquite grill and offers traditional cuisine and Never Land pool views. The Coffee House, Captain's Galley, and Croc's Bits 'n' Bites provide snacks and quick meals for guests on the go. Room service is available. (For more information about hotel dining, see the *Good Meals, Great Times* chapter.)

The convention and meetings area, adjacent to Goofy's Kitchen and linked to the lobby via a photo-lined passageway, deserves a look for its Disney-related artwork, including a floor-to-ceiling collage of Disney collectibles and milestones. Created entirely

from old toys, souvenirs, name tags, and other assorted memorabilia, it commemorates the colorful and unique history of Disneyland. The photo hall of fame depicts celebrities, members of royalty, and political figures who have visited the resort.

The hotel can provide safe-deposit boxes, currency exchange, and child-care referrals. An ATM is on the premises. Airport buses bound for the Orange County and Los Angeles airports make regular stops at the hotel, as do tour buses, city and county buses, and buses traveling to and from downtown Los Angeles.

Rates for doubles run $195 to $235, depending on the view and season, plus $15 for each extra adult (no charge for children under 18 staying in their parents' room); no charge for rollaways or cribs. For the outstanding concierge-level rooms and amenities, add $65 to $75. Suites are $335 to $2,400 (for the Marina Suite). Parking costs $5 per day for hotel guests ($15 for valet); others pay $2 per hour, with a $15 maximum for 24 hours. Disneyland Hotel; 1150 Magic Way; Anaheim, CA 92802; 714-956-6425 (for reservations and information) or 714-635-2300 (front desk); *www.disneyland.com.*

DISNEY'S GRAND CALIFORNIAN HOTEL:
This 751-room hotel is in a prime location—smack-dab in the middle of the Disneyland Resort. It even has its own private entrance to Disney's California Adventure theme park and easy access to Downtown Disney.

A border of trees surrounds the six-story hotel, built as a tribute to the Arts and Crafts tradition of the early 1900s—a style made famous by the striking designs of architect Frank Lloyd Wright. Rich cedar and redwood paneling decorates the cavernous lobby, where display cabinets filled with original art and quality reproductions introduce guests to that rich period of art. The lobby's great hearth has a perennially lit fire. Furnishings throughout the

hotel have warm colors and intricate textures. Even the hotel staff wears period costumes.

Each of the 703 deluxe guestrooms and 48 suites features a 27-inch TV, a safe large enough to fit a laptop computer, lighted wardrobe, desk with two-line telephone, a computer and fax-accessible data port, iron and board, and small refrigerator. The bathroom has marble surfaces, a makeup mirror, and a hair dryer.

Most of the guestrooms in the hotel feature two queen beds, though 80 have a king bed, and 160 have one queen bed plus a bunk bed with a trundle (these rooms sleep five). The carved wooden headboards are designed to resemble vines on a trellis, the bedspreads have a stained-glass-like design, and Bambi appears subtly in the shower curtain pattern.

Guest services include 24-hour room service, laundry and dry cleaning, a full-service business center, and a bridal salon. The concierge level offers upgraded amenities and services. Guests can relax at the Fountain Pool or frolic in Redwood Pool (the two are connected), with its themed slide; or they can enjoy the two whirlpools, children's pool, clothing boutique and gift shop, child-care center known as Pinocchio's Workshop, and Grizzly Game Arcade. The 4,000-square-foot

Hot Tip!

Don't touch anything in a Grand Californian room's mini-bar unless you're sure you want it—you'll be charged whether or not you take the item.

fitness center incorporates a weight room, exercise classes, a couple of massage rooms, dry and steam saunas, and lockers.

Among the varied dining options are the Napa Rose, which features California cuisine and wines, and the Storyteller's Cafe, open for breakfast, lunch, and dinner in an Old California setting and the backdrop for a character-hosted breakfast. A quick-service eatery, Whitewater Snacks, supplies specialty coffees, fast food, and baked goods; the poolside bar is good for a quick meal or snack. The Hearth-stone Lounge doubles as a breakfast spot each morning, dispensing coffee and pastries to guests heading into the park.

The hotel can provide safe-deposit boxes and currency exchange. An ATM is on the premises. Airport buses bound for Orange

County and Los Angeles airports stop here, as do tour buses, city and county buses, and buses traveling to and from Los Angeles.

Rates for regular rooms run $260 to $310, depending on the view and season, plus $15 for each extra adult (no charge for children under 18 staying in their parents' room); concierge rooms are $395; presidential suites, $2,650. There are no rollaway beds, but a sleeping bag with a pad can be supplied; no charge for cribs. Self-parking is $5 per day (this optional daily fee also includes local phone calls, daily newspaper delivery, and fitness center access); valet parking is $15 Disney's Grand Californian; 1150 Disneyland Drive; Anaheim, CA 92802; 714-956-6425 (for reservations and information) or 714-778-6600 (front desk); *www.disneyland.com*.

DISNEY'S PARADISE PIER HOTEL: When Disney's California Adventure rose on the plot of land across the street from the Disneyland Pacific Hotel, that property got a face-lift and a new name—Disney's Paradise Pier Hotel. Its facade now reflects the ambience and breezy, carefree California style of the Paradise Pier district of the new park, which it overlooks. This property, the smallest of the Disneyland Resort hotels, is popular with business people and families alike. It underwent an extensive refurbishment in 2004 and boasts spiffed-up rooms and an inviting new pool area.

The hotel's two high-rise towers—one 15 stories, the other 14 stories—are juxtaposed to create a central atrium, which cradles the lobby and a larger-than-life character sculpture. Mickey's familiar silhouette shows up extensively in the hotel's decor—in the artwork, the ceramics, and even the upholstery.

Each of the 502 rooms, including 12 suites, features Disney-themed furnishings, one king-size bed or two queen beds, plus a foldout twin sofa bed in the sitting area (a particular convenience for families). The rooms on the cabana level open onto a large recreation area that also includes a sundeck, swimming pool, whirlpool, children's play area, and snack bar. If you plan to spend a lot of time in or beside the pool, consider a concierge-level room on the third floor for direct access.

Two shops, including the spacious and well-stocked Mickey in Paradise, a coffee bar with its own Mickey cappuccino machine, and two restaurants are on the ground level of the hotel. Disney's PCH Grill offers California cuisine and has a popular character breakfast, Minnie & Friends. The hotel's other restaurant, Yamabuki, has a full sushi bar (refer to *Good Meals, Great Times*). Room service offers PCH Grill specialties. The hotel also has an exercise room, a small concierge lounge, and an ATM. A glass-enclosed elevator provides a bird's-eye view of both the lobby and Disney's California Adventure.

Guests at the hotel have an exclusive entrance into the Paradise Pier section of Disney's California Adventure. The hotel is also connected to the Disneyland Resort and Downtown Disney by a landscaped walkway. Guests can also get to Disneyland by taking the monorail from the Downtown Disney station. Both Disneyland Park and Disney's California Adventure are within a 10- to 15-minute walk. Free shuttles to the theme parks are available, too (offered seasonally).

Rates for doubles run $195 to $235, depending on the view and the season (no charge for kids under 18 sharing their parents' room), plus $15 per extra adult; no charge for rollaways or cribs. For concierge rooms and various amenities, add another $65 to $75. Suites run $875 to $1,300. Self-parking is $5 per day (prices include local calls, weekday newspaper delivery, and exercise room access); valet parking is $15. Disney's Paradise Pier Hotel; 1717 Disneyland Dr.; Anaheim, CA 92802; 714-956-6400 (for reservations and information) or 714-999-0090 (front desk); *www.disneyland.com*.

Disneyland Good Neighbor Hotels

With fewer than 2,500 rooms available at the Disneyland Resort and tens of thousands of guests pouring through the theme park turnstiles each day, it's no wonder that a majority of visitors must stay in one of the establishments located off Disney property. To make it easier for guests to narrow down their off-property choices, the folks at Disney have selected several local hotels and motels that meet the Disney standard and anointed them the "Disneyland Good Neighbor" properties. Before receiving the Disney seal of approval, hotels are graded on amenities, services, decor, guest satisfaction, price, and location.

Ranging from national chains to smaller operations, the Good Neighbor hotels proliferate along Harbor Boulevard, which flanks the resort on the east. From Harbor, it's easy to walk to the Disneyland Resort. A few properties are on Ball Road, the resort's northern boundary. Katella Avenue borders the resort to the south and leads to the Anaheim Convention Center and the city's major convention hotels. Divided into the categories of Suite, Superior, Moderate, and Economy, there are 36 Good Neighbor hotels in all. In the following pages we describe some of our favorites. For a rundown of the Good Neighbor properties not described in this listing, see "The Rest of the Best" on page 51.

Prices: Expect to pay $100 to $200, or more, per night for a hotel room for two adults and two children (kids usually stay in their parents' room for free), $50 to $120 for a motel room, and $25 to $55 for tent or RV camping. Prices drop a bit in winter; they are highest in the summer and over holidays. The room tax in Anaheim is 15 percent.

Additional costs: When comparing accommodation costs, consider hidden zingers, like parking. Big hotels usually charge for it ($6 to $10 a day; more for valet service). Most also charge an additional fee when more than two adults occupy a room. The cutoff age at which there is no charge for children varies; it's often 17 or 18 but can be as low as 12. Be sure to inquire about telephone rates when you check in—hotel surcharges are notoriously huge.

Savings: You can save money by staying in a hotel that offers complimentary breakfast and shuttle service to Disneyland. Discounts are sometimes offered to those who belong to an automobile or retirement association.

Individual needs: What's essential for one vacationer—and worth the extra cost—might seem frivolous to another: room service, on-site restaurants, live music, a suite, a kitchen, concierge service and amenities, large swimming pool, exercise room, or a place that accepts pets.

Good Neighbor Hotels

1 Embassy Suites Anaheim North
2 Anaheim Residence Inn by Marriott
3 Hilton Suites Anaheim/Orange
4 Embassy Suites Buena Park
5 Hawthorn Suites Orange
6 Homewood Suites by Hilton
7 Hawthorn Suites LTD, Anaheim
8 Sheraton Anaheim
9 Anaheim Garden Grove
10 Hilton Anaheim
11 Anaheim Marriott
12 Hyatt Regency Alicante
13 Hyatt Regency Orange County
14 Courtyard by Marriott Buena Park
15 Best Western Park Place Inn
16 Park Inn International
17 Anaheim Fairfield Inn by Marriott
18 Best Western Anaheim Inn
19 Hilton Garden Inn
20 Coast Anaheim Hotel
21 Candy Cane Inn
22 Howard Johnson Plaza-Hotel
23 Best Western Stovall's Inn
24 Carousel Inn & Suites
25 Portofino Inn & Suites
26 Radisson Hotel Maingate Anaheim
27 Best Western Pavilions
28 Clarion Hotel Anaheim
29 Hampton Inn & Suites
30 Holiday Inn Anaheim at the Park
31 Holiday Inn Hotel & Suites
32 Tropicana Inn & Suites
33 Anaheim International Inn Travelodge
34 Ramada Inn Maingate
35 Anaheim Ramada Inn

Packages: The Walt Disney Travel Company offers packages in conjunction with each of the Good Neighbor hotels—representing poten-tially big savings for travelers. Refer to "Travel Packages" in the *Getting Ready to Go* chapter of this book or simply contact the Walt Disney Travel Company directly at 714-520-5050.

Note: The following recommended establishments accept major credit cards and offer nonsmoking rooms and rooms for travelers with disabilities, unless otherwise indicated. Call the properties directly to inquire about deposit requirements and cancellation policies. Rates given were correct at press time but are subject to change and should always be confirmed by phone.

Suite Hotels

ANAHEIM RESIDENCE INN BY MARRIOTT: At first glance, the two- and three-story stucco buildings with tile roofs could easily be mistaken for a condominium complex. The well-maintained grounds are landscaped with hibiscus, bougainvillea, lemon, sweet gum, and pepper trees, plus park-style benches and, we're convinced, the only remaining orange tree still standing in the city of Anaheim.

Inside the inn, the living-room-like lobby is inviting, with comfortable couches, chairs, cocktail tables, fireplace, and television. Facilities include a swimming pool that's open 24 hours, a kids' pool, a whirlpool, Ping-Pong tables, and a single court for badminton, basketball, or volleyball. There is also a self-serve guest laundry.

The suites are spacious, and feature a 25-inch TV, pay-per-view movies, and Nintendo; a breakfast bar; and a fully equipped kitchen with a dishwasher, stove, microwave, and full refrigerator. Several room configurations are available.

Complimentary services include grocery delivery, housekeeping, shuttle transportation to the Disneyland Resort and the convention center (neither is really within walking distance), a full breakfast buffet daily, and a social hour Monday through Thursday from 5 P.M. to 7 P.M. The hotel will accept one small pet in a suite for a flat charge of $75.

Rates for a single studio start at $139 (maybe even $99, if you're lucky and the occupancy rate is low when you visit); a slightly larger studio with 2 queen beds called the Studio Queen, at $149; and a multiroom

family suite, at $199. A rollaway costs $10; no charge for cribs. Lower long-term rates are also available.

Anaheim Residence Inn by Marriott; 1700 S. Clementine St.; Anaheim, CA 92802; 714-533-3555 or 800-331-3131; or visit the hotel's website at *www.rimhospitality.com*.

PHOTO BY KEITH GROSHANS

Superior Hotels

ANAHEIM MARRIOTT: Across the street from the Anaheim Convention Center and the Hilton, the Marriott is a favorite among conventioneers. Most of the 1,032 rooms, located in two towers and two four-story wings, have balconies. Each room has one king-size bed or two doubles and cable TV. The hotel restaurants—JW's Steakhouse and Cafe Del Sol—are popular with locals and guests alike. For a quick bite, drop by the Pizza Hut or Starbucks on the premises.

There are two pools, surrounded by lounge chairs (one of the pools is partially covered), as well as two whirlpools and a health club with an exercise room and two saunas. Guests enjoy the poolside and lobby bars, and concierge services.

The hotel is a couple of long blocks from the Disneyland Resort—for most it is not within walking distance. Shuttle service to the Disney theme parks is provided for a fee; transportation to area airports is also available for a fee.

Rates for two start at $119 (there is no charge for children under 18 sharing their parents' room); suites start at $220; $10 per additional adult. Rollaway beds and cribs are free. Special packages, including some for families, and discounted weekend rates are available. Self-parking costs $13 per day; valet parking is $20 per day. Pets are accepted at the hotel.

Anaheim Marriott; 700 W. Convention Way; Anaheim, CA 92802; visit the hotel's website at *www.marriotthotels.com/LAXAH*; or call 714-750-8000 or 800-228-9290.

HILTON ANAHEIM: The 14-story glass exterior of Southern California's largest hotel reflects the Anaheim Convention Center, just steps away, and the three-story atrium lobby invites the outdoors (and swarms of conventioneers) inside. The Hilton has 1,572 rooms, including 95 suites, decorated in soft, light colors, with wicker furniture and California art. Atop the hotel, the Executive Floor provides special services and amenities, as well as complimentary continental breakfast and hors d'oeuvres in its lounge.

PHOTO BY KEITH GROSHANS

The hotel's outdoor recreation center, on the fifth floor, features a heated swimming pool, four whirlpools, and three acres of sundecks and rose gardens. There is a Starbucks Coffee on the premises. Other dining options include the Casablanca-style Cafe Oasis, serving three meals a day; and Pavia, with Italian cuisine and live entertainment. Don't overlook the sushi bar and the sports bar with big-screen TV in the lobby. Note that the restaurants tend to be especially crowded at lunchtime and during convention breaks.

Add to that a self-service post office, business center, and two levels of shops. The 25,000-square-foot Sports and Fitness Center has and exercise equipment, a pool, basketball court, whirlpool, steam baths, sauna, exercise classes, spa facials, body treatments, and massage. There's even an outdoor driving range.

Orange County Walk of Stars, the sidewalk entrance to the hotel, highlights notables such as Gene Autry, Steve Martin, and Buzz Aldrin. Rates for a double room range from $79 to $299, plus $20 per extra adult (no charge for children under 18 when sharing their parents' room); suites run a bit higher. Ask about special packages. There's no charge for cribs or rollaways. Self-parking costs $11 per day, valet parking $17. Pets are permitted.

Hilton Anaheim; 777 Convention Way; Anaheim, CA 92802; 714-750-4321 or 800-222-9923; *www.anaheimhilton.com.*

HYATT REGENCY ORANGE COUNTY: The hotel, located in Garden Grove, is four (long) blocks south of the Disneyland Resort. A recent renovation and expansion resulted in 241 new suites, plus a restaurant and lounge. Its dramatic, 17-story atrium encloses palm trees, fountains, and greenery, and houses the California Grill restaurant, Starbucks, Pizza Hut Express, specialty shops, and a bar. Each of the hotel's 654 guestrooms features either a king-size bed or two double beds and cherry-wood furniture that complements the modern interior design.

Each room includes amenities such as coffeemakers, hair dryers, iron with board, plus cable TV. The one- and two-bedroom Family Suites also have a living room, wet bar, up to three TVs, refrigerator, and microwave. Suites can accommodate up to 8.

Kids Suites include a room for the little ones, complete with bunk beds, activity table, and the Disney Channel. The parents' room has a king bed, 27-inch TV, fridge, and microwave.

The hotel's impressive recreational facilities, located on a 25,000-square-foot, third-story roof, include two pools, whirlpool, exercise room, and two rooftop tennis courts. Complimentary transportation to the Disneyland Resort is provided, and airport shuttle service is available.

Room rates run $89 to $249, with weekend rates of $99 to $125 (no charge for children under 18 occupying their parents' room), plus $25 for each additional adult; $110 to $1,095 for suites. There is no charge for rollaway cribs. Self-parking is $12 per day; valet parking, $15.

Hyatt Regency Orange County; 11999 Harbor Blvd.; Garden Grove, CA 92840; 714-750-1234; *www.hyattoc.com.*

SHERATON ANAHEIM: With its turrets, towers, and Tudor design, this 489-room hotel looks more like a castle, surrounded by grounds that incorporate two peaceful courtyards, a rose garden, fountain, pond, and small waterfall. A stream runs through the lobby, which has a comfortable seating area around a stone fireplace. The hotel also has a restaurant, gift shop, bar, and deli that is open long hours. The reception staff and concierge get high marks for their helpfulness.

The hotel has 450 rooms and 39 suites. The rooms—all large (500-plus square feet)—have two queen- or one king-size bed, cable TV, in-room movies, voice mail, irons, ironing boards, hair dryers, and coffeemakers. Each suite has a sitting area with a sofa bed and wet bar.

The hotel has an arcade, heated pool, whirlpool, exercise room, guest laundry, and conference rooms. It provides room service, valet service, a business center, and frequent complimentary shuttle service to the Disneyland Resort. Airport transportation is available. Rates for doubles run $95 during off-season to $195 during peak season (no charge for children under 18 sharing their parents' room); $150 to $345 for suites, plus $20 for rollaways; no charge for cribs. Be sure to request the best available rate when confirming pricing. A refrigerator is available on advance request for $20 per stay.

Sheraton Anaheim; 900 South Disneyland Drive; Anaheim, CA 92802; 714-778-1700 or 800-331-7251; *www.sheratonanaheim.com.*

Moderate Hotels

ANAHEIM FAIRFIELD INN BY MARRIOTT: Fronted by palms and pines, this handsome, affordable 467-room hotel is situated across from the Disneyland Resort. All of its rooms were recently refurbished, and are awash in bright colors and Disney artwork. The rooms are in two towers (one tower is nine stories high; the other, eight). Each room features a king-size bed or two queen beds, sofa bed, cable TV, an iron and board, hair dryer, refrigerator, and coffeemaker. The hotel is served by a family-style eatery called Millie's Restaurant & Bakery.

Other facilities include a heated pool, whirlpool, gift shop, and Cafasia Snack Shop and Game Room. There is complimentary transportation to the Disneyland Resort. The rooms may be occupied by up to five people, and rates range from $74 to $129; cribs are available.

Anaheim Fairfield Inn by Marriott; 1460 S. Harbor Blvd.; Anaheim, CA 92802. Call 714-772-6777 or 800-228-2800, or visit the hotel website at *www.anaheimfairfieldinn.com.*

BEST WESTERN PARK PLACE INN: This three-story, 199-room inn is located directly across from the Disneyland Resort pedestrian entrance. The lobby is spacious, with a high ceiling and two cozy seating areas, a fireplace, and windows looking onto Harbor Boulevard.

A gift shop sells Disney souvenirs, while Disney tickets may be purchased through the guest relations staff. Room configurations include a king-size bed and sleeper sofa, two queen-size beds and a sleeper sofa, or two double beds. Rooms are equipped with a refrigerator, microwave, iron with board, and coffeemaker (at no additional cost).

Among the facilities are a pool with an adjacent whirlpool, and a guest laundry. Rates, which include continental breakfast at the inn or pancakes at Captain Kids, run $89 to $139 for a standard double room; mini suites run $99 to $149 (there is no charge for children under 18 sharing their parents' room). Rollaway beds cost $15; there is no extra charge for cribs.

Best Western Park Place Inn; 1544 S. Harbor Blvd.; Anaheim, CA 92802; 714-776-4800 or 800-854-8175, ext. 4; or visit the hotel's website at *www.parkplaceinnandminisuites.*

CANDY CANE INN: There's a lot to like about this sweet, two-story hotel with a fountain out front, relaxed ambience, wrought-iron touches, and flowers everywhere. Located just down the street from the Disneyland Resort's main entrance (a manageable walk for adults and non-toddlers), the Candy Cane Inn is family-run and well-maintained.

Each of the 172 rooms, which are set far back from the street, has a refrigerator, coffeemaker, iron, hair dryer, and two queen beds with down comforters, dust ruffles, and European pillow shams. Add to that the guest laundry, swimming pool, gazebo-covered whirlpool, and kids' wading pool. A complimentary continental buffet breakfast is served daily. Premium rooms also have microwaves, free video rentals, breakfast delivered to the room, and late check-out. Sightseeing services are available, as well as complimentary shuttle service to and from the Disneyland Resort. Transportation to local airports can be arranged. Parking is free.

Rates for a double room with two queen-size beds range from $87 to $159, depending on the season. Rollaways are $10; no charge for cribs. The inn is conveniently located across the street from a small shopping area with fast-food eateries and one-hour photo processing.

Candy Cane Inn; 1747 S. Harbor Blvd.; Anaheim, CA 92802. Call 714-774-5284 or 800-345-7057, or visit *www.candycaneinn.net.*

HOLIDAY INN ANAHEIM AT THE PARK: About half a mile north of Disneyland's main entrance, this five-story hotel has one of the best landscaped pool areas in Anaheim, and the pool is heated and open 24 hours a day.

All 253 guestrooms have coffeemakers, voice mail, pay-per-view movies, hair dryers, and irons. Each of the five Kids Suites has a microwave, refrigerator, and bunk beds. Other services and facilities include a fitness center, car rental, free parking, a gift shop, restaurant, room service, lobby bar, foreign currency exchange, guest laundry, and valet dry cleaning. It no longer offers a complimentary shuttle to the Disneyland Resort. Four kids ages 12 and under can eat free from a child's menu when accompanied by a paying adult.

Rates for one to four people run $70 to $129, depending on the season and occupancy (there is no charge for kids under 17 sharing their parents' room). Rollaways are $13; cribs are free.

Holiday Inn Anaheim at the Park; 1221 S. Harbor Blvd.; Anaheim, CA 92805; 714-758-0900 or 800-545-7275; or visit the website *www.holiday-inn.com/anaheim-park*.

HOWARD JOHNSON ANAHEIM HOTEL:

This property has some of the lushest landscaping of any place in Anaheim, except for the Disney hotels, and that's a major reason to stay here. Flowers and trees proliferate; a central fountain anchors the four two-story units. The hotel is close to the Disneyland Resort and local eateries. For a fee, it offers shuttle service to and from the Disneyland Resort.

The 320 rooms are divided among six buildings on six acres. Most have two queen beds, and all have a refrigerator, Sony PlayStation, and free high-speed Internet access. Ninety percent of the rooms are nonsmoking. The rooms are relatively spacious, though the bathrooms are a bit on the small side.

There are two outdoor heated pools, a whirlpool, and a kids' wading pool (which is connected to a "spray zone"), as well as two laundry rooms, a gift shop, and an arcade. The hotel-partner restaurant, Mimi's Café, is next door. Babysitting can be arranged. Rates range from $59 to $134, depending on the season. There is no charge for parking. Rollaways are $7; cribs are free. Ask about family packages.

Howard Johnson Anaheim hotel; 1380 S. Harbor Blvd.; Anaheim, CA 92802; 714-776-6120 or 800-422-4228; *www.hojoanaheim.com*.

PARK INN & SUITES: Directly across the street—and a relatively short walk away—from the Disneyland Resort, this hotel, with its shingled roof, clock tower, turrets, and tidy window boxes, looks like something out of a

Bavarian village. Each of the 121 rooms and suites has a refrigerator, coffeemaker, hair dryer, and an iron with board. The inn offers complimentary continental breakfast. It also has a pool (with a view of Disneyland's Matterhorn), two gift shops, and a guest laundry facility.

> ## Hot Tip!
> If you stay in the 1400 or 1500 block of Harbor Boulevard, you can cross the street and walk to the parks from your hotel.

Although there's no in-house restaurant, many eating places, including Millie's restaurant, are within walking distance. Millie's also provides room service to all Park Inn guestrooms. In-room dining is available daily from 6 A.M. to 10 P.M.

Deluxe standard rooms, most with two queen-size beds, start at $115 year-round; suites start at $149 and can accommodate up to six people, but they have only one bath. Rollaways are $15; cribs are free. The Inn provides complimentary shuttle to Disneyland upon request.

Park Inn & Suites; 1520 S. Harbor Blvd.; Anaheim, CA 92802; 714-635-7275 or 800-670-7275; *www.parkinn-anaheim.com*.

COAST ANAHEIM HOTEL: This 14-story tower is easy to spot, and the 491 rooms and eight suites have full or small balconies that provide a nice view of the pool or the Disneyland Resort (and a view of the fireworks). All rooms offer either one king or two queen beds, pay-per-view movies available anytime, video games, irons, coffeemakers, hair dryers, and baths with separate sinks.

A large gift shop is on the premises, as is a lobby bar, coffee shop, snack shop, and an espresso bar. Popular with groups, the Overland Stage restaurant (with authentic furnishings from a Mississippi riverboat) serves steak, seafood, and pasta for dinner only and offers a children's menu. The hotel also has a large L-shaped pool, whirlpool, and a poolside bar.

Shuttle service is available (for a fee) to the Disneyland Resort. Room rates run $79 to $159 for doubles, depending on occupancy and season; suites start at $340. Rollaways cost $15 extra; cribs are available free of charges.

Coast Anaheim Hotel; 1855 S. Harbor Blvd.; Anaheim, CA 92802; 714-750-1811 or 800-663-1144; or visit *www.coasthotels.com.*

Economy Hotels

BEST WESTERN STOVALL'S INN: What makes the inn unique is its topiary garden. The property features 290 guestrooms, complimentary continental breakfast, fitness room, business center, and a pair of pools (one is heated), two whirlpools, a wading pool, and a gift shop. Room configurations include two queen-size or one king-size bed or two double beds and a bathroom with a separate sink and plenty of counter space. Refrigerators are available for $8 a day. Disney park-hopper passes may be purchased at the front desk.

A shuttle bus takes guests to Disneyland for a fee. Room rates for up to five people run $79 to $119 in season, $69 to $109 the rest of the year. Rollaways are $15; cribs are free.

Best Western Stovall's Inn; 1110 W. Katella Ave.; Anaheim, CA 92802; 714-778-1880 or 800 854 8175; *www.bestwestern.com/stovallsinn.*

TROPICANA INN & SUITES: This establishment is right at the pedestrian crosswalk into the Disneyland Resort. Each of its 200 tropically infused rooms has a TV, coffeemaker (with coffee supply), refrigerator, microwave, hair dryer, separate vanity, iron, in-room movies, and either a king-size bed or two queens. Each morning, a free refreshment (coffee, juice, and pastry) is served in the hospitality room.

The inn has no restaurant, but an on-site shop sells fruit, fried chicken, breakfast items, snacks, and other food; a gift shop sells souvenirs. McDonald's, IHOP, Millie's, Denny's, and other eateries are within walking distance. Millie's provides room service. It's about a five-minute walk to Disneyland.

The inn has a heated outdoor pool and guest laundry. The inn provides a shuttle to Disneyland on request. Room rates start at $78. Suites accommodate four to six people. Suite rates range from $98 to $195. Some suites come with kitchens.

Tropicana Inn; 1540 S. Harbor Blvd.; Anaheim, CA 92802; 714-635-4082 or 800-828-4898; *www.tropicanainn-anaheim.com.*

The Rest of the Best

Here's a roundup of the remaining Disneyland Good Neighbor hotels. They feature amenities and rates similar to those described in this chapter. However, some of the properties are located a bit farther from the Disneyland Resort.

Note: Hotels and motels boasting "Good Neighbor" status are subject to change during the year; call 714-520-5050 for the most current list of participating properties.

Suite Hotels
- Embassy Suites Anaheim; 3100 E. Frontera St.; Anaheim; 714-632-1221
- Embassy Suites Buena Park; 7762 Beach Blvd.; Buena Park; 714-739-5600
- Hawthorn Suites LTD Anaheim; 1752 S. Clementine St.; Anaheim; 714-535-7773
- Hawthorn Suites Orange; 720 The City Dr. South; Orange; 714-740-2700
- Hilton Suites Anaheim/Orange; 400 N. State College Blvd.; Orange; 714-938-1111
- Homewood Suites by Hilton; 12005 Harbor Blvd.; Garden Grove; 714-740-1800

Superior Hotels
- Anaheim/Garden Grove Crown Plaza Resort; 12021 Harbor Blvd.; Garden Grove; 714-867-5555
- Courtyard by Marriott Buena Park; 7621 Beach Blvd.; Buena Park; 714-670-6600

- Doubletree Hotel Anaheim/Orange County; 100 The City Dr.; Orange; 714-634-4500
- Hilton Garden Inn; 11777 Harbor Blvd.; Garden Grove; 714-703-9100

Moderate Hotels
- Best Western Anaheim Inn; 1630 S. Harbor Blvd.; Anaheim; 714-774-1050
- Carousel Inn & Suites; 1530 S. Harbor Blvd.; Anaheim; 714-758-0444
- Clarion Hotel Anaheim; 616 Convention Way; Anaheim; 714-750-3131
- Hampton Inn & Suites; 11747 Harbor Blvd.; Garden Grove; 714-703-8800
- Portofino Inn & Suites; 1831 S. Harbor Blvd.; Anaheim; 714-491-2400
- Radisson Hotel Maingate Anaheim; 1850 S. Harbor Blvd.; Anaheim; 714-750-2801

Economy Hotels
- Anaheim International Inn Travelodge; 2060 S. Harbor Blvd.; Anaheim; 714-971-9393
- Anaheim Ramada Inn; 1331 E. Katella Ave.; Anaheim; 714-978-8088
- Best Western Pavilions; 1176 W. Katella Ave.; Anaheim; 714-776-0140
- Holiday Inn Hotel & Suites; 1240 S. Walnut; Anaheim; 714-535-0300
- Ramada Inn Maingate; 1650 S. Harbor Blvd.; Anaheim; 714-772-0440

On the Coast

When it comes to upscale and elegant lodging, Orange County's coastal resorts are especially tempting—and they're only about a half-hour drive from the Disneyland Resort. Imagine spending the day in the park and then returning to your hotel for a stroll on the beach at sunset. Most coastal hotels do not offer regularly scheduled shuttle service to the Disneyland Resort (or anywhere else, for that matter), as the Anaheim hostelries do, so you will need a car.

Laguna Beach

INN AT LAGUNA BEACH: Perched dramatically on a cliff overlooking Laguna Beach, the inn is within walking distance of Heisler Park, Main Beach, the Laguna Art Museum, and many galleries, shops, and cozy cafes. Completely nonsmoking inside, the recently renovated inn has 70 rooms, 52 of which have ocean views.

Each room is furnished with a ceiling fan, air-conditioning, a TV, VCR (with selections from a video library), coffeemaker, hair dryer, an iron, a small refrigerator, bathrobes, CD players, and feather beds. Some rooms have two queen beds and a bathtub; others, a king bed, queen sleeper sofa, balcony, and shower. Four corner deluxe rooms, two of which are quite large, provide stunning views of the coastline. Beach towels and umbrellas are in the room and may be used for the length of your stay.

Hot Tip!

Stay in Laguna if small inns and early-morning walks along the beach appeal to you. Choose Newport if you prefer resort hotels and nightlife. It's easier to get rooms in Newport than in Laguna on summer weekends.

There is one pool and a whirlpool. In-room facials and massages are available on request. Continental breakfast is complimentary and is delivered to your room; the inn treats guests to cookies and refreshments from 5 P.M. to 9 P.M. daily. On-site parking is available for a fee.

Rates in summer run from $159 to $301 for village-view rooms and $269 to $559 for ocean-view rooms. The rest of the year, expect to pay $99 to $229 for village-view rooms and $199 to $499 for ocean view. Ask about special travel packages. Inn at Laguna Beach; 211 N. Coast Hwy.; Laguna Beach, CA 92651; 800-544-4479; *www.innatlagunabeach.com.*

RITZ-CARLTON, LAGUNA NIGUEL: This magnificent Mediterranean villa-style resort sits on 18 acres, high on a bluff that overlooks the Pacific Ocean and Orange County's southern coast. The views from the lounge and from many of the 363 guestrooms and 30 suites are sensational. On a clear day you can see Catalina Island, 37 miles away, and at night the sound of the surf lulls you to sleep. Each guestroom has French doors and a balcony or patio. The hotel's marble floors, Persian carpets, crystal chandeliers, and museum-quality 18th- and 19th-century European and American art and antiques make a visit here worthwhile even if you can't stay overnight.

In addition to a two-mile stretch of sandy beach (which is open to the public), the hotel has two pools and two whirlpools, a nearby 18-hole golf course designed by Robert Trent Jones, Jr., four tennis courts, table tennis, and a beach volleyball court.

It also has a fitness center with yoga classes, lockers, whirlpool, two saunas or coed steam room, exercise room, massage center, and beauty salon.

The Dining Room, which is one of Orange County's finest restaurants (and the only one to currently boast a Five Diamond rating), warrants a visit in its own right, and the Club Grill and Bar features music and dancing. The Terrace Restaurant offers three meals a day, as well as a Friday night seafood buffet and Sunday champagne brunch. Afternoon tea is served in the library, and room service is available around the clock. Other hotel amenities include concierge and valet service, as well as a shuttle to and from the golf course and the beach.

Rates for doubles range from $325 to $535, depending on location and view (or $425 to $665 for Club rooms, with the addition of five culinary treats throughout the day); cribs are free. Suites start at $525. Parking is valet only, $25 a day for overnight guests, $9 for other visitors. The hotel is a 40-minute drive south from the Disneyland Resort. Ritz-Carlton, Laguna Niguel; One Ritz-Carlton Dr.; Dana Point, CA 92629; 949-240-2000 or 800-241-3333; *www.ritzcarlton.com*.

SURF & SAND: Perched beside 500 feet of sandy beachfront less than a mile from the shops, galleries, and restaurants of Laguna Beach, this stylish hotel has 165 rooms, almost all with king-size beds and private balconies. The accommodations fill three buildings.

Decorated with furnishings the color of sand dunes, all provide in-room movies, CD players (management can supply CDs at no charge), robes, and a marble bath with a hair dryer.

The nine-story Ocean Towers have the biggest and the priciest, except rooms at the hotel (the one- and two-bedroom suites are larger and cost more). Because of its location, guests staying in the three-story Surfside building often have the sensation of being afloat when the surf rolls in. The five-story Seaview Terrace overlooks the pool and beach.

Casual Splashes restaurant has indoor and outdoor seating, serves breakfast, lunch, and dinner, and features primarily Mediterranean cuisine. Adjacent to it, Splashes Bar is particularly popular at sunset; both have direct access to the beach. The hotel also has a medium-size pool (with beach access, as well), a well-stocked gift shop, and a spa. The Aquaterra spa purports to blend the "healing therapeutic essences of the ocean and land." Room service and concierge service are available.

A member of Preferred Hotels & Resorts Worldwide, the Surf & Sand is situated across the road from several art galleries and is approximately a 40-minute drive south from the Disneyland Resort.

Rates for doubles range from $285 to $450, depending on the location, time of year, and time of week; suites start at $600 in winter and $800 in summer. The hotel offers valet parking for $18 a day; there is no self-parking available. Surf & Sand; 1555 S. Coast Hwy.; Laguna Beach, CA 92651; 949-497-4477 or 800-524-8621; *www.surfandsandresort.com*.

Where to Rent a Beach Bungalow

Newport Beach is simply brimming with cottages, condominiums, and duplex apartments waiting to be your beach home away from home. Some include patios with barbecue facilities, and many are conveniently situated right on the sand, within easy strolling distance of local restaurants and shops. For additional information, contact the Newport Beach Conference & Visitors Bureau; 949-719-6100 or 800-942-6278; *www.newportbeach-cvb.com*.

Newport Beach

BEST WESTERN BAY SHORES INN: The inn has that special ambience unique to small, family-run places (this one's been in the Pratt family for 25 years). Guests are encouraged to hang out in deck chairs on the roof; check out free videos; use the complimentary beach towels, umbrellas, boogie boards, pails, and beach toys; and grab fruit, coffee, or tea from the kitchen whenever the urge strikes. The three-story building has an elevator, a sundeck, breakfast room, and free parking. There's no pool or restaurant on the property, but the bay, ocean, and popular Crab Cooker restaurant are just a stroll away. The entire property is nonsmoking.

Most of the 25 rooms are furnished with a single queen bed, though a couple have two queens or two doubles. All feature corner armoires, hair dryers, as well as air-conditioning, though the last is hardly necessary, given the constant ocean breeze. Double-paned windows muffle noise from the street. The Bay Suite has two queen beds (plus a pull-out couch in the living room), a balcony with a bay view, a kitchen, two baths, and a fireplace. Two one-bedroom annex suites contain two queen beds but no kitchen or view. Each suite sleeps six.

Rates include a breakfast of fresh muffins, pastries, bagels, toast, and hot or cold cereal; they range from $109 to $199 for a double room, depending on the season. Either annex suite runs $199 to $419; the Bay Suite is $259 to $469. Rollaways and cribs are not available. The hotel is about 20 minutes from the Disneyland Resort. Best Western Bay Shores Inn; 1800 W. Balboa Blvd.; Newport Beach, CA 92663; 949-675-3463 or 800-222-6675; *www.thebestinn.com.*

HYATT NEWPORTER: This local landmark (it was the first resort hotel in the Newport area), with a terra-cotta exterior and French doors and windows, exudes a California-Mediterranean air of laid-back luxury. Its 403 guestrooms come in several settings: some wrap around a courtyard, others look onto the golf course or Newport Bay, still others face one of the hotel's attractive pools. There are also four bungalows, each with three bedrooms, three baths, a fireplace, and a private yard with a swimming pool.

Besides a nine-hole golf course, three large swimming pools, and three whirlpools, the hotel has volleyball and shuffleboard courts, a health-and-fitness center, and 26 acres of lush, landscaped grounds. Guests have privileges at the adjoining private Palisades Tennis Club, which has 16 courts that are lighted for night play. The Jamboree Grill serves breakfast, lunch, and dinner in a gardenlike setting and on a terrace. Sunday brunch features fresh seafood, carved meats, sushi, and a selection of tempting desserts. Room service is not available.

The hotel provides complimentary transportation to Balboa Island, Fashion Island, and John Wayne Airport, where shuttle service to the Disneyland Resort is available. Rates for doubles run from $145 to $245; suites start at $400. There is no charge for children under 18 sharing their parents' room; $25 daily per extra adult; no charge for rollaways or cribs. Self-parking is $7, valet parking, $13. Pets are no longer allowed. The hotel is about a half-hour drive south from the Disneyland Resort. Hyatt Newporter; 1107 Jamboree Rd.; Newport Beach, CA 92660; 949-729-1234 or 800-233-1234; *www.hyattnewporter.com.*

NEWPORT BEACH MARRIOTT HOTEL AND TENNIS CLUB: The attributes of this 586-room property are many, but foremost among them are the views of Balboa Bay and the Pacific Ocean, the eight tennis courts (lighted for night play), two good-size swimming pools, two whirlpools, and the location across the street from Newport Center Fashion Island, with its 150 boutiques, department stores, and eateries.

The hotel boasts a fine restaurant with an open-air terrace, plus a pleasant bar. It also has concierge service, a gift shop, free transportation to John Wayne Airport, underground parking (for a fee), and a health club that is free to all hotel guests. The guestrooms are located in two towers (one of which has a top-story cocktail lounge with a fabulous view of the Pacific Ocean) and in two low-rise wings; room configurations feature double, queen-, or king-size beds.

Small pets are permitted. Rates run $149 to $189 for doubles and $350 and up for suites; no charge for children under 13 sharing their parents' room or for cribs or rollaways. The hotel is a half-hour drive south from the Disneyland Resort. Newport Beach Marriott Hotel and Tennis Club; 900 Newport Center Dr.; Newport Beach, CA 92660; 949-640-4000 or 800-228-9290; *www.marriott.com.*

Bed & Breakfast Inns

Economical, intimate, congenial. These are a few reasons fans give for choosing to stay in B&Bs. Guestrooms are often furnished with antiques, they may have fireplaces or fabulous ocean views, and private baths have become the norm. B&Bs get the day off to a fine start by supplying a filling breakfast in a serene setting. Most of Orange County's B&Bs are clustered along the coast.

BLUE LANTERN INN: On a bluff overlooking the Pacific, this upscale guesthouse has a slate roof, leaded glass doors, and cobblestoned pathways lined with flowers. Each of the 29 rooms features casual California decor, a fireplace, large bathroom with whirlpool tub, refrigerator, coffeemaker, television, VCR, telephone, and robes. Most have a private patio or balcony, with views of the Dana Point yacht harbor or the Pacific Ocean. The staff provides turndown service.

Complimentary breakfast is served in the sunroom, as are wine and cheese later in the day. Guests chat and play games around a fireplace in the lobby's sitting area or in the library. Teddy bears proliferate in the public areas (and are for sale); the guestrooms, on the other hand, are more sophisticated and nearly bear-free. The inn has an exercise room; it also makes bikes available to guests.

Rates for doubles range from $155 to $500. It's one block west of the Pacific Coast Highway, well within walking distance of several restaurants, and about a half-hour drive from the Disneyland Resort. Because of the location, it's a particularly good choice for those who plan to visit points in both Anaheim and San Diego. Blue Lantern Inn; 34343 Street of the Blue Lantern; Dana Point, CA 92629; 949-661-1304 or 800-950-1236; *www.foursisters.com*.

CASA LAGUNA INN: This has got to be one of Southern California's best-kept secrets, tucked atop a hill overlooking the ocean, just south of Laguna's galleries and restaurants. More enclave than inn, it has five patios, where guests enjoy a large buffet breakfast and afternoon refreshments and hors d'oeuvres—unless they choose to socialize in the inn's landmark Mission House (1920). Also on the grounds is a heated pool landscaped with exotic flowers, and a bell tower with an observation deck.

The 20 rooms and suites are individually decorated with a mix of turn-of-the-century furnishings in wicker and wood. Each one has a private bathroom with shower (some have a whirlpool tub), air-conditioning, high-speed Internet access, cable TV, CD and DVD player (with use of available disks), telephone, and small refrigerator. There is a business center, and a massage therepist. The one-bedroom Cottage, which dates from 1932, features original stained glass, a sitting room with a fireplace, a living room area with a piano, and a private wraparound deck. The Cottage and some suites have kitchens. All suites (and some rooms) have fireplaces.

The courtyard-room rates for doubles are $130 to $195; the ocean-view rooms, $160 to $250; suites, $195 to $375; and the Cottage, which sleeps up to four, $295 to $450. Kids under 12 stay for free in their parents' room. There is free parking behind the inn, which is across the highway from white-sand Victoria Beach and Moss Point Beach. It's about a 45-minute drive south from the Disneyland Resort. Casa Laguna Inn; 2510 S. Coast Hwy.; Laguna Beach, CA 92651; 949-494-2996 or 800-233-0449; *www.casalaguna.com*.

DORYMAN'S OCEANFRONT INN: Situated across the street from the ocean and pier in a charming part of Newport Beach, this B&B is elegant, romantic, and Victorian. Each of the ten guestrooms is beautifully appointed with French and American antiques, a queen- or king-size bed, a fireplace, and modern amenities, including Italian marble showers that double as sunken tubs, a pedestal sink or one tucked into in oak cabinet, plus television and telephone. Half the rooms overlook the ocean, and a couple of them have whirlpool tubs. Rose petals and candles are two of the more luxurious touches. Champagne may be purchased.

The inn has lamp- and skylighted passageways, wood paneling, a breakfast room, and a patio (three rooms open directly onto it) that is perfect for sunbathing and sunrise and sunset watching. Rates range from $195 to $380. Take the elevator to the second floor, where the reception area and the rooms are located. The inn is a half-hour drive south from the Disneyland Resort. Doryman's Oceanfront Inn; 2102 W. Oceanfront; Newport Beach, CA 92663; 949-675-7300.

EILER'S INN: The reception area of this secluded New Orleans-style inn fills a corner of the living room, a comfortable gathering spot with couches, local art, a large coffee table, and six fireplaces; wine and cheese are served here daily from 5 P.M. to 6 P.M., and a classical guitarist performs on Saturday.

Twelve rooms occupy two floors and surround a flower-filled, brick courtyard. Each has country decor complete with antique chest and mirror, floral bedspread and wallpaper, and a private bath with shower (some baths are short on counter space; no TVs or telephones in the rooms). Most rooms have a king or queen bed; two have two double beds. Three rooms provide an ocean view.

The inn also has a sundeck and a small game and TV room. Breakfast—an event, with homemade breads or cakes, boiled eggs, fruit, fresh-squeezed juice, and hand-ground coffee—is served in the courtyard or beside the fireplace. Innkeepers supply iced tea and coffee throughout the day; they also keep a stash of fruit and candy at the reception desk.

Rates for doubles range from $95 to $165, depending on the room and time of the year and week (they tend to be higher during the summer and on Friday and Saturday year-round). The suite, which has a living room,

bedroom, and kitchenette, goes for $185 to $255; add another $20 for each person in the suite beyond two (there is a sofa bed in the room). The inn is four blocks from the center of town; it's a 40-minute drive south from the Disneyland Resort. Limited parking. Eiler's Inn; 741 S. Coast Hwy.; Laguna Beach, CA 92651; 949-494-3004; *www.eilersinn.com*.

SEAL BEACH INN AND GARDENS: On a quiet street a block from the beach and the heart of picturesque Seal Beach, this bed-and-breakfast is only a 10-minute drive from much livelier Long Beach. All 23 rooms are filled with fine Victorian antiques, framed prints, Oriental carpets, and luxurious fabrics. Accent pieces include brass chandeliers from old houses in New Orleans and stained-glass windows from Scotland. Most rooms have built-in bookcases, whirlpools, and fireplaces; some of the larger rooms can accommodate more than two guests.

A red telephone booth from England, lampposts that stood on the streets of Long Beach in the 1930s, and a 300-year-old iron fountain from France decorate the grounds. Behind the inn is a small heated swimming pool, and colorful gardens bloom throughout the year.

Breakfast is served in the Tea Room on tables covered with lace cloths. In the late afternoon, tea and snacks are served beside the fireplace, and guests read vintage books and play chess, checkers, or Scrabble in the adjoining library. The inn's staff provides concierge service, helping plan daily itineraries and making reservations at area restaurants.

Rates start at $170; the elegant penthouse goes for $399. For a real treat, ask about the Gondola Getaway packages. The inn is a 25-minute drive southwest from the Disneyland Resort. Seal Beach Inn & Gardens; 212 Fifth St.; Seal Beach, CA 90740; 562-493-2416 or 800-443-3292; *www.sealbeachinn.com*.

Disneyland Park

When you wish upon a star, your dreams come true. So says the song, and it's always possible in Disneyland Park (also known as the Magic Kingdom), Walt Disney's own dream come true. He envisioned "a place of warmth and nostalgia, of illusion and color and delight." The result: a place where imagination is given free rein, grins and giggles are encouraged, and everyone can see the world through a child's eyes.

The undisguised pleasure on the faces of park-goers reveals that they have fallen under the spell of a turreted pink castle; the oompah of a band marching down Main Street, U.S.A.; the sound of a train conductor's voice calling "All aboard!"; a close-up encounter with Mickey and Minnie; or a nighttime spectacle more fantastic than the most elaborate dream.

Those who first entered Disneyland as kindergartners now return with their own children—or even grandchildren—to find the park of their memories unchanged in spirit and heart. Attractions have come and gone since the park opened in 1955, of course, and whole new "lands" have been added.

But the enchantment guests experience when they walk through the portals of "The Happiest Place on Earth" remains constant. That may well be Disneyland's most enduring accomplishment.

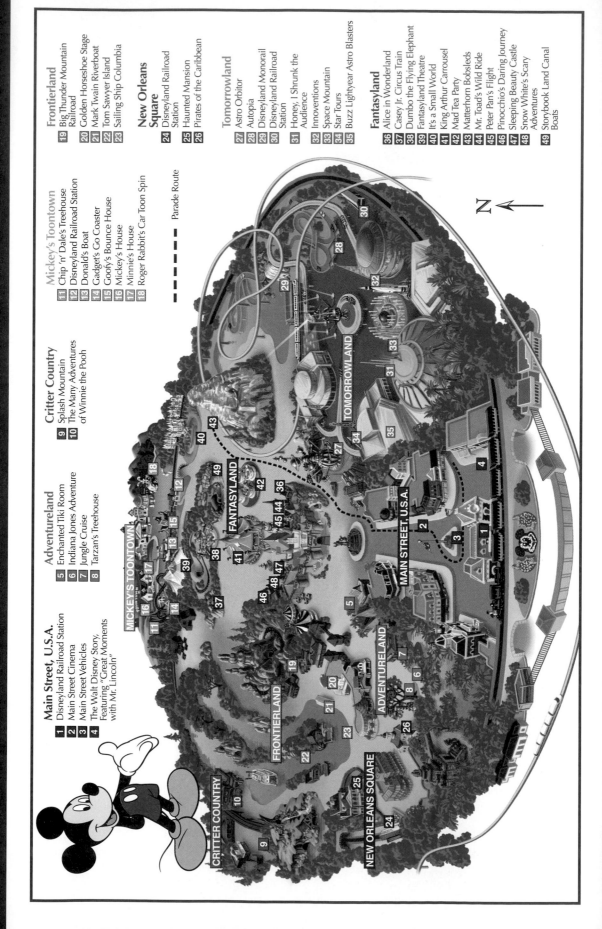

Main Street, U.S.A.
1 Disneyland Railroad Station
2 Main Street Cinema
3 Main Street Vehicles
4 The Walt Disney Story, Featuring "Great Moments with Mr. Lincoln"

Adventureland
5 Enchanted Tiki Room
6 Indiana Jones Adventure
7 Jungle Cruise
8 Tarzan's Treehouse

Critter Country
9 Splash Mountain
10 The Many Adventures of Winnie the Pooh

Mickey's Toontown
11 Chip 'n' Dale's Treehouse
12 Disneyland Railroad Station
13 Donald's Boat
14 Gadget's Go Coaster
15 Goofy's Bounce House
16 Mickey's House
17 Minnie's House
18 Roger Rabbit's Car Toon Spin

- - - - Parade Route

Frontierland
19 Big Thunder Mountain Railroad
20 Golden Horseshoe Stage
21 Mark Twain Riverboat
22 Tom Sawyer Island
23 Sailing Ship Columbia

New Orleans Square
24 Disneyland Railroad Station
25 Haunted Mansion
26 Pirates of the Caribbean

Tomorrowland
27 Astro Orbitor
28 Autopia
29 Disneyland Monorail
30 Disneyland Railroad Station
31 Honey, I Shrunk the Audience
32 Innoventions
33 Space Mountain
34 Star Tours
35 Buzz Lightyear Astro Blasters

Fantasyland
36 Alice in Wonderland
37 Casey Jr. Circus Train
38 Dumbo the Flying Elephant
39 Fantasyland Theatre
40 It's a Small World
41 King Arthur Carrousel
42 Mad Tea Party
43 Matterhorn Bobsleds
44 Mr. Toad's Wild Ride
45 Peter Pan's Flight
46 Pinocchio's Daring Journey
47 Sleeping Beauty Castle
48 Snow White's Scary Adventures
49 Storybook Land Canal Boats

Getting Oriented

Disneyland Park's layout—a basic hub-and-spokes configuration—is simple, but it was innovative when the park opened in 1955. The design makes getting around easy, though it's not altogether effortless, since the numerous nooks, crannies, and alleyways can be a bit confusing at first.

The hub of the theme park's wheel is Central Plaza, which fronts Sleeping Beauty Castle. From it extend five spokes leading to eight "lands": Main Street, U.S.A.; Adventureland; Frontierland; New Orleans Square; Critter Country; Fantasyland; Mickey's Toontown; and Tomorrowland.

As you face Sleeping Beauty Castle, the first bridge to your left takes you to Adventureland; the next one, to Frontierland and New Orleans Square. To your right, the first walkway goes to Tomorrowland, and the next one—known as Matterhorn Way— leads directly into Fantasyland, and on to Mickey's Toontown. If you cross the Castle's moat and walk through the archway, you'll also end up in Fantasyland. Critter Country occupies its own cul-de-sac extending north from New Orleans Square.

Study the map at left to familiarize yourself with the layout of Disneyland before you actually set foot in it. When you arrive at the park, ask for a Disneyland guidemap, which contains the same map, along with information about the times and locations for the day's scheduled entertainment and where to see the characters. It also supplies a list of special services available in the park.

PARKING

Guests are directed to park in Disney's Mickey and Friends parking structure or in one of three lots: Pinocchio, on Disneyland Drive beside the Disneyland Hotel; Simba, behind and adjacent to Disney's Paradise Pier Hotel; and Timon, a remnant of the original Disneyland parking lot off Harbor Boulevard. (Disney's California Adventure stands on what used to be the rest of that lot.) If one parking area is full, a cast member will direct you to one that isn't. Courtesy tram service transports guests from the parking deck and the Timon lot only.

Parking areas open an hour before the park does, but getting a space can take a half hour if there's a long line of park-goers, all with the same idea of getting a head start on the day.

Parking Fees: Guests arriving in regular passenger vehicles pay $8 to park. (The fee for vans and RVs is $10; for buses, $15.) You may leave the lot during the day and return later the same day at no additional charge. (Hold on to your parking stub as proof of payment.)

Lost Cars: Even if you take careful note of where you parked, you might have trouble remembering the exact spot when you return later. Hundreds more vehicles will likely be parked around yours. If this happens, contact a cast member and tell him or her approximately when you arrived. With that information, parking lot personnel can usually figure out the car's general location, and someone will then comb the lanes for it on a scooter.

GETTING AROUND

The Disneyland Railroad's five narrow-gauge trains make a 20-minute loop around the perimeter of the park, stopping at stations in Main Street, U.S.A.; New Orleans Square; Mickey's Toontown; and Tomorrowland. Horse-drawn streetcars, horseless carriages, and a motorized fire engine make one-way trips up and down Main Street.

To travel outside Disneyland park, consider the sleek monorail, which glides between Tomorrowland and Downtown Disney. From Downtown Disney, you can walk to any of the three on-property hotels—the Disneyland Hotel, Disney's Paradise Pier Hotel, and Disney's Grand Californian. Disney's California Adventure park is just a few steps from the entrance to Disneyland (the two parks require separate admission, unless you have a Three-, Four-, or Five-Day or Resort Park Hopper Ticket).

Park Primer

BABY FACILITIES

The Baby Care Center, on Main Street, U.S.A., by First Aid, provides changing tables, high chairs, toddlers' toilets, and a nursing area. Baby food can be warmed here, and baby powder, diapers, formula, and food are sold. There are no napping facilities or baby-sitting services.

FIRST AID

First Aid is located at the north end of Main Street, next door to the Main Street Photo Supply Co. A registered nurse is on duty during park operating hours.

GUIDED TOUR

Guests who are familiar with Disneyland but would like to know more about it should try the guided tour "A Walk in Walt's Footsteps." This recently tweaked walking tour allows guests to experience the Happiest Place On Earth from its founder's perspective.

Packed with anecdotes, history, and culture, it includes a sneak peek at the lobby of the legendary Club 33 restaurant in New Orleans Square, a luncheon on the balcony of the Disney Gallery, a visit to the Enchanted Tiki Room (the first attraction to feature Disney's pioneering Audio-Animatronics technology), and a collectible pin.

Tickets for the tour cost $49 for adults and children, plus park admission. They are available at the ticket booths at the main entrance or at City Hall. The tour lasts about 3½ hours.

HOURS

Disneyland is open daily. Weekday hours are generally from 10 A.M. to 8 P.M., with extended hours during the summer. Saturday hours are typically 9 A.M. to midnight. The hours on Sundays are usually about 9 A.M. to 9 P.M. For specific park hours, call 714-781-4565, or check online at *www.disneyland.com*.

During the busy summer and Christmas holiday seasons, it's especially wise to arrive first thing in the morning so that you can visit the popular attractions before the lines get long. If you arrive at Disneyland too late, the parking structure and surrounding lots could be more crowded than usual; this is almost always the case in the summer months and during the last week of December.

For more timing tactics, see "Hot Tips" in this chapter and "Crowd Patterns" in the *Getting Ready to Go* chapter.

INFORMATION

Cast members at Disneyland Information Centers in City Hall and at Central Plaza can answer any questions you might have (or help plot your day so that you can make the most efficient use of your time and see what attractions truly interest you). Specifics on special services and safety considerations have been compiled in Disneyland's guidemap; ask for it when you enter the park.

Information Board: An invaluable resource for planning the day, the Information Board is set up permanently at the north end of Main Street, U.S.A. Located in a grassy spot near the Plaza Pavilion and the entrance to Adventureland, it lets you know how long the waits are for most of the popular attractions, what (if anything) is not operating that day, and where and when park entertainment will take place. The board is updated every hour. Cast members who are stationed there will also answer specific questions and provide information about the restaurants and hotels in the Disneyland Resorts. They can help guests locate their favorite Disney characters in the park, too.

MONEY MATTERS

Cash and traveler's checks are accepted at all food and merchandise locations throughout Disneyland. American Express, MasterCard, Visa, JCB Card, and the Discover Card are accepted at all shops, cafeterias, fast-food eateries, snack bars, and full-service establishments (cash only at most vending carts). Traveler's checks are available for AAA members at the AAA tour and Travel Services Kiosk. Contact the AAA Kiosk at 714-563-7470.

Personal checks with your name and address printed on them, drawn on U.S. funds, and accompanied by a government-issued photo ID, are also accepted as payment for meals and merchandise.

Disneyland Resort hotel guests may charge almost any purchase made in the theme park back to their hotel bill if they gave a credit card number at check-in. Keep in mind that this service is not available at most Downtown Disney locations.

Guests may purchase Disney Dollars in $1, $5, and $10 denominations from any park entrance ticket booth, the Bank of Main Street, and City Hall. Disney Dollars are accepted at the three Disney hotels, Downtown Disney, California Adventure, and throughout Disneyland. They can be redeemed for real currency at any time.

There are several ATMs here. The first one, encountered when first entering the park, is located beside the Bank on Main Street.

PACKAGE STORAGE

There's no need to lug bags around. You can store bulky packages at the Newsstand at the entrance to Disneyland (on the right as you exit the park). Package Express delivery service is no longer offered.

SAME-DAY RE-ENTRY

Guests who wish to leave the park and return later the same day may do so by getting their hand stamped upon exiting. The stamp will survive numerous hand washings. Keep in mind that you will need both your park ticket and a hand-stamp for re-entry.

SMOKING POLICY

At Disneyland park, smoking is only permitted in designated smoking areas; refer to a park guidemap for specific locations. It is prohibited inside all attractions, waiting areas, shops, and indoor and outdoor dining areas.

STROLLERS & WHEELCHAIRS

Strollers and wheelchairs may be rented for $7 inside the turnstiles of Disneyland park, with a $20 deposit and major credit card. Electric Convenience Vehicles (ECVs) cost $30 for the day, with a $20 deposit and major credit card. Lost strollers may be replaced at the main entrance and at The Star Trader shop, in Tomorrowland.

SECURITY CHECK

Guests entering Disney theme parks are subject to a security check. Backpacks, parcels, purses, etc., may be searched by security personnel before guests are permitted to enter.

Expect car trunks to be searched when entering Disney parking facilities.

Guests checking into Disneyland Resort hotels are asked to present a valid government-issued photo ID.

Ticket Prices

Although prices are always subject to change, the following will give you an idea of what you can expect to pay. Note that prices and ticketing structure are likely to increase in 2004. For current prices, call 714-781-4565 or visit *www.disneyland.com.*

	Adults	Children*
One-Day Ticket	$49.75	$39.75
Three-Day Ticket	$129	$99
Four-Day Ticket	$159	$129

*3 through 9 years of age; children under 3 free

Main Street, U.S.A.

This pretty thoroughfare represents Main Street America in the early 1900s, complete with the gentle clip-clop of horses' hooves on pavement, melodic ringing of streetcar bells, and strains of nostalgic tunes such as "Bicycle Built for Two" and "Coney Island Baby."

The sounds of brass bands, a barbershop quartet, and ragtime piano fill the street. An old-fashioned steam train huffs into a handsome brick depot. Rows of picturesque buildings line the street. Authentic gaslights, which once lit up Baltimore and St. Louis, flicker at sundown in ornate lampposts lining the walkways, and the storefronts—painted in a palette of pastels—could not be more inviting. Walt Disney was a master of detail: throughout Main Street, even the doorknobs are historically correct.

To make the buildings appear taller, a set designer's technique called forced perspective was employed. The first floor is seven-eighths scale (this allows guests to enter comfortably); the second story is five-eighths scale; and the third, only half size. The dimensions of the whole are small enough for the place to seem intimate and comforting, yet the proportions appear correct. (Forced perspective was also used to make the Matterhorn and Sleeping Beauty Castle seem taller than they are.)

The shops that line Main Street, U.S.A., draw guests back repeatedly during their Disneyland visit (see the "Shopping" section of this chapter and you'll understand why).

The following attractions are listed in the order in which you'll encounter them while walking from the main entrance up Main Street to the Central Plaza, toward Sleeping Beauty Castle.

Birnbaum's Best

BIRNBAUM'S ★BEST★ Stamps like this one indicate the attractions that we find superlative in one (and usually more) of the following ways: state-of-the-art technology, theming, beauty, novelty, thrills and spills (make that splashes), and overall whimsy. Each "Birnbaum's Best" promises to deliver a dynamite Disneyland experience!

CITY HALL: Before strolling up Main Street, stop briefly at the Information Center at City Hall, on the west side of Town Square, to get entertainment schedules, as well as help making dining reservations, or advice to help you plan your Disneyland day. City Hall is also a great meeting place if members of your party separate and plan to congregate later.

FIRE STATION: Next door to City Hall, this was Walt Disney's home away from home during the construction of Disneyland. His apartment, on the top floor, is decorated just as he

left it, but is not open to the public. A light burns in the window in his memory. Kids love—and are welcome—to climb on the fire wagon parked inside the Firehouse. It's authentic (from the early 1900s) and provides a great photo opportunity.

BANK OF MAIN STREET: The bank offers foreign-currency exchange and sells Disney Dollars. There is an ATM inside.

DISNEYLAND RAILROAD: Walt Disney loved trains so much he actually built a one-eighth-scale model, the Carolwood Pacific, in the backyard of his home. So it was only natural that his first theme park include a railroad—five narrow-gauge steam trains that circle Disneyland park in about 20 minutes, making stops in Main Street, U.S.A.; New Orleans Square; Mickey's Toontown; and Tomorrowland.

Hot Tip!

The Disneyland Railroad is wheelchair-accessible at New Orleans Square, Mickey's Toontown, and Tomorrowland stations.

Main Street just wouldn't be Main Street without the sound of the trains chugging in and out of the station and the conductors calling "All aboard!"

Two of the locomotives were built at the Walt Disney Studios, while three had other lives before coming to Disneyland. All five trains are powered by oil-fueled steam boilers and must stop several times a day to fill up on water. They are powered by diesel boilers and run on 100 percent pure steam pressure.

Guests who ride the train between Tomorrowland and Main Street, U.S.A., are in for a couple of surprises. In 1958, Walt Disney added a diorama of the Grand Canyon, depicted from its south rim on a seamless, hand-woven canvas that is 306 feet long and 34 feet high, and covered with 300 gallons of paint. The fauna and foliage depict deer, a mountain lion, a golden eagle, wild turkeys, skunks, porcupines, and desert mountain sheep, surrounded by quaking aspens and piñons and ponderosa pines, with a snowfall, a storm, a sunset, and a rainbow thrown in for good measure. The accompanying music is the "On the Trail" section of American composer Ferde Grofé's Grand Canyon Suite.

Adjacent to the Grand Canyon, yet eons away, the Primeval World diorama—a scene of misty swamps, deserts, rain forests, erupting volcanoes, and 46 prehistoric creatures inspired by Disney's 1940 film *Fantasia*—opened in 1966, after an interim stop at the Ford Pavilion at the New York World's Fair.

THE WALT DISNEY STORY, FEATURING "GREAT MOMENTS WITH MR. LINCOLN": A JOURNEY TO GETTYSBURG: The Disneyland Opera House makes the perfect backdrop for a tribute to the life and accomplishments of Walter Elias Disney. A 15-minute film about him is shown continuously, and the actual offices he used in the Burbank studio for 26 years are on view. His briefcase and models of his personal planes, the Mickey I and the Mickey II, rest in this office, just as they did when he worked there. Adjacent to it, in his formal office, is the baby grand on which Leopold Stokowski previewed music for *Fantasia*. Other memorabilia include letters from celebrities and politicos.

Note that the offices and all of the memorabilia may not be on display during your visit.

Mr. Lincoln: Besides Walt Disney, the other star here is the Audio-Animatronic version of America's 16th president. This classic attraction was updated in the summer of 2001. The show begins by immersing guests in the firsthand perspective of an 1863 Union soldier involved in a Civil War battle. His story is told through period photographs and "3-D" audio technology.

The presentation climaxes with Abraham Lincoln's emotional Gettysburg address. Mr. Lincoln stands up and discourses on liberty and the American Spirit—all the while nodding, gesturing, turning, and shifting his weight in a realistic fashion. The sound system is Disney-imagineered "binaural audio."

MAIN STREET VEHICLES: Main Street's motorized fire wagon, horseless carriages, and horse-drawn streetcars give the thoroughfare a real touch of nostalgia, while at the same time giving guests a lift from one end of the street to the other. The fire truck is modeled after those that might have been discovered on an American main street in the early 1900s, except that it has seats where the hose was meant to be carried.

The horse-drawn streetcars, inspired by those in 19th-century photographs, carry 30 passengers each. Most of the horses that pull the cars are Belgians (characterized by their white manes and tails and lightly feathered legs) and Percheron draft horses.

PHOTO BY KEITH GROSHANS

Save Time in Line!

For those of us who'd prefer not to waste time standing in line for theme park attractions, Disney's Fastpass is nothing short of a miracle. Basically, the system allows guests to forgo the task of waiting in an actual line for a number of theme park attractions.

How? Simply by walking up to the Fastpass booth (located near the entrance of participating attractions) and slipping their park ticket into the Fastpass machine.

In return, guests get a slip of paper with a time printed on it (in addition to the safe return of their park ticket). That time—for example, 4:05 P.M. to 5:05 P.M.—represents the "window" in which guests are invited to return to the attraction and practically walk right on—without standing in a long line!

Once you use your Fastpass to enter an attraction (or the time on it has passed), you can get a new Fastpass time for another attraction. It's also possible to get a Fastpass for a second attraction two hours after the first one is issued.

For example, if one pass was issued at 2 P.M. you can get a Fastpass for another attraction at 4 P.M. Sound confusing? It won't be once you've tried it.

Disney's Fastpass service is free and available to everyone bearing a valid theme park ticket. It should be available during peak times of the day and all peak seasons. We've placed the Fastpass logo (**FP**) beside the listing for all of the attractions that were participating at press time. However, since more attractions are scheduled for inclusion, check a park map for an up-to-the-minute listing of Fastpass attractions.

Note that all Disney attractions continue to offer the option of standing in a traditional line. If you happen to enjoy the standing-in-line experience, by all means, go for it. Otherwise, take our advice: Fastpass is the way to go!

MAIN STREET CINEMA: This small, standing room only theater features a classic Mickey Mouse cartoon.

PENNY ARCADE: This place is now more of a candy shop than arcade, but the air of nostalgia remains. Those who have frequented it in the past will be happy to find Esmeralda front and center, as before, ready as always to tell your fortune. The arcade still has Mutascopes, machines that feature hand-cranked moving pictures and require a penny to operate. Fans of the classic electrocution machine will be happy to know that it is right out front.

Save some change for the arcade's nine penny presses. You insert a penny (plus a few other coins to pay for the service), and the penny will be flattened and imprinted with the image of Sleeping Beauty Castle or the face of one of the Disney characters.

CENTRAL PLAZA: Main Street, U.S.A., ends at Central Plaza, the hub of the park, and four of the park's lands are directly accessible from here. At its center stands the Walt and Mickey Partners statue. It's one of the park's most popular picture spots.

One of Disneyland's two Information Centers is located here, near the entrance to Adventureland. Besides the information desk, there is a handy Information Board, updated hourly, that posts wait times for many attractions, which attractions offer Fastpass, what (if anything) is not operating that day, and where and when park entertainment will take place.

PLAZA GARDENS: Visiting performers fill the small stage here in the afternoons, and guests dance to live bands Saturday evenings year-round and Friday evenings in summer. This is a fine spot to bring a snack and relax.

Adventureland

For someone who grew up in Marceline, Missouri, around the turn of the twentieth century, as Walt Disney did, the far-flung regions of the world must have seemed most exotic and exciting. So it's not surprising that when he was planning his new park, he designated one area, called Adventureland, to represent all the (then) remote and mysterious corners of the world.

The original South Seas–island ambience all but disappeared with the opening of the Indiana Jones Adventure in 1995, and Adventureland became a 1930s jungle outpost. Today the entrance to the Jungle Cruise is a walk-through headquarters, with period photographs and radios playing big-band music interrupted by news flashes about Professor Jones's latest exploits and discoveries. Shops here now sell wares that appeal to modern-day adventurers. And it's not at all uncommon to see guests wandering around in hats à la Indy.

ENCHANTED TIKI ROOM: Introduced in 1963, this was the first of the park's Audio-Animatronic attractions and the precursor of more elaborate variations, such as "Great Moments with Mr. Lincoln" and the above-mentioned Dr. Jones. Housed in a vaguely Polynesian complex situated at the entrance to Adventureland, the 15-minute show has been given a spiffy face-lift to mark Disneyland's 50th anniversary.

The stars are four feathered emcees (José, Michael, Pierre, and Fritz), backed up by a sextet of pastel-plumed, long-eyelashed parrots, and an eclectic chorus of orchids, carved wooden tiki poles, tiki drummers, singing masks, bird-of-paradise flowers, macaws, Amazon parrots, toucans, fork-tailed birds, cockatoos, and several other species.

The 225 performers all sing and drum up a tropical storm with so much animation that it's hard to resist a smile. Their repertoire

includes "In the Tiki, Tiki, Tiki Room" (the show's theme song), "The Hawaiian War Chant," "Let's All Sing," and "Aloha to You."

JUNGLE CRUISE: The spiel delivered by the skipper on this seven-minute river adventure has its share of corny jokes, but your navigator may turn out to be a natural comic with a funny delivery. Just remember that the bad jokes are all part of the fun.

As jungle cruises go, this one is as much like the real thing as Main Street, U.S.A., is like life in a real small town—long on loveliness and short on the visual distractions and minor annoyances that constitute the bulk of human experience. There are no mosquitoes, no Montezuma's revenge. And the Bengal tiger and two king cobras at the ancient Cambodian ruins, and the great apes, gorillas, crocodiles, alligators, elephants, hippos, and lions in the water and along the shores represent no threat to passersby—though according to maintenance crews, they are almost as much trouble as real ones.

Movie buffs should note that Bob Mattey, who helped develop these jungle creatures, also worked on the giant squid from the Disney film *20,000 Leagues Under the Sea*, the man-eating plants in many *Tarzan* movies, and the menacing mechanical shark in *Jaws*.

The large-leafed upright tree in the Cambodian ruins section of the attraction is a Ficus religiosa, the same species of tree under which Buddha received enlightenment in India many centuries ago.

TARZAN'S TREEHOUSE: The 70-foot-high *Disneydendron semperflorens grandis*, or "large, ever-blooming Disney tree," which cradled the Swiss Family Treehouse from 1962 to mid-1999, now embraces another lofty dwelling: Tarzan's

Treehouse, inspired by the book by Edgar Rice Burroughs and Disney's animated feature *Tarzan*. Overlooking the Jungle Cruise and the Temple of the Forbidden Eye (the setting for Indiana Jones's misadventures), this moss- and vine-covered "high-rise apartment" shelters Tarzan; his adoptive mom, the ape Kala; and his companion, Jane.

An interactive play area at the base of the tree has been designed around the scientific equipment that Jane and her father brought to the jungle. (Guests are welcome to experiment with some of it.) Nearby, a makeshift wooden staircase crafted from shipwreck salvage and a weathered suspension bridge provide easy access to the treehouse itself.

Jane's drawings, displayed throughout the compound, reveal the amazing story of Tarzan's survival and coming-of-age in the wild. (But could there be trouble in paradise? That lout of a leopard, Sabor, is lurking in the tree!) By the time guests plant their feet on terra firma once more, they will have hit new heights, not unlike a certain high-flying hero himself, and gotten acquainted with some of the characters—human and animal—who have shared in his exploits.

BIRNBAUM'S BEST

INDIANA JONES™ ADVENTURE: FP Hidden deep within the dense jungles of India, the Temple of the Forbidden Eye was built long ago to honor the powerful deity Mara. According to legend, Mara could "look into your very soul" and grant the "pure of heart" one of three gifts: unlimited wealth, eternal youth, or future knowledge. But legend also issues a stern warning: "A terrible fate awaits those who gaze upon the eyes of Mara!" Dr. Jones would only comment, "Records indicate that many have come, but few have returned."

Now you can take an expedition through the ancient temple ruins in this attraction based on the George Lucas/Steven Spielberg film trilogy. The whole experience, including the pre-show and queue area, can easily take more than an hour (without a Fastpass), though the ride itself lasts about 3½ minutes. You follow the jungle path through Dr. Jones's cluttered encampment, then enter the temple via the path marked by his original team. In the queue area, a newsreel tells of Jones's latest expedition. What it does not reveal is that he has entered the temple and disappeared.

Following in his footsteps, you will see warning signs that indicate there still may be booby traps that have not yet been disarmed. (The fun is in paying no heed to the warnings and letting the spikes fall where they may.) Inside the temple, guests board 12-passenger vehicles reminiscent of 1930s troop transports. One person takes the wheel and serves as the expedition driver, but not until all are securely fastened in their seats for the twists and turns ahead. Hold on to your hat!

The search for Indiana Jones is on, and an encounter with the fearsome Mara is unavoidable. The trip reveals a world of mummies, glowing fires, falling lava, worrisome snakes, and poisonous darts.

Surprises lurk around every bend, and escape is only temporary (just as in the movies), as you suffer an avalanche of creepy crawlies, traverse a quaking suspension bridge, and, best of all, find yourself face-to-face with a gigantic rolling ball that threatens to flatten everyone in its path. At the end of the ride, Indy himself is waiting for you, with a flippant parting remark such as "That wasn't so bad" or "Next time you're on your own."

Thanks to the wizardry of Disney Imagineers, no two rides are exactly the same, so each time you enter the Temple of the Forbidden Eye, the experience will be slightly different.

Note: Pregnant women and guests who suffer from heart conditions, motion sickness, weak backs, and other limitations should not ride. Kids must be at least 3 years old or at least 46 inches tall to board; those under 7 must be accompanied by an adult. Spooked by snakes? There are more than a few in here. They're not real, but still creepy. Just a warning.

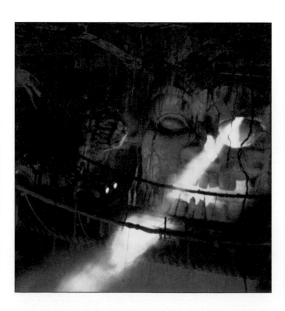

New Orleans Square

PHOTO BY JILL SAFRO

Though New Orleans Square did not figure in the Disneyland layout until 1966, it's certainly among the park's most evocative areas. This would be true even if it were home only to the superb Haunted Mansion and Pirates of the Caribbean. But there's also its picturesque site on the shores of the Rivers of America, and its architecture, a pastiche of wrought iron, pastel stucco, French doors, and beckoning verandas.

Not to be missed are the pleasant open-air dining spots; the romantic Blue Bayou restaurant overlooking the moonlit lagoon stretch of Pirates of the Caribbean; the unique assortment of shops; and the music—lively jazz and Dixieland, performed in traditional New Orleans style.

As you sit here on a warm evening, snacking on fritters and hot chocolate, images of Disneyland-as-amusement-park evaporate. Just as Main Street, U.S.A., makes the theme park a great place to shop, New Orleans Square makes it a fine spot to spend a few relaxing hours. Those click-click sounds emanating from the railroad station are the Morse code version of the actual speech Walt Disney gave on the opening day of Disneyland back in 1955.

The attractions that are described on the following pages are listed in the order in which you would encounter them while strolling from east to west in Disneyland's New Orleans Square.

BIRNBAUM'S ★BEST★ PIRATES OF THE CARIBBEAN: FP

One of the most swashbuckling adventures you'll find at Disneyland, this 16-minute boat ride transports guests through a series of sets portraying a rowdy pirate raid on a Caribbean village. Bursting with cannon fire, stolen loot, a gluttonous feast, and a raucous band of unruly mercenaries, Pirates of the Caribbean has entertained more people than any theme park attraction in history. It was the last attraction on which Walt Disney worked extensively.

The experience begins with a short excursion through a bayou, where will-o'-the-wisps glow just above the grasses. Fireflies twinkle nearby, while stars spangle the twilight-blue sky overhead. The attention to detail nearly boggles the mind. The Audio-Animatronic cast of 64 human figures and 55 animals includes drunken pigs whose legs actually twitch in their soporific contentment, chickens so realistic that even a farmer might be fooled at first, and a piccolo-playing pirate whose fingers move and cheeks puff as he toots a little ditty. Notice the realistic details, like the hairs on the leg of one swashbuckler perched atop a bridge overhead.

The attraction's theme song, "Yo-Ho, Yo-Ho; a Pirate's Life for Me," manages to transform what is actually a picture of some blatant buccaneering into a rousing time for all. A must—again and again.

FP = Fastpass attraction (see page 64)

THE DISNEY GALLERY: The stairways on either side of the entrance to Pirates of the Caribbean lead to this French Quarter–style suite of rooms, originally designed to be the private apartment of Walt Disney. Dignitaries often visited the park, and he wanted an elegant place in which he and his brother Roy could meet and greet them. Today, the gallery has changing exhibits of original artwork, focusing mainly on the concepts and drawings for specific Disney projects. Cast members give gallery tours upon request.

The inviting interior patio is climate controlled year-round because Walt Disney planned to do a lot of entertaining there. In the evenings, the balcony holds up to 20 guests for VIP seating for Fantasmic! (Reservations are necessary; for information, see "Entertainment" at the end of this chapter.)

Study the grillwork surrounding the balcony; the initials W.D. and R.D. (for Walt and Roy Disney) are woven into the design.

BIRNBAUM'S ★BEST **HAUNTED MANSION:** FP In a British radio interview, Walt Disney once explained how sorry he felt for those homeless ghosts whose hauntable mansions had fallen to the wrecker's ball. Feeling that these lost souls sorely needed a place of their own, he offered this Haunted Mansion, unquestionably one of Disneyland's top attractions. From its stately portico to the exit corridor, the special effects are piled on to create an eerie, but never terrifying, mood. Just frightfully funny.

Judicious applications of paint and expert lighting effects heighten the shadows that play ghoulishly on the walls outside. The jumble of

PHOTO BY KEITH GROSHANS

trunks, chairs, dress forms, and other assorted knickknacks in the attic are left appropriately dirty, and extra cobwebs, which come in convenient liquid form, are strung with abandon. The eerie music and the slightly spooky tones of the Ghost Host often set small children to whimpering, and soon their Mickey Mouse ears have been pulled tightly over their eyes. Still, the spirits that inhabit this house on the hill—999 in all—are a tame lot for the most part, though they are always looking for occupant number 1,000.

Hot Tip!

Haunted Mansion Holiday kicks off in October and runs through December. It features Jack Skellington from Tim Burton's *The Nightmare Before Christmas*, as well as holiday decor galore. Silly, seasonal sight gags abound.

What makes the seven-minute attraction so special is the attention to, and abundance of, details—so many that it's next to impossible to take them all in during the first, or even the second or third, time around. In the Portrait Chamber, a roomful of fearsome-looking gargoyles that adjoins the chandeliered and lace-curtain-adorned foyer, it's fun to speculate on whether the ceiling moves up or the room moves down. (It's one way here and the opposite way at the mansion's counterpart at Walt Disney World's Magic Kingdom.)

Once in your Doom Buggy, look for the bats' eyes on the wallpaper, the tomb-sweet-tomb plaque, and the rattling suit of armor in the Corridor of Doors. Can you spot a Hidden Mickey in the haunted dining room?

Then there are the dead plants and flowers and broken glass in the Conservatory, where a hand reaches out of a half-open casket; the terrified cemetery watchman and his mangy mutt in the Graveyard; the ghostly teapot that pours spectral tea; the ectoplasmic king and queen on the teeter-totter; the bicycle-riding spirits; the transparent musicians; and the headless knight and his supernatural Brunhilde. Nice stuff all.

The mansion was constructed in 1963, based on studies of houses around Baltimore; the attraction itself opened in 1969. The music "Grim Grinning Ghosts" was composed especially for the Haunted Mansion attraction.

Frontierland

This is the America experienced by the pioneers as they pushed westward: rough wilderness outposts, dense forests, rugged mountains delineating the skyline, and rivers lapping at the shore.

The sights in Frontierland are just about as pleasant as they come at Disneyland, and the atmosphere as relaxing. That's especially true in the afternoon, when the riverboat *Mark Twain*, with its elaborate wooden lacework trim, pulls majestically away from its dock for a cruise along the Rivers of America.

The following Frontierland attractions are described in the order in which visitors encounter them while moving counterclockwise from the Central Plaza gateway toward Big Thunder Mountain.

FRONTIERLAND SHOOTIN' EXPOSITION:
This shooting gallery, set in an 1850s town in the Southwest Territory, is completely electronic. Eighteen rifles are trained on Boothill, a mining town complete with a bank, jail, hotel, and stables. They fire infrared beams that trigger silly results whenever they strike the red reactive targets. The most challenging target is the moving shovel, which, when struck, causes a skeleton to pop out of a grave.

Note: Disneyland tickets do not include use of the arcade. Pay 50 cents for 20 shots—then fire away.

BIRNBAUM'S BEST **BIG THUNDER MOUNTAIN RAILROAD:** FP Hold onto your hats and glasses, because this here's the wildest ride in the wilderness. Inspired by peaks in Utah's Bryce Canyon, Big Thunder Mountain is entirely a Disney creation. The name comes from an old Indian legend about a sacred mountain in Wyoming that thundered whenever men tried to excavate its gold. The attraction took five years of planning and two years of construction, and it cost about as much to build as the rest of the original Disneyland attractions put together—$16 million.

As roller coasters go, this one is relatively tame. It's short on steep climbs and precipitous drops that put hearts in throats and make stomachs protest, but long on tight curves that provoke giggles of glee. Adding to the appeal of this thrill ride is the scenery that the runaway mine train passes along the way: a pitch-black bat cave, giant stalactites and stalagmites, a waterfall, a natural-arch bridge that affords fine views over the Big Thunder landscape, and mine walls ready to cave in.

The queue area sets the scene of the quaint mining town, with two hotels, a newspaper office, dance hall, saloon, and general store. If you listen closely, you may hear a local barmaid flirting with a miner to the tune of "Red River Valley" or "Listen to the Mockingbird."

As you proceed toward the loading area, notice the brownish stone walls on each side of you. They were created from a hundred tons of real gold ore from the former mining town of Rosamond, California, which also yielded the ten-foot-tall stamp mill designated Big Thunder Mine 1880.

This is an extremely popular ride, so try to get to it first thing in the morning, during a parade, or just before park closing, when the lines are shorter. For the best of both worlds, ride twice—once by day, to see the scenery, and again after dark, for the pleasure of hurtling through the cool night (you might catch a glimpse of the Fantasmic! show).

Note: Pregnant women and guests who have heart conditions, motion sickness, weak backs, and other limitations should not ride. Children must be at least 3 years old and a minimum of 40 inches tall to board. Kids under 7 years old must be accompanied by an adult.

MARK TWAIN RIVERBOAT: One of the original Disneyland attractions and the first paddle wheeler built in the United States in half a century, this five-eighths-scale vessel circumnavigates Tom Sawyer Island. Along the way, it passes the River Belle Terrace, the Royal Street Veranda, the docks for the Tom Sawyer Island Rafts, piney Critter Country, a waterfall, abandoned railroad tracks, and lovely dense woods full of the alders, cottonwoods, maples, and willows that might have been found along the Missouri frontier more than a century ago. Moose, elk, and (real) ducks complete the passing scene.

On a busy day, this 14-minute ride offers a pleasant respite from the crowds. And if you manage to get one of the few chairs in the bow, the *Mark Twain* also provides a rare opportunity to put your feet up.

GOLDEN HORSESHOE STAGE: Tongue-in-cheek humor and western flair are the key ingredients in the musical and specialty acts featured at this entertainment venue. The hall itself is resplendent with chandeliers, polished floors and banisters, and a long brass railing. Supposedly, it was inspired by the Golden Horseshoe Saloon, which flourished in a bygone era in New York City. Walt Disney kept a private box here, just to the left of the stage, on the upper level.

Billy Hill & the Hillbillies, brothers who mix bluegrass music and wacky comedy, are regular performers at the Golden Horseshoe Stage (for specifics, see page 94). Performance times vary. Check a guidemap's entertainment schedule or drop by an Information Center when you arrive at the park.

There is no assigned seating inside; all of the seats are good, though those up front or on the balcony are perhaps the best.

SAILING SHIP COLUMBIA: A full-scale replica of the ten-gun, three-masted "Gem of the Ocean," the *Columbia* operates seasonally and on higher-attendance days at Disneyland. The original ship, constructed in Plymouth, Massachusetts, in 1787 and christened the *Columbia Rediviva* ("freedom reborn"), was

the first American craft to circumnavigate the globe. (Back then, that took three years to do.)

Disney's *Columbia*, dedicated in 1958 and renovated in 1984, was the first of its kind to be built in more than a century, and it circumnavigates the Rivers of America in 15 minutes. It has a steel hull and a deck planked with Douglas fir, and measures 110 feet from stem to stern, with an 84-foot mainmast. Usually moored at Fowler's Harbor, opposite the Haunted Mansion, the ship towers majestically over the treetops below.

Below Decks: The *Columbia*'s maritime museum, open only when the ship is operating, illustrates the way sailors lived on the original vessel during its later voyages, as reported in the ship's log and in letters between the captain and the owners.

TOM SAWYER ISLAND: The landfall that the *Mark Twain*, the *Columbia*, and Davy Crockett's Explorer Canoes circle as they ply the Rivers of America was at one time the highest point in Disneyland. Its treehouse, complete with spyglasses and peepholes, lets would-be branch dwellers gaze out over the treetops to the *Mark Twain* when it's docked across the river. But the treehouse is only one of the many wonders on Tom Sawyer Island.

Hot Tip!

Cool, dark, and spooky inside, the labyrinthine Injun Joe's Cave is one of the best spots on Tom Sawyer Island.

On another wonder, the floating Barrel Bridge, it's nearly impossible to maintain a stride more decorous than a lurch. Nearby, kids scramble up a small hill studded with log steps. Then there's Castle Rock Ridge—a group of boulders that includes the mightily spinning Merry-Go-Round Rock, the aptly named Teeter-Totter Rock, and (inside the Ridge) the spacious Pirate's Den and smaller Castle Rock Dungeon. The latter is full of niches and cul-de-sacs just the right size for the island's youngest explorers, but

Hot Tip!

Select one member of your party to be a Fastpass representative—someone who'll gather the park tickets and get Fastpass assignments for the group.

so narrow and low-ceilinged in places that grown-ups who don't bend down or turn sideways risk getting stuck, just like Winnie the Pooh.

At the island's southernmost point, there's a perpetually creaking old mill; at the opposite end stands Fort Wilderness.

Small signs point to places of interest on the island, and even though the footpaths are decidedly well-trodden, any time spent here is worthwhile, and could encompass some of your happiest getaway moments at Disneyland.

Note: Tom Sawyer Island closes early to allow for Fantasmic! preparation. Check at the dock for excursion times, particularly the last departure.

Disneyland Park Fastpass Attractions

Long lines got you down? Not to worry— most of the major Disneyland attractions now offer Fastpass. (For an explanation of this time-saving, line-skipping system, turn to page 64.) Here's a list of those "E-ticket" crowd pleasers (keep in mind that attractions may be added to the list at any time—check a park guidemap for last-minute inclusions):

ADVENTURELAND
Indiana Jones Adventure

NEW ORLEANS SQUARE
Pirates of the Caribbean
Haunted Mansion

FRONTIERLAND
Big Thunder Mountain Railroad

CRITTER COUNTRY
Splash Mountain
The Many Adventures of Winnie the Pooh

FANTASYLAND
Matterhorn Bobsleds

MICKEY'S TOONTOWN
Roger Rabbit's Car Toon Spin

TOMORROWLAND
Star Tours; Autopia; Space Mountain

Critter Country

PHOTO BY KEITH GROSHANS

Lush shady forests of pines, locusts, white birches, coastal redwoods, and evergreen elms surround Critter Country, one of the most pleasant corners of Disneyland. In 1972, this land debuted as Bear Country, the backwoods home of the since departed Country Bear Playhouse. From 1956 through 1971, the area was called the Indian Village, complete with teepees and a dance circle, and was part of Frontierland.

In 1989, the zone welcomed foxes, frogs, geese, rabbits, crocodiles, and many of the other critters that make up the Audio-Animatronic cast of Splash Mountain. To make the new furry residents feel at home, Disney Imagineers rechristened the area Critter Country. Observant guests will spot scaled-down houses, lairs, and nests tucked into hillsides and along the river.

Attractions are described here according to their east-to-west locations.

BIRNBAUM'S ★BEST★ **SPLASH MOUNTAIN:** **FP** The fourth peak in Disneyland's mountain range of thrill rides— along with Big Thunder Mountain, the Matterhorn, and Space Mountain—Splash Mountain is unlike the other three attractions, where passengers ride roller coaster–style cars down tubular steel tracks. In this nine-minute

ride, they board hollowed-out logs and drift on a waterborne journey through backwoods swamps and bayous, down waterfalls, and finally (here's where the speed picks up), over the top of a steep spillway at the peak of the mountain into a briar-laced pond five stories below.

Hot Tip!

If you want to get soaked on Splash Mountain, sit in the front of the car; the spray has less of a dampening effect in back.

Splash Mountain is based on the animated sequences in Walt Disney's 1946 film *Song of the South*, and the principal characters from the movie—Brer Rabbit, Brer Fox, and Brer Bear—appear in the attraction courtesy of Audio-Animatronic technology. In fact, Splash Mountain's stars and supporting cast of 103 performers number almost as many as those in Pirates of the Caribbean, which has 119 Audio-Animatronic characters.

Comparisons to Pirates of the Caribbean are particularly apt, as Splash Mountain was consciously designed to be a "How do we top this?" response to the popular, long-running pirate adventure. Splash Mountain breaks new ground on several counts. Besides setting a record for total animated characters, it also boasts one of the world's tallest and sharpest flume drops (52½ feet at a 47-degree angle). It's one of the fastest rides ever operated at Disneyland Park.

One other twist makes Splash Mountain unique in the annals of flumedom: After hurtling down Chickapin Hill, the seven-passenger log boats hit the pond below with a giant splash—and then promptly sink under-water (or seem to), with just a trace of bubbles left in their wake.

Splash Mountain's designers didn't only borrow the attraction's characters and color-saturated settings from *Song of the South*. They also included quite a bit of the film's Academy Award–winning music. In fact, the song in the attraction's finale, "Zip-a-Dee-Doo-Dah," has become something of a Disney anthem over the years. The voice of Brer Bear is performed by none other than Nick Stewart, the same actor who spoke the part in the film when it was released in 1946.

Keep in mind: the hotter the day, the longer the lines, so go early or late.

Note: You must be at least 40 inches tall and 3 years old to ride the Splash Mountain attraction. Children under 8 must be accompanied by an adult.

DAVY CROCKETT'S EXPLORER CANOES:
Of all the boats that circle the Rivers of America, these 35-foot fiberglass craft may offer the most fun, at least for the stalwart. They are real canoes, and, no, they are definitely not on tracks. Though the helmsman and the sternman may be strong enough to handle the rowing, guests' contributions are also vital when it comes to completing the 2,400-foot voyage.

Note: This attraction operates only on certain days, and it closes at dusk. Check at the landing for excursion times.

Hot Tip!
Davy Crockett's Explorer Canoes is an attraction that operates seasonally. In other words, they might not be open during your visit. To learn if the canoes will be bobbing in the Rivers of America during your trip, visit *www.disneyland.com* before you leave home.

THE MANY ADVENTURES OF WINNIE THE POOH AND THE BLUSTERY DAY: FP
There's a new critter in town and he goes by the name of Winnie the Pooh. In this colorful new attraction, everyone's favorite honey-lovin' cub treats Magic Kingdom guests to a wild and whimsical 3½-minute tour of his home turf.

The attraction features a most unlikely form of transportation: beehives! They whisk (and bounce) guests through Hundred Acre Wood, where the weather's most blustery. The wind is really ruffling the feathers of one of the locals. It seems Owl's treehouse has been shaken loose and just may topple to the ground—and onto the beehives below.

Similar sight gags abound, from a bubble-blowing Heffalump (hey, this is Disneyland) to a treacherous flood that threatens to sweep Tigger, Piglet, and the rest of the gang away. When Pooh saves the day, it's time to cele-brate—and everyone is invited to the party.

Note that, like other Fantasyland attractions, The Many Adventures of Winnie the Pooh has a few scenes that take place in near darkness. Some youngsters may find these moments a bit unsettling. (If they can handle the likes of Mr. Toad's Wild Ride and Pinocchio's Daring Journey, they should be fine in the Hundred Acre Wood.)

FP = Fastpass attraction (see page 64)

DISNEYLAND PARK

Fantasyland

Walt Disney called this a timeless land of enchantment. Village lanes twist between houses built of half-timbers, brick, stone, and stucco, often embellished with brightly colored folk paintings. The skyline, dominated by the peak of the Matterhorn, bristles with chimneys and weather vanes, turrets and towers. At the center of it all, as if deposited here by an itinerant carnival, is the King Arthur Carrousel.

When Walt Disney created Snow White's Scary Adventures, Mr. Toad's Wild Ride, and Peter Pan's Flight, the black light and glow-in-the-dark paints he used (so popular during the psychedelic sixties) were great novelties. But in recent decades the palette of available hues and the spectrum of special-effects techniques have taken quantum leaps forward, and Fantasyland has benefited from these remarkable advances. Thanks to fiber optics, rear projection, holography, and other advanced special-effects techniques (developed in the course of constructing Epcot at Walt Disney World and Tokyo Disneyland), it has become even more of a visual treat.

Note: Parents of young children should be aware that some of Fantasyland's attractions take place in the dark. These include Peter Pan's Flight, Mr. Toad's Wild Ride, Alice in Wonderland, Snow White's Scary Adventures, and Pinocchio's Daring Journey.

Attractions are described here as you come upon them when moving roughly counterclockwise from Sleeping Beauty Castle.

SLEEPING BEAUTY CASTLE: Rising above the treetops at the end of Main Street, U.S.A., it could be a figment of your imagination or a mirage created by Tinker Bell's pixie dust. Closer inspection proves this architectural confection is as real as the swans in the moat surrounding it. A composite of medieval European castles, primarily in the French and Bavarian styles, Sleeping Beauty Castle, the gateway to Fantasyland, is constructed of concrete, with towers that rise 77 feet above the moat. Trimmed in 22-karat gold leaf, it appears shiny even on gray days. The structure seems larger than it really is due to the use of forced perspective, down to the bricks.

From the Central Plaza, you're actually looking at the back of the castle; Walt Disney decided it was prettier that way and had the builders turn it around. The drawbridge, lowered when the park first opened in 1955, is like a real one—though it's been raised (and lowered again) only once since then. That historic event took place in 1983, at the rededication ceremony for the "new" Fantasyland.

Outside the castle, juniper is planted around the water's edge; it's one of the few green plants that the swans won't eat. One of the two graceful trees to the right of the drawbridge bears hundreds of tiny yellow flowers in spring, and the other is covered with fragile lavender flowers for several weeks in early summer.

ARIEL'S GROTTO: The Little Mermaid spends most of the day in a grotto just a few steps north of her father's garden. Here she visits with guests, who often ask her to sign their autograph books or pose for a photograph. She's happy to oblige. You can take as many shots as you like with your own camera or purchase a five-by-seven ($12.95) or eight-by-ten ($16.95) photo taken by one of Disneyland's photographers. The photos may be picked up at the Main Street Photo Supply Co.; allow a few hours for processing.

TRITON GARDEN: This tiny oasis, located between the castle and the entrance to Tomorrowland, is filled with landscaped walkways, tide pools, rock outcroppings, and succulent plants. But the big lure at Triton Garden is the jets of water that leap from rock to rock and catapult over the bridge. Kids can't resist matching wits with them. At night, the interplay of lights, colors, and fountain spray transforms the garden into a particularly beautiful spot.

PHOTO BY KEITH GROSHANS

SNOW WHITE GROTTO: Tucked off Matterhorn Way, at the eastern end of the moat around Sleeping Beauty Castle, this is one of those quiet corners of the park easily overlooked by guests. If you stand by the wishing well, you might hear Adriana Caselotti, the original voice of Snow White, singing the lovely melody "I'm Wishing," written for Disney's Oscar-winning 1937 film.

While Snow White sings, jets of water rise and fall in the waterfall fountain on the other side of the walkway, and a quartet of small fish rises up from the bottom of the pool at the base of the cascade to swim around in little circles. Any coins tossed into the well go to charity.

BIRNBAUM'S ★BEST★ **PETER PAN'S FLIGHT:** This attraction is one of the park's loveliest—and most popular. Based on the novel by Sir James M. Barrie about the boy who wouldn't grow up, by way of Walt Disney's 1953 animated feature, the ride's special effects soar to celestial heights.

Pirate ships carry travelers through the clouds and into a sky filled with tiny fiber-optic stars.

Water ripples and gleams softly in the moonlight; the lava on the sides of a volcano glows with almost the intensity of the real thing. After an ephemeral few minutes, the ships seem to drift through a waterfall and back into reality, an unloading area that is all the more jarring after the magic of the trip through Never Land.

Of the approximately 350 miles of fiber optics found throughout Fantasyland, the majority are used in this ride. The twinkling London scene is an enlarged model of an authentic map of the city.

MR. TOAD'S WILD RIDE: Based on the 1949 Disney film *The Adventures of Ichabod and Mr. Toad*—which was inspired by Kenneth Grahame's classic novel *The Wind in the Willows*—this zany attraction, housed in an English manor bristling with ornate chimneys that really smoke, takes guests on a riotous ride from the perspective of the eccentric but lovable Mr. Toad.

Unfortunately, he is as inept a driver as you might expect a toad to be. During the excursion, you crash through the fireplace in his library, scattering embers everywhere; burst through a wall full of windows; careen through the countryside; charge headlong into a warehouse full of TNT; lurch through the streets of London; then ram into a pub and veer out again. During the two-minute journey, you'll also be berated by a judge in court, nearly collide head-on with a railroad train, and even be banished to a fiery inferno.

Did You Know?

There is a shadow of Sherlock Holmes (complete with pipe and cap) in the second-story window of the manor that houses Mr. Toad's Wild Ride.

ALICE IN WONDERLAND: Traveling in oversize caterpillars, visitors fall down the rabbit hole and embark upon a bizarre adventure in that strange world known as Wonderland. They come face-to-face with Tweedledum and Tweedledee, a garden filled with singing roses, the Cheshire Cat, the Queen of Hearts and her playing-card soldiers, the White Rabbit, and other characters from Lewis Carroll's beloved story *Alice in Wonderland*.

At the end of the nearly four-minute ride, the giant "un-birthday" cake explodes, providing a suitable climax to this sweet interlude.

MAD TEA PARTY: The sequence in Walt Disney's 1951 release *Alice in Wonderland* in which the Mad Hatter hosts a tea party for his "un-birthday" is the theme for this attraction—a group of colorful oversize teacups whirling wildly on a spinning tea table. Festive Japanese lanterns hang overhead. The park's original thrill ride back in 1955, it lasts only 1½ minutes, so if the line is long, come back later.

Note: The teacups may look mild, but it's a good idea to let a reasonable interval pass after eating before you take one for a spin.

BIRNBAUM'S ★BEST★ MATTERHORN BOBSLEDS: Though it's 100 times smaller than the actual peak, Disney's version of the Matterhorn is still a credible reproduction. The use of forced perspective makes the snowy summit look much loftier than the approximately 147 feet it does reach. Even the trees and shrubs help create the illusion. Those at the timberline are far smaller than the ones at the bottom.

The ride itself, like the more sophisticated Space Mountain and Big Thunder Mountain Railroad attractions, has to be counted among the most thrilling at Disneyland. At the time the Matterhorn Bobsleds were dedicated, in 1959, they were considered an engineering novelty because their dispatch system allowed more than one car to be in action at once.

The ride begins with a long climb into the frosty innards of the mountain, then makes a speeding, twisting, turning descent through a cloud of fog and past giant icicles and ice crystals. The wind howls as you hurtle toward a brief but inevitable encounter with the Abominable Snowman. The speed of the downhill flight away from the creature seems greater than it really is because much of the journey takes place inside tunnels. Splashdown is in an alpine lake.

Note: Pregnant women, children under 3, and guests who suffer from weak backs, heart conditions, motion sickness, and other physical limitations should not take the ride.

STORYBOOK LAND CANAL BOATS: This seven-minute cruise through Monstro the Whale and past miniature scenes from classic Disney animated films is not one of Disneyland's major attractions, yet few who take the trip deny that the journey is one of the park's sweetest, filled with intricate, evocative settings. No detail was spared, from the home of the Three Little Pigs to the Old English village of Alice in Wonderland (where the White Rabbit boasts his very own mailbox) to the London park that Peter Pan and Tinker Bell flew over with Wendy, John, and Michael Darling on their way to Never Land.

Other storybook locales include the marketplace where Aladdin met Princess Jasmine, the Seven Dwarfs' home and jewel mine, and Cinderella's castle. At the end of the cruise, the boat drifts past Geppetto's village, Prince Eric and Ariel's castle, and King Triton's castle.

PHOTO BY JILL SAFRO

IT'S A SMALL WORLD: The background music for this attraction is cheerful and singsong, sometimes maddeningly so. It does grab

your attention, starting with the cheery facade, embellished with stylized representations of the Eiffel Tower, the Leaning Tower of Pisa, Big Ben, the Taj Mahal, and other landmarks. The 30-foot-tall clock with the loud ticktock and the syncopated swing is frosting on the architectural cake. The whirring of gears that marks every quarter hour alone warrants a trip to the attraction's plaza on the edge of Fantasyland and next to Toontown.

Boats carry guests into a land filled with more than 300 Audio-Animatronic dolls representing children from 100 regions of the world. It's a pageant for the eyes, even if the ears grow weary. (If you find yourself humming "It's a Small World" for the next several hours, you can blame Richard M. and Robert B. Sherman, the Academy Award–winning composers of the music for *Mary Poppins*, among many other Disney scores.)

Topiary figures in the shapes of a giraffe, elephant, rhinoceros, lion, horse, and other friendly beasts bid guests a fond farewell at the end of the ride.

Note that It's a Small World is transformed inside and out between Thanksgiving and New Year's to become as close to a winter wonderland as you're likely to find in Southern California. The dolls even sing "Jingle Bells" along with "It's a Small World."

CASEY JR. CIRCUS TRAIN: One of the key sequences in the movie *Dumbo*, in which an engine named Casey Jr. pulls a circus train up a steep hill, became the inspiration for this 3½ minute train ride that circles Storybook Land. The Storybook Land Canal Boats are better for viewing the landscaping and miniature details there, but it's worth a ride inside one of the wild-animal cage cars. Each train has two of them—plus a real caboose. Listen as the engine chugs, "I think I can," and then, "I thought I could," as it negotiates the hill.

DUMBO THE FLYING ELEPHANT: As beloved a symbol of Fantasyland as Sleeping Beauty Castle, this ride reminds all who see it of the baby elephant immortalized in the 1941 Disney film. Dumbo discovers, after drinking from a bucketful of champagne, that his inordinately large ears, which have been such a source of embarrassment, actually enable him to fly.

PHOTO BY JILL SAFRO

A mechanical marvel, Dumbo the Flying Elephant is full of filigreed metalwork, with cogs, gears, and pulleys galore. Brass pipes spew water from the base, and music is supplied by a vintage band organ housed in a small, ornate structure nearby. That figure atop the ride is Timothy Mouse, who became Dumbo's manager after the little elephant was hired to be a star by the same circus folk who once teased him. The topiary figures pay tribute to the little guy with the floppy ears.

SNOW WHITE'S SCARY ADVENTURES:

Ornamental stone ravens perch on carved stone skulls atop a stone tower, and hearts pierced through with swords lie at the base of the twisted pillars that support this brooding building. All this might lead you to expect an attraction as frightfully elaborate as the Haunted Mansion. It isn't. That said, the two-minute ride includes several fairly jarring scenes. In one, the Queen changes into a scary old hag before your eyes; in another, this wicked witch has the nerve to tempt you with a poisoned apple.

After passing a brief and joyful scene in the Seven Dwarfs' cottage, the cars travel through a creepy dungeon, visit a workshop where the Queen labors over her bubbling caldron, and then venture into the Frightening Forest, where moss-draped trees point talon-like branches at passersby. The visit to the jewel mines, where the Seven Dwarfs labor, is more beautiful than scary, because of the emeralds, rubies, and sapphires glowing benignly in the darkness.

It all ends in true storybook fashion: As the evil Queen attempts to roll a stone down the side of a mountain to crush the dwarfs below, she gets struck by lightning (via a strobe

PHOTO BY KEITH GROSHANS

effect) and tumbles over the edge of a cliff, leaving Snow White, the handsome prince, and their seven sidekicks to live happily ever after, as depicted in the mural near the exit. The music is taken from rare recordings used to create the film's original sound track.

Note: This attraction can be too intense for small children.

PINOCCHIO'S DARING JOURNEY:
Based on Disney's 1940 animated feature, this is a three-minute morality play of sorts, with Jiminy Cricket serving as host and guide. Pinocchio, who is the creation of the toymaker Geppetto, pays a visit to Pleasure Island and then discovers the right way to live.

As the ride vehicles move from the cheerful land of popcorn and Ferris wheels to the seamy world of Tobacco Road, Pleasure Island hues are replaced by drab shades of brown and gray. Here, little boys are turned into donkeys and sold to the salt mines.

Pinocchio escapes that fate, nearly becomes supper for Monstro the Whale, and winds up back home in the care of Geppetto—another happily-ever-after ending. The final scene, in which the Blue Fairy turns into a cloud of sparkles and then disappears, leaving a smattering of pixie dust on the floor, is partially accomplished via fiber optics.

Note: This attraction may be a bit frightening to toddlers (not to mention those of us who may be spooked by the concept of turning into a donkey).

KING ARTHUR CARROUSEL:
Guests come upon this graceful park landmark as they stroll toward the Sleeping Beauty Castle passageway into Fantasyland. One of the few attractions in the park that is an original rather than a Disney adaptation, the carrousel contains 72 horses—all movable, as Walt Disney wished. Carved in Germany over a century ago, no two alike, they are as pampered as the live Belgian horses on Main Street. The ornamentation on them is gold, silver, and copper leaf.

The faces on the inside and outside of the carousel are gold leaf. The shields on the lances supporting its big overhead canopy are those of the Knights of the Round Table and other, less illustrious, crests. Nine hand-painted panels on top of the carrousel's main face re-create the story of Sleeping Beauty.

King Arthur Carrousel was completely refurbished in 2003.

Mickey's Toontown

Disneyland lore tells us that when Mickey Mouse burst onto the movie scene in 1928 in *Steamboat Willie*, the first sound cartoon, his success was so great that his busy schedule demanded he practically live at the Walt Disney Studios. Thirty cartoons later, in the early 1930s, he was one tired mouse, so he moved into a quiet residence in a "toon only" community south of Hollywood. Over the years, many toon stars gravitated to Mickey's Toontown, as it quickly became known. Minnie Mouse, Pluto, Goofy, Roger Rabbit, Chip, Dale, and Gadget all live here, and Donald Duck docks his boat, the Miss Daisy, on Toon Lake.

> ## Hot Tip!
>
> There are no full-service restaurants in Toontown, just a few fast-food places with window service, and limited outdoor seating. So don't plan on having a big meal here.

One afternoon in the early 1950s, while Mickey and his close friend Walt Disney were relaxing on Mickey's front porch, Walt revealed his idea for a theme park that would appeal to "youngsters of all ages." Mickey suggested that he build it next to the secret entrance to Toontown, and the rest is history. Disneyland opened to the public in 1955, but little did anyone realize when they were drifting through It's a Small World that they were right next door to Mickey's Toontown.

In 1990, Mickey and his friends decided to open up their neighborhood and their homes to non-toons, and in preparation, all of Toontown received a new coat of ink. The grand opening took place in January 1993, marking the first new "land" to debut at Disneyland since Critter (originally Bear) Country opened in 1972.

Legend aside, the development of Toontown was a real challenge: to create a three-dimensional cartoon environment without a single straight line. Yet as topsy-turvy as it is, Mickey's Toontown is a complete community, with a downtown area, including a commercial center and an industrial zone, plus a suburban neighborhood. The best part is that everything is meant to be touched, pushed, and jumped on. Kids do just that, while adults relish the attention to detail and the assortment of gags. Much of what's here is interactive, from the mousehole covers to the public mailboxes.

This booming toontropolis is home to ten attractions, two shops, and three fast-food eateries. The rides are described in the neighborhood sections that follow; the shops, in the "Shopping" section later in this chapter; and the eateries, in the *Good Meals, Great Times* chapter of this book.

Guests enter this colorful land by walking under the Toontown train depot. The attractions are listed as they are encountered when strolling counterclockwise.

Downtown Toontown

In Toontown's "business" zone, an animated taxi teeters off the second-floor balcony of the Cab Co. A runaway safe has crashed into the sidewalk, and crates of rib-ticklers, ripsnorters, slapsticks, and wisecracks wait for passersby to lift the lids. At the Fireworks Factory, a plunger sets off quite a response when pressed; it's a good thing the Toontown Fire Department is located right next door.

Lift the receiver of the police phone outside the Power House (home to all sorts of electrifying gizmos—open the door at your own risk), and you might hear a voice over the toon police car radio, announcing, "Someone put mail in the box, and the box doesn't like it. Please respond post haste." Or step on the mouse-hole cover near the post office, and you might hear, "How's the weather up there?" or, "Is it time to come out now?"

You never know what to expect once inside Toontown—but it's all bound to be "goofy."

BIRNBAUM'S BEST **ROGER RABBIT'S CAR TOON SPIN: FP** This chaotic, rollicking ride combines the technology of the Mad Tea Party teacups (cars here spin 360 degrees) and the tracks of

PHOTO BY JILL SAFRO

Fantasyland attractions, such as Mr. Toad's Wild Ride. Benny the Cab and Roger Rabbit join the dizzying chase, which takes guests through the back alleys of the toon underworld made famous in the film *Who Framed Roger Rabbit*. The mission of each car is to save Jessica Rabbit from the evil weasels while avoiding the dreaded Dip.

ROGER'S FOUNTAIN: In this funny fountain, a statue of Roger Rabbit is suspended in midair, afloat on a column of water erupting from a broken fire hydrant that he has seemingly crashed into. He's still holding the steering wheel from the cab he was driving. Surrounding the hydrant, four floating cab tires serve as inner tubes for fish spouting arcs of water into the air.

JOLLY TROLLEY: Transportation around Mickey's Toontown is supplied by a rocking-and-rolling trolley that weaves its way on figure-eight rails. Providing a one-way ride to or from either end of Mickey's Toontown, it stops outside Roger Rabbit's Car Toon Spin and Mickey's House. A large gold windup key on top of the engine turns as the trolley makes its rounds.

POST OFFICE: Each kooky mailbox actually speaks in the voice of the character whose mail it receives—Mickey Mouse, Minnie Mouse, Roger Rabbit, Jessica Rabbit, Donald Duck, and Goofy. It can be quite a cacophony.

Outside, the letter box pipes in with comments like, "Don't just stand there—mail something!"

Toon Square

Located between the downtown area and the residential section of Toontown, this district is home to local businesses and institutions, including the Toontown Skool, the Department of Ink & Paint, and the 3rd Little Piggy Bank. Toontown's three eateries— Clarabelle's Frozen Yogurt, Pluto's Dog House, and Daisy's Diner—stand side by side on the square.

CITY HALL: Toon residents emerge from this municipal building and proceed to the bandstand out front to greet guests, entertain with their antics, and provide more relaxing photo opportunities than are often available elsewhere in Disneyland.

When a character is about to arrive, the colorful "Clockenspiel" above City Hall comes to life: Mallets ring bells, toon hands pull whistles, and figures of Roger Rabbit and Mickey Mouse pop out of cannons, blowing horns that, in turn, produce bouquets of flowers.

GOOFY'S GAS: From the looks of it, any traveler would think twice about refueling at this station. On the other hand, it does house Toontown's public restrooms and telephones, and that's an important location to know (though we don't recommend making any important business calls here).

Pedestrians can now refuel here, too. A candy stand, called Goofy's Tuneup Treats, (open seasonally) offers sweet snacks. It's also a convenient locale to purchase souvenirs. The water fountain beside the station dispenses funny but refreshing H_2O.

Mickey's Neighborhood

The homes in this district sit at the base of the 40-foot-tall Toon Hills, which have their own version of the famous Hollywood sign. The attractions are described as a guest would pass them while walking counterclockwise from Mickey's Fountain.

MICKEY'S FOUNTAIN: A statue of the world's most famous mouse stands at the center of a pool surrounded by toon-style musical instruments, creating a whimsical centerpiece for the Toontown residential area.

MINNIE'S HOUSE: It's hard to miss Minnie's house. This lavender-and-pink creation has a

sweetheart theme for the sweetheart inside. Here guests can peek at Minnie's living room with its chintz sofa and sophisticated magazines (*Cosmousepolitan* and *Mademouselle*) on the coffee table.

There are messages from Goofy and Mickey on the answering machine in the hallway. Guests are invited to create new fashions for Minnie on the computer in her dressing room.

In Minnie's kitchen, a cake in the oven rises when a knob is turned, pots and pans clank out a melody when the stove is switched on, and the dishwasher churns when a button is pushed. The Cheesemore refrigerator is stocked with an assortment of dairy products, including Golly Cheeze Whiz, and the shopping list left on the outside of the fridge hints at this mouse's cheeses of choice. Be sure to check out the cookies on her kitchen table (and be prepared for a little trick, courtesy of Ms. Mouse).

> ## Hot Tip!
> Toontown closes two hours before the rest of Disneyland Park on nights when the park is presenting a fireworks show.

As you leave Minnie's House, you'll pass the wishing well in her yard. Don't think you're hearing things: It's been known to share a few parting thoughts.

MICKEY'S HOUSE: A path leads from Minnie's backyard to the front door of Mickey's House. The welcoming yellow dwelling with a tile roof, huge green door, and green shutters is home to the toon who started it all. Not only is Mickey's face on the mailbox out front, but his welcome mat is in the instantly recognizable shape of three circles— his head and ears.

In the living room stands a player piano and a curio cabinet filled with all manner of memorabilia, including Mickey's baby shoes and a picture of him with his friend Walt Disney, as well as some of Pluto's treasures—a huge bone and a half-eaten shoe. In the laundry room, the washing machine chugs merrily away, and laundry supplies, such as Comics Cleanser and Mouse 'n' Glo, are at the ready.

From here, make your way through the greenhouse and into Mickey's backyard, where you'll see Pluto's doghouse and a garden with mysteriously disappearing carrots.

MICKEY'S MOVIE BARN: Ever industrious, Mickey has transformed the old barn in back of his house into a workplace, and guests are welcome to visit him here. The first stop is the Prop Department, where costumes and props from some of his famous cartoons are stored.

In the Screening Room, a bumbling Goofy projects movie clips from remakes currently in progress, among them *Steamboat Willie* and *The Sorcerer's Apprentice*. Mickey is hard at work on a soundstage, but happy to take a break. Guests enter in small groups for a photo and autograph session with the "famouse" star.

Note: You can't get to Mickey's Movie Barn without going through his house. This attraction is a must for die-hard fans of the Mouse.

CHIP 'N' DALE TREE-HOUSE: Just past Mickey's House stands the home of that jolly chipmunk duo, Chip and Dale. Styled to look like a redwood tree, this high-rise accommodates kids, but not adults. A spiral staircase leads to the lofty perch, whose windows provide a fine view of Toontown.

GADGET'S GO COASTER: Gadget is the brilliant inventor from the TV cartoon *Chip 'n' Dale's Rescue Rangers*. So it's only fitting that some of her handiwork is within view of their treehouse. Gadget, the ultimate recycler, has created this coaster from an assortment of gizmos that once served other purposes. Giant toy blocks are now support beams for the

tracks; hollowed-out acorns have become the cars of the train; and bridges have been created from giant combs, pencils, paper clips, and such. The thick steel tracks give the impression of a tame ride, but there are a few thrills, right up to the final turn into the station. This experience is exciting but brief (1 minute), so if the line is long, save it for later.

Note: Kids must be at least 3 years old before they can ride Gadget's Go Coaster. Those under 7 must be accompanied by an adult. Pregnant women are advised to skip the trip.

MISS DAISY: Donald Duck's houseboat, named for his fair feathered friend, is docked in Toon Lake, adjacent to Gadget's Go Coaster. Parents can relax in a shaded seating area near a waterfall while their children explore the boat, which looks a whole lot like its owner.

See if you can recognize Donald's eyes in the large portholes of the pilothouse, his jaunty blue sailor's cap in the roof of the cabin, and his face in the shape of the hull. Would-be sailors can climb the small rope ladder or the spiral staircase up to the pilothouse to steer the wheel that turns the compass or to toot the boat's whistle.

GOOFY'S BOUNCE HOUSE: Located beside the *Miss Daisy*, this abode is just for kids. Inside, they can literally bounce off the walls, the furniture, and even the fireplace. Since the windows are made of netting, parents get a good view of the goings-on. The garden outside Goofy's house boasts an odd assortment of delights: stalks of popcorn, spinning flowers, unusually watery watermelons, jack-o'-lanterns, and squished squash.

Note: Kids must be at least 3 years old but no taller than 52 inches. Cubbyholes are provided for shoes. Remove glasses, hats, and other items that may break or cause injury to your child or another bouncer.

TOON PARK: This tiny enclave next to Goofy's Bounce House supplies a safe play area for toddlers. Adjacent seating gives parents and other guests an inviting place to rest and enjoy the youngsters' antics.

Tomorrowland

PHOTO BY JILL SAFRO

When Walt Disney was alive, the future seemed simple: We would all dress in Mylar and travel in flying saucers. The Tomorrowland he created in the fifties was set in the distant year of 1987, part Buck Rogers and part World's Fair. The latest incarnation of Tomorrowland, rededicated in May 1998, is based on a classic vision of the future, one that looks at it from the perspective of the past. The result is an innocent and hopeful place (imagine, for instance, a planet that renews itself!), one more in keeping with the rest of Disneyland than with the sterile, less positive future world often depicted in contemporary films.

Visit Tomorrowland today, and you enter a visually engaging terrain, where the palette of colors is not otherworldly but warm and earthy. Futuristic boulders and dreamlike architecture coexist with apple, orange, lemon, and pomegranate trees that line pathways created from gray, mauve, and burgundy bricks. This landscape fires the intellect as much as the imagination.

Galileo Galilei, Leonardo da Vinci, Jules Verne, H. G. Wells, and certainly Walt Disney would have felt at home here. Aldous Huxley probably wouldn't have.

Three of Tomorrowland's most recent additions are also at Walt Disney World, in Florida: Honey, I Shrunk the Audience; Innoventions; and Astro Orbitor (which has an identical twin at Disneyland Paris). Other well-loved Tomorrowland attractions remain, among them Space Mountain, Star Tours, and Autopia, and all of them have undergone cosmic face-lifts.

A replica of the Moonliner, a Tomorrowland icon from 1955 to 1966, sits on a pedestal near the site of its predecessor. Sleek monorail trains still glide to and from the Downtown Disney district, while traditional Disneyland Railroad trains continue to chug their way into the Tomorrowland station, a reminder that the past is, indeed, prologue.

The following attractions are described as you encounter them when proceeding counterclockwise from the Main Street entrance to Tomorrowland.

ASTRO ORBITOR: Towering above the entrance to Tomorrowland, this big whirligig with spinning orbs and speeding starships is a fitting symbol for Tomorrowland. Astro Orbitor, modeled on a drawing made by Leonardo da Vinci almost five centuries ago, is the successor to Rocket Jets, which gave Disneyland guests a lift for 30 years. Each ride vehicle accommodates two passengers (or two adults and one small child), who can maneuver it up and down while spinning clockwise for 1½ minutes, reveling in sweeping views of Tomorrowland, Central Plaza, and Sleeping Beauty Castle.

Note: The minimum age to ride is 1 year. Young children have to be in the company of an adult.

BIRNBAUM'S ★BEST★ **BUZZ LIGHTYEAR ASTRO BLASTERS:** The Evil Emperor Zurg is up to no good—and it's up to that Space Ranger extraordinaire Buzz Lightyear and his Junior Space Rangers (that means you) to save the day.

So goes the story line of Tomorrowland's brand-new video-game-inspired spin through toyland. The adventure is experienced from a toy's point of view. Guests begin their 4½-minute tour of duty as Space Rangers at Star Command Action Center. This is where Buzz

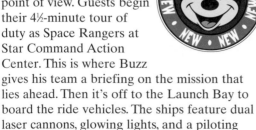

gives his team a briefing on the mission that lies ahead. Then it's off to the Launch Bay to board the ride vehicles. The ships feature dual laser cannons, glowing lights, and a piloting joystick.

In addition to Buzz and the evil Emperor, you may recognize some other toy faces swirling

Hot Tip!

To maximize your scoring potential at the Buzz Lightyear attraction, aim for targets that are moving or far away. They yield the most points.

about—the little green, multi-eyed alien squeaky toys, best known for their awe of "the claw." The squeakies have been enlisted to help in the fight against Zurg.

Once Junior Space Rangers blast off, they find themselves surrounded by Zurg's robots, who are mercilessly ripping batteries from toys. As Rangers fire at targets, beams of light fill the air. For every target hit, you will be rewarded with sight gags, sound effects, and points. The points, which are tallied automatically, are accumulated throughout the journey. Although the vehicles follow a rigid "flight" path (they're on a track), the joystick allows riders to maneuver the ships, arcing from side to side or spinning in circles while taking aim at your surroundings.

When the star cruiser arrives at Zurg's spaceship, it's showdown time. Will good prevail over evil? Or has time run out for the toy universe? And will you score enough points to be a Galactic Hero? (Most people improve their scores with a little practice.)

BIRNBAUM'S ★BEST★ **STAR TOURS:** 🅵🅿 Inspired by George Lucas's blockbuster series of *Star Wars* films, this is one of the most intriguing attractions at Disneyland. It offers guests the opportunity to ride on droid-piloted StarSpeeders, the exact same type of flight simulator used by military and commercial airlines to train pilots. Once aboard the spacecraft, guests embark on a harrowing flight into deep space and encounter giant ice crystals and laser-blasting fighters. It goes without saying that seat belts are definitely required.

The indoor queue area is air-conditioned. During the pre-show, guests watch as the beloved *Star Wars* characters R2-D2 and C-3PO, here employees of a galactic travel agency, bustle about in a hangar area, servicing the Star Tours fleet of spacecraft.

Riders board the 40-passenger craft for what is intended to be a leisurely trip to the Moon of Endor. The flight is out of control from the start, as the rookie pilot proves that Murphy's Law applies to the entire universe.

The sensations are extraordinary and the technology quite advanced.

Note: Passengers must be free of back problems, heart conditions, motion sickness, and other physical limitations to ride. Guests not meeting the minimum height requirement of 40 inches and children under age 3 will not be permitted to board. Pregnant women should not ride. The least bumpy seats are near the center of the compartment; for thrills, sit in the back.

STARCADE: This arcade adjoining Space Mountain is by some accounts one of the best in Orange County. There are easily 200 games—many of them created by Sega, Namco, and Midway—incorporating motorcycles, race cars, skateboards, snowboards, bicycles, jet skis, snow skis, horses, spacecraft, and tanks. Most represent whatever happens to be hottest at the moment. Certainly noteworthy is the R360, a turbulent 360-degree pilot game. A dozen air-ball machines and a wall of pinball machines are on the upper level. There are also two penny presses.

Costs range from 25 cents to $4 per game. There are $1, $5, and $10 change machines, as well as a cashier, on the premises.

BIRNBAUM'S **★BEST★** **HONEY, I SHRUNK THE AUDIENCE:** The latest in 3-D film techniques link up with state-of-the-art chicanery when Rick Moranis, Marcia Strassman, and the kids reprise their roles from the movie *Honey, I Shrunk the Kids*. In this 18-minute misadventure, Professor Wayne Szalinski manages to unleash all sorts of mayhem.

In the pre-show area, guests watch a movie about the development of the Imagination Institute. Then they are welcomed to the Institute and given an overview of what will happen inside, where Professor Szalinski is to receive the Inventor of the Year Award and demonstrate some of his latest inventions.

On the way into the 575-seat theater, guests receive "protective goggles" (3-D glasses) to shield their eyes in case any flying debris comes their way during the demonstrations. One misguided mishap leads to another when the Shrinking Machine and then the Dimensional Duplicator go on the fritz. The theater is accidentally shrunk, and when the professor's young son picks it up to show his mom, the audience is left shaken up but screaming for more.

To add to the mix, in-your-face experiences are provided by a gargantuan dog, a menacing viper, an army of mice (don't say we didn't warn you), and a monster cat that morphs into a lynx and then into a lion. Eventually, everyone and everything returns to normal, sort of.

Note: Honey, I Shrunk the Audience is known to frighten small children and more than the occasional grown-up (especially those afraid of snakes or mice).

INNOVENTIONS: This two-level pavilion housed in the former Carrousel Theater is Tomorrowland's largest attraction, providing a look at a future so near that some of the products showcased are already on the market. Guests hop aboard a slowly rotating base at one of five themed "pods"—home, transportation, work and school, sports and fitness, and entertainment—and enter the foreseeable future as it relates to that particular area.

After receiving a quick introduction from the wisecracking, Audio-Animatronic Tom Morrow (voice courtesy of the actor Nathan Lane, who also sings new lyrics to "Great Big Beautiful Tomorrow"), guests are free to explore the world of Innoventions at their own pace, stepping on and off the moving base to visit other areas, watch live demonstrations, and test new products (none of them for sale) at leisure.

A central atrium leads to the second level and The World of Computers, where the exhibits are sponsored by some companies involved in developing new products and technologies: Compaq, Honeywell, Kaiser Permanente, AT&T, General Motors, among others. (Company participation changes from

time to time.) The second floor of this building, where the exit is located, had not been open to the public since 1974. Now you can walk around almost the entire perimeter.

Note: Parents, hold on to kids' hands, or the rotating floor might deposit them in a different area from you. There is no time limit at Innoventions; experience it at your own pace.

TOMORROWLAND AUTOPIA: FP The only attraction from the original Tomorrowland, Autopia was coined "The Freeway of the Future" back in 1955. Kids have always loved guiding the small sports cars around the twisting roadways (for them, a top speed of seven miles per hour is thrilling). Now pint-size motorists and their parents encounter a souped-up version of the original ride.

The separate Tomorrowland and Fantasyland roadways now comprise a single attraction (yes, there were two Autopias; the one in Fantasyland opened in 1959 to accommodate spillover crowds). Guests now enter through a single boarding area in Tomorrowland and watch an entertaining pre-show on a large video screen that presents the world from a car's point of view. Drivers (and one passenger per vehicle) travel in restyled cars through 21st-century terrain, experiencing a series of happy roadside surprises along the way. At the ride's end, they receive a commemorative driver's license as a memento. A shop proffers auto-related toys and assorted souvenirs.

Note: Kids must be at least 52 inches tall and at least 7 years old to drive alone. Pregnant women and guests with back or neck problems should not ride.

SPACE MOUNTAIN: FP When Space Mountain first opened in 1977, it quickly rocketed to the top of just about everyone's list of favorite attractions. It's popularity is sure to soar to new heights as the attraction is "relaunched" during Disneyland's "Happiest Celebration on Earth" fiftieth anniversary party.

While the classic facade and essence of Space Mountain remain intact, the experience is decidedly 21st century. Brave voyagers board new vehicles in a realistic launch port. After shooting through a disorienting tunnel, riders will have a close encounter with a meteorite. After that, it's all about screeching through the darkness, past spinning stars and whirling galaxies. Add to that an edgy, instrumental sound track (which is synchronized to each car) and you've got one out-of-this-world attraction.

In the evening, Space Mountain becomes even more surreal, with a classic rock sound track and psychedelic light show. Far out!

If your courage fails you, just ask an attendant to direct you to the nearest "chicken exit."

Note: Pregnant women and guests who have weak backs, heart conditions, motion sickness, and other physical limitations should sit this one out. Children younger than 8 year must be

accompanied by an adult (kids under 3 are not permitted to ride). Guests must be at least 40 inches tall to experience Space Mountain.

DISNEYLAND MONORAIL: Who doesn't love the monorail? America's first daily operating monorail was a novelty when it was introduced at Disneyland in 1959. A decade later it was replaced with four sleek Mark V five-car trains, and it's always a thrill to see them gliding through the park. Straddling a concrete beamway, the monorail has rubber tires, which enable it to glide quietly, as well as braking wheels atop the beam, and guiding and stabilizing wheels on either side.

The 2½-mile-long "highway in the sky" is a distinctive and integral part of Tomorrowland. The nine-minute round-trip ride takes guests around the periphery of Tomorrowland, across the resort to Downtown Disney and its diverting activities, and then back to Tomorrowland.

Hot Tip!

A trip on the monorail yields panoramic views of Disney's California Adventure theme park and its neighbor, the Grand Californian resort. However, it does not stop at either place.

For a special experience, inform the cast member on the boarding ramp that you'd like to sit up front in the pilot's cabin. It can usually accommodate up to five passengers. If all the seats are taken, you can always wait for the next monorail and try your luck again.

Note that by boarding the monorail in Tomorrowland, you are actually leaving the Disneyland park. Be sure to get your hand stamped. You'll need to show it and a valid ticket to re-enter the park.

Trips are all "one way." You'll be asked to disembark at the Downtown Disney station. This is the spot to reboard when you're ready to head back to the Disneyland park. Know that walking is also an option—as Disneyland and Disney's California Adventure are about a 5-minute stroll away.

Note that the monorail is considered more of an attraction than a mode of transportation. It takes about the same amount of time (maybe even less) to walk from the Downtown Disney station to the Disneyland park.

Tomorrowland Icons

MOONLINER: Beside Redd Rockett's Pizza Port, this two-thirds-scale, 53-foot-high replica of an early Tomorrowland icon stands 50 feet from the site of the original rocket. It is set on a 12-foot pedestal that doubles as a refreshment stand, called The Spirit of Refreshment. Water vapor wafts from its nozzles, but the only thing that is "launched" here is bottled beverages (and then only by request).

THE OBSERVATRON: This quirky icon for Tomorrowland towers above the area, constantly beaming electronic messages into space. Every 15 minutes, it comes to life in an orchestrated medley of music and motion. Radio Disney has taken up permanent residence underneath it.

Shopping

Until you get to know Disneyland, you might not expect that anyone would visit just to go shopping. But among Southern Californians, it's a top draw for the quality merchandise and appealing gift items. Mickey Mouse paraphernalia, such as key chains, mugs, T-shirts, hats, and other such souvenirs, is found here in abundance, of course, but there are some surprises, such as character-inspired costumes for kids, Mickey Mouse desk accessories for the office, and upscale items, such as art collectibles, jewelry, and products for the home.

Main Street, U.S.A.

CANDY PALACE: An old-fashioned pageant in pink and white, this shop is alluring at any time of day, but never more than when the candymakers are at work in the glass-walled kitchen confecting candy canes, chocolate-covered strawberries, caramel apples, toffee, fudge, and other temptations for anyone with a sweet tooth. The products made on the premises are for sale, along with a bounty of chocolates, hard candies, and licorice.

CHINA CLOSET: If you're in the market for figurines, picture frames, or snow globes, this is the place to go.

CRYSTAL ARTS: Glasses and pitchers, trays, and other mementos can be engraved (for free) and monogrammed while you wait, or you can purchase them unornamented. The shop also sells glass miniatures, bells, and paperweights.

DISNEY SHOWCASE: Informally known as Pin Trading Central, this shop features an array of Disney pins and souvenirs.

DISNEYANA: Collectors and the simply curious alike will discover rare and unusual Disney merchandise here, such as limited-edition art and hand-painted cels inspired by Disney animated classics. Popular pieces include crystal, bronze, and pewter figurines, and striking porcelain sculptures from the Walt Disney Classics Collection.

Note: Disney Imagineers and artists often drop by the shop to sign reproduction artwork or recently published books.

DISNEY CLOTHIERS, LTD.: Disney character merchandise has always been popular, but if you want something a little more stylish, this is where to find it. The spot caters to fashion-conscious shoppers with a love for Disney gear. Almost every item in the selection of men's, women's, and children's clothing and accessories sold here incorporates Disney characters in some way.

EMPORIUM: Much like an old-time variety store, this large and bustling shop offers an

PHOTO BY JILL SAFRO

incredible assortment of wares, and it is home to the popular Disneyland logo merchandise. Decorative figurines, clothing, plush toys, character hats, and a wide variety of souvenirs make up the bulk of the stock.

THE MAD HATTER SHOP: This hat shop stocks Mickey Mouse ears in black and various colors, plus a good assortment of other toppers just for fun or to protect tender skin from the sun.

MAIN STREET MAGIC SHOP: Small but well stocked with gags and tricks—and books about how to pull them off —this shop has the wherewithal to inspire budding illusionists. In

Hot Tip!

Much of the merchandise sold in the Disneyland Resort is not available elsewhere. So if you love it, buy it here. If you regret not making a purchase, call the Disneyland order line at 800-362-4533.

the market for an invisible pooch? A magic wand? An ice cube with a bug in it? This place has it all.

MAIN STREET PHOTO SUPPLY CO.: If a roving Disneyland photographer snaps your mug, this is the place to pick up the print. You can also find film, frames, and photo albums. They may have extra lens caps on hand, too.

PHOTO BY TILL SALVENS

MARKET HOUSE: This Disney version of an old-fashioned general store sells cookies, licorice ropes, jelly beans, chocolates, and hard candy—all goodies you would expect to find in a turn-of-the-century store. Kitchen accessories, dinnerware, and gourmet foods, all loaded with Disney character (and characters), are Market House favorites.

NEW CENTURY JEWELRY: Among the delicate offerings here are 14-karat-gold charms of Tinker Bell, Donald Duck, and Minnie Mouse. The marcasite character jewelry is subtle and sophisticated.

NEW CENTURY TIMEPIECES: Merchandise in all shapes and sizes, including Mickey Mouse watches and alarm clocks, along with other character-laden novelty clocks, beckons from the polished wood cases at this shop.

PENNY ARCADE: Adjacent to the Gibson Girl Ice Cream Parlor is a virtual Coney Island of food and fun. Jars of "penny"-style candy, available by the piece, fill ornate shelves, and scrumptious saltwater taffy, which you won't find anywhere else in the park, is available by the scoop in more than a dozen flavors, including licorice, peppermint, and

root-beer float. To add to the carnival atmosphere, old-fashioned arcade games that still cost a penny to play and a Welty Orchestrion line the walls.

SILHOUETTE STUDIO: Working at the rate of about 60 seconds per portrait, Disneyland's silhouette artists truly are a wonder to behold.

20TH CENTURY MUSIC COMPANY: This little place carries a rather extensive selection of classic Disney music. A special kiosk allows guests to purchase recordings they may have had as kids and burn them onto a CD. At press time, more than 40 archived titles were available, including the 1957 recording of *Alice in Wonderland*, 1961's *Babes in Toyland*, and tunes from the more recent *Disney Afternoon*. Each CD includes a reproduction of the old album cover.

New Orleans Square

CRISTAL D'ORLEANS: Glasses and chandeliers, decanters and ashtrays, pitchers and paperweights are typical treasures here. All engraving, and some monogramming, is free of charge.

THE DISNEY GALLERY: Located above the entrance to Pirates of the Caribbean in several rooms originally designed as an elegant apartment for Walt Disney, the gallery displays original drawings and designs for Disneyland, as well as artwork from Disney Art Editions featuring classic Disney animation. Changing exhibits feature the works of Disney Imagineers, long stored in vast archives.

Selected pieces of artwork have been reproduced in limited editions and are for sale, along with note cards and postcards, most of which are exclusive to the gallery. Don't overlook the small interior courtyard, a nice escape from the hustle and bustle.

Note: Disney Imagineers and artists often drop by The Disney Gallery to sign reproduction artwork or recently published books.

JEWEL OF ORLEANS: This jewel of a store specializes in one-of-a-kind estate pieces—carefully chosen rings, cameos, watches, brooches, and cuff links—some date from 1850 to 1990, but most are Art Deco, from the 1920s and 1930s. Diamonds, rubies, opals, emeralds, sapphires, pearls, and garnets, all in artistic settings, twinkle from the display counters. Prices range from about $125 to $24,000.

Hot Tip!

The best places to find character costumes are in Fantasyland, at the Castle Princess Shop and the Princess Boutique. Disney Clothiers, Ltd., on Main Street, U.S.A., carries character clothing for infants and toddlers.

LE BAT EN ROUGE: Need to cross a few Disney-villain-related items off your shopping list? You've come to the right place. Also lining the shelves are tchochkes and thingamabobs with a Haunted Mansion Holiday theme.

LA BOUTIQUE DE NOEL: Filled with the Christmas spirit year-round, this shop is a repository of holiday collectibles. Santa Claus figures, wooden soldiers, Christmas stockings, ornaments, and decorations prove irresistible any time of year. Open seasonally.

LA MASCARADE: The elegance and allure of New Orleans have been captured in the intriguing Guissipe Armani sculptures and Disney figurines on display in this charming open-air market. An eclectic mix of both vintage pieces and fine reproductions makes this spot well worth a lingering look or two.

L'ORNEMENT MAGIQUE: The whimsical designs of the artist Christopher Radko fill this tiny shop. Cruella De Vil, Winnie the Pooh, the Seven Dwarfs, and Peter Pan have all inspired ornaments, and each year Radko creates a design exclusively for Disneyland. Open seasonally.

PIECES OF EIGHT: Wares with a pirate theme are purveyed at this shop beside the Pirates of the Caribbean exit. There are pirate rings, ships' lanterns, stocking caps, and fake

Hot Tip!

Each afternoon a Disney princess reads stories to children at the Princess Boutique.

knives, swords, and skulls in plastic and rubber. You'll also discover T-shirts, key chains, glasses, and other souvenir items imprinted with the Pirates of the Caribbean logo. For the right price, you can fill up a bag with pirate booty.

Frontierland

BONANZA OUTFITTERS: Mosey in and try on something fit for living legends. You'll find everything from apparel to western-inspired household and gift items. With Pioneer Mercantile right next door, this is truly one-stop shopping for western gear and getups for the whole family.

PIONEER MERCANTILE: This shop carries all manner of paraphernalia inspired by the pioneer period in American history and this country's folk heroes. Young buckeroos will be delighted with the videos and books about the Wild West, and every budding Pocahontas or Pecos Bill will find authentically styled costumes, along with western character plush toys to be their sidekicks.

WESTWARD HO TRADING COMPANY: It's on the right side as you enter Frontierland from Central Plaza. Hitch up your wagon and come on in. A huge assortment of candies awaits you here: tempting candy bars, yummy fudge sold by the piece or the pound, and "scoop your own" jelly beans.

The Mickey, Minnie, Donald, and Goofy cookie tins make wonderful souvenirs long after the last morsel has been savored. (It's downright dangerous to come here on an empty stomach.)

Critter Country

POOH CORNER: All manner of Pooh merchandise awaits, including plush toys, note cards, photo albums, cookie jars, bookends, watches, infants' apparel, children's clothing, sleep shirts, and bedroom slippers. There's a candy kitchen, too.

POOH & YOU PHOTOS: Pooh and his pals can be found in Critter Country. You can take photos with your own camera or buy a five-by-seven ($12.95) or an eight-by-ten ($16.95) taken by a Disneyland photographer.

Adventureland

ADVENTURELAND BAZAAR: The plush jungle animals corralled here include lions, tigers, and panda bears (oh, my!).

INDIANA JONES ADVENTURE OUTPOST: This outfitter can supply the most daring expeditions with all manner of safari apparel, notably Indy's trademark headgear, as well as other rough-and-ready wear and "artifacts" related to the ever-popular Indiana Jones.

SOUTH SEAS TRADERS: This is the spot to browse for safari-themed items such as T-shirts, shorts, jackets, windbreakers, bags, belts, and a selection of straw and safari hats.

TROPICAL IMPORTS: This emporium is almost always irresistible to youngsters. The reason: rubber snakes, spiders, lizards, frogs, and bugs by the barrel- or basketful. The squeamish will prefer the selection of plush jungle animals.

Fantasyland

CASTLE PRINCESS SHOP: Gowns and crowns dazzle the eyes of every young princess who enters this royal boutique, tucked inside Sleeping Beauty Castle, just to the left of the entrance to Fantasyland. From wish-upon-a-star-perfect costumes to jewelry and other courtly keepsakes, this little shop has made more than a few special dreams come true.

Get Your Ears Done Here

Since Disneyland first opened in 1955, there has been no more coveted souvenir of the park than a pair of Mickey Mouse ears personalized with the lucky owner's name—or that of a family member. They can be embroidered for no additional charge at both locations of the Mad Hatter, in Fantasyland and in Main Street, U.S.A., as well as at the Gag Factory in Toontown and at The Star Trader and The Hatmosphere in Tomorrowland. The shops do not embroider company names on hats.

FANTASY FAIRE GIFTS: On Disneyland's parade route, near the entrance to the Fantasyland Theatre, this open-air stand stocks special souvenirs spun from the tales and sights in Fantasyland.

GEPPETTO'S TOYS AND GIFTS: Situated alongside Pinocchio's Daring Journey, this is the place to find Disney fairy-tale figures, Marie Osmond dolls, Bob Baker Marionettes, and teddy bears from Boyd's Bear Collection, as well as Annette Funicello Bears, created by the former Mouseketeer. The popular Engel-Puppen dolls (Snow White and Belle among them) are custom-made to your specifications; their creator, the German doll maker Helmut Engel, often stops by to chat with guests and sign certificates for the dolls they have chosen. Each one comes with its own dress; three additional costumes made famous by Disney leading ladies are available for separate purchase. Open seasonally.

HERALDRY SHOPPE: At this tiny shop in the castle, you can trace your family name through centuries and continents and have its history printed up (a great gift idea). Or choose from hand-painted marble or bronze shields, coat-of-arms certificates, rings, T-shirts, and hats emblazoned with your family crest.

IT'S A SMALL WORLD TOY SHOP: The whimsical structure near the entrance to It's a Small World stocks an assortment of Barbie dolls and accessories, Hot Wheels, and Disney-licensed Mattel toys, dolls, and plush toys featuring the Disney characters.

LE PETIT CHALET GIFTS: As cozy as a warm cup of cocoa on a winter evening, this small Swiss shop, nestled at the base of the Matterhorn, is the repository of traditional Disneyland gifts and souvenirs.

MAD HATTER: Always a great place for hats and plush character caps—and Mouse ears, of course (they'll embroider them for you). The large selection of novelty headgear includes Donald's sailor cap, a hat sporting Goofy's ears, Jiminy Cricket's and Uncle Sam's top hats, and floppy jester caps.

PRINCESS BOUTIQUE: At the western end of Sleeping Beauty Castle, this is the main stop at Disneyland for serious toy and costume shopping. Youngsters will go for the inexpensive souvenirs and perhaps cajole parents or grandparents into springing for one of the fantasy costumes. These outfits can transform young guests into Minnie Mouse, Peter Pan, Alice in Wonderland, Buzz Lightyear, or even the nasty Captain Hook. Children's books, videos, games, dolls (including Madame Alexander and Marie Osmond), and the like complete the offerings.

PRINCESS PHOTOS: Capture a magic moment with Belle, Cinderella, Snow White, or Sleeping Beauty outside the queue area for Pinocchio's Daring Journey. You can snap as many photos as you like with your own camera or indulge in a five-by-seven ($10) or an eight-by-ten ($15) photo taken by a Disneyland photographer.

STROMBOLI'S WAGON: Located near the Village Haus, this stand offers sundry souvenirs—everything from Disney plush toys to Mickey Mouse sunglasses. Some of the smaller items available here include character key chains, pens, buttons, and candy. The shop is named after the villain in *Pinocchio*.

VILLAINS LAIR: This wickedly tempting den, across the castle courtyard from the Tinker Bell Toy Shoppe, is dedicated to well-known doers of dastardly deeds—Maleficent, Ursula, Cruella De Vil, and other beloved Disney baddies.

Mickey's Toontown

GAG FACTORY: A Laugh-O-Meter outside this shop gives some indication of the fun to be found inside, along with an assortment of character merchandise—plush toys, stationery, souvenirs, T-shirts, novelty headwear, and candy—all featuring the Fab Five (Mickey, Minnie, Donald, Pluto, and Goofy) and their friends. Take a moment to admire the toon architecture, especially the pillars at the back of the store.

MICKEY & ME PHOTOS: Trying to get your photo taken with Mickey on busy days can be challenging, but if you follow this insider tip, it's a piece of cake: Mickey can often be found working in the Movie Barn behind his house in Toontown, and he's always happy to stop what he's doing to greet his guests and pose for pictures. You can take as many photos as you like with your own camera (at no charge)

or opt for a five-by-seven ($10) or eight-by-ten ($15) shot taken by a Disneyland photographer who works on the set with Mickey. Note that the line to meet the Mouse is often a long one. But to his legions of loyal fans, it's well worth the wait.

Tomorrowland

THE HATMOSPHERE: Caps, hats, visors, Mouse ears, and headbands with ears—the headgear here ranges from the rudimentary to the ridiculous. Mouse ears make lasting Disneyland souvenirs, especially if your name is embroidered on them. (There is no extra charge to have the Mouse ears personalized with Disney's signature gold-colored thread.)

AUTOPIA WINNER'S CIRCLE: Located near the Autopia attraction exit, this open-air shop specializes in merchandise with an automotive theme. Here you'll find everything from a toy car to an antenna topper for a real one.

THE STAR TRADER: The Star Trader is the repository of everything from T-shirts and jewelry to back scratchers and shoehorns, not to mention jewelry, mugs, key chains, candy, and much more—all emblazoned with the likenesses of the Disney characters.

Toys in the likeness of Buzz Lightyear, Woody, and the gang from *Toy Story* can usually be found here, along with hundreds of stuffed animals. In the section over by the Star Tours attraction exit, the *Star Wars* legends have come to collectible life.

Walk of Magical Memories

Now you can own a little piece of Disneyland—10 inches of it, to be exact. For $150 you can purchase and personalize one of the hexagonal bricks that line the esplanade between Disneyland and California Adventure. Inscriptions and Disney logos mark special occasions or salute family names and hometowns. For more information, or to purchase a brick, call 800-760-3566.

Entertainment

Together with Walt Disney World, Disneyland books more entertainment than any other organization in the world. What follows is typical of the variety you can expect. Check a park guidemap for daily offerings.

Performers & Live Shows

Performers stroll, march, croon, and pluck their way through Disneyland every day—so frequently that all you usually have to do to find them is follow your ears.

Main Street, U.S.A.

CORNER CAFE PIANIST: Rod Miller is often on hand to tickle the ivories on the snow-white upright piano at this centrally located eatery (he's been with Disney for 30 years!). The piano has also been known to play all by itself. Daily.

DAPPER DANS: The official greeters of Main Street, U.S.A., this classic singing quartet performs standards such as "In the Good Old Summertime" and "Coney Island Baby" in perfect four-part harmony. They may be found strolling on the sidewalk or pedaling their bicycle built for four. Five days a week.

DISNEYLAND BAND: A presence in the park since opening day in 1955, Disneyland's signature musical group specializes in turn-of-the-century band music, but it can play just about anything. The band performs inside the main entrance when the park opens, in Town Square (at the south end of Main Street), and at other locations.

Inquire at City Hall for a show schedule. Five days a week.

FIREHOUSE SAX QUARTET: This group of saxophonists plays standards from the early 1900s, as well as classic Disney tunes. Though they usually perform near the Firehouse in town square, they occasionally jump aboard the fire truck and take the show on the road.

FLAG RETREAT: The flag at Town Square is lowered just before sunset each day (times may vary; check at City Hall for specifics). The ceremony is best when Disney's All-American Collegiate Band is on hand. The band plays several rousing marches and "The Star-Spangled Banner" as the finale, bringing guests to their feet, hands over hearts, in a moving patriotic moment. On the band's days off, the music is a sound track. Even on these days, it's a rewarding experience. Usually presented daily.

MAIN STREET MERCHANTS ASSOCIATION MUNICIPAL BRASS BAND: The local merchants have "banded" together to "drum up" some business for their shops on Main Street. The sounds of this neighborhood brass band can be heard on Main Street three days a week. Check a park map for the schedule.

Adventureland

ALADDIN & JASMINE'S STORYTALE ADVENTURES: The story of Aladdin is re-created by Aladdin and Jasmine themselves, with the help of a few "guest stars" picked from the audience. Hosted by two storytellers,

Dancing

Bands play several sets at Club Buzz on Saturdays year-round and nightly during peak seasons. In addition, Plaza Gardens Stage, adjacent to Central Plaza, hosts the "Jump, Jive, Boogie Swing Party" on Friday evenings in summer, and "Big Band Bonanza" on Saturdays. Guests have been known to spin like teacups around the dance floor.

Barker Bob and Kazoo, the tale unfolds in front of Aladdin's Oasis. Fridays, Saturdays, and Sundays year-round; daily in summer. Check a park map or at the theater for showtimes.

TRINIDAD TROPICAL STEEL DRUM BAND: Enjoy the calypso beat of this colorful group that performs near the entrance to the Jungle Cruise. You can catch them on weekends throughout the year.

New Orleans Square

BAYOU BRASS BAND: The hip, funky sounds of contemporary New Orleans brass bands have arrived at Disneyland, courtesy of this lively six-piece band. Three days a week.

GLORYLAND BRASS BAND: New Orleans funeral processions are unique experiences—soulful, energetic, and always musical. The Gloryland Brass Band embodies the spirit of this tradition. Two days a week. Presented seasonally.

ORLEANS STREET BAND: The "second line" tradition comes to life each time this group hits the Square. The musicians perform a classic New Orleans street-band repertoire with exuberance and style. Two days a week.

ROYAL STREET BACHELORS: Their style is early traditional jazz and blues, with a mellow four-beat sound similar to that once commonly heard in the Storyville section of the Crescent City. Five days a week.

VARIETY ACTS: In New Orleans Square, street performers and personalities of every kind serve up sights and sounds inspired by blues, jazz, Cajun, and zydeco traditions. Specialty acts include mimes, tap dancers, and street-corner musicians. Five days a week.

Frontierland

BILLY HILL & THE HILLBILLIES: Dishing up a lively mix of bluegrass and comedy on the Golden Horseshoe Stage, these four brothers, all named Billy and all first-rate musicians, never take themselves–or their guests–too seriously. Five days a week

LAUGHING STOCK CO.: Sheriff Clem Clodhopper has no desire to marry Mayor McGillicuddy's daughter, Sally Mae, but neither of them will take "no" for an answer. An old-time serial in three parts is played out as the dysfunctional trio finagles to get Sally Mae hitched to someone (anyone), even an unsuspecting park guest. Four days a week.

Fantasyland

SNOW WHITE—AN ENCHANTING NEW MUSICAL: In what is easily the most elaborate musical production ever staged at Disneyland park, this stage show brings to life the characters and melodies from the classic Disney film *Snow White and the Seven Dwarfs*.

A product of an impressive team of creative forces—including Broadway theater veterans—the high-caliber, high-energy musical was specially crafted as theater for families with young children. (That said, if your child is spooked by the image below, consider prepping him or her ahead of time. Rest assured, it all ends happily.)

The show is presented several times a day inside the Fantasyland Theater. Check a park guidemap for the schedule.

SWORD IN THE STONE CEREMONY: A lucky child is appointed king or queen of the realm by pulling a magic sword named Excalibur from the stone in front of King Arthur Carrousel. Merlin the Magician presides over the proceedings. Weekends year-round; daily in summer.

Tomorrowland

CLUB BUZZ—LIGHTYEAR'S ABOVE THE REST: By day, this futuristic dining and entertainment venue presents "Calling All Space Scouts: A Buzz Lightyear Adventure." The ever-popular Buzz stars in this interactive mix of music, humor, and action. He is joined by the evil Emperor Zurg, Space Cadet Starla, and some of those Little Green Men. Call it dinner theater Tomorrowland style. Shows are presented daily.

Club Buzz hosts live bands on select nights. Check a park guidemap for location and showtimes.

WIZARD ACROBAT SHOW: These spry performers fly through the air with the greatest of ease. Four days a week.

Parades

No Main Street is complete without a parade, and Disneyland has plenty. The usual route runs between Town Square and the promenade in front of It's a Small World—or vice versa. The direction and route can vary, so it's wise to ask at the Information Center at City Hall or Central Plaza.

DISNEYLAND PARADE OF DREAMS: Meant to evoke memories and spark inspiration, this new parade winds its way down Main Street twice a day. As it does, gymnasts, trampoline performers, and aerial artists dazzle guests, as do dozens of familiar Disney characters.

The parade, which lasts about 20 minutes, brings dream themes to life through music. It is usually presented two times daily. Check a park

guidemap's entertainment schedule for current details and showtimes.

A CHRISTMAS FANTASY PARADE: Rows of toy soldiers right out of *Babes in Toyland* march down Main Street, accompanied by dancing gingerbread men, skating snowflakes, and whirling snowmen and women. Mrs. Claus and the Seven Dwarfs, Pinocchio and Geppetto, Buzz and Woody, the Little Mermaid, Daisy Duck and Clarabelle, and even Scrooge McDuck and Cinderella's wicked stepfamily are all part of the fun. Mickey and Minnie, in a horse-drawn carriage, and Santa Claus himself, with Pluto filling in for Rudolph, put in an appearance at the end of the parade. It takes place daily from Thanksgiving Day through New Year's Day.

Where to Watch the Parades: The best vantage points from which to see the parades are the platform of the Disneyland Railroad's Main Street depot, Town Square near the flagpole, and the curb on either side of Main Street. If you'd like to avoid crowds, any viewing location other than Main Street will be better.

Two other options are the terrace outside the Plaza Inn (but be aware that the seating is limited here) and the tables in the courtyard of the Carnation Cafe, where the view may be partially obstructed. Better still, plan to catch a later parade on nights when more than one is scheduled.

You can also stand on either side of the promenade area in front of It's a Small World, whose multicolored facade provides a whimsical only-at-Disneyland backdrop. Wherever you decide to station yourself for the parade, plan to arrive about an hour beforehand to claim your piece of turf.

Fireworks

REMEMBER. . . DREAMS COME TRUE:
This impressive new fireworks show, presented nightly in summer, on New Year's Eve, and on other select occasions ignites the sky with a kaleidoscope of colors over Sleeping Beauty Castle. At about 9:30 P.M., Tinker Bell flies in to start the spectacular light show in fantastic fashion. That's followed by the stories of the wishes of classic Disney characters, from Cinderella to Aladdin—all to the accompaniment of a medley of Disney tunes and other musical favorites. More than 200 pyrotechnic shells are fired, one every couple of seconds, in time to the music.

Where to Watch: One of the best areas is about midway down Main Street, U.S.A., near the Main Street Photo Supply Company. (Be sure to face the castle!)

Special Occasions

Though plenty of special events take place in the park year-round (some require special-admission tickets), Disneyland does not celebrate holidays in a major way, except for Halloween (see page 68) and the period between Thanksgiving and New Year's, when the entire park glows with holidays themes.

(We have witnessed the yuletide holiday decorations in place as early as October.)

A Christmas Fantasy Parade, a Disney holiday favorite, takes place throughout this season. Live music and hundreds of performers bring to life beloved holiday traditions of the past. **It's a Small World Holiday** celebrates yuletide customs around the world. The singing dolls add "Jingle Bells" to their repertoire in numerous languages, and the ticktock clock in the whimsical facade dons a Santa hat. **Main Street, U.S.A.,** is decked out in traditional red and green, including hundreds of poinsettias and a huge white fir decorated with several thousand lights and ornaments, and surrounded by oversize holiday packages. Carolers hold forth at the **Fantasyland Theatre**. On two nights at the beginning of the season, a candlelight procession ending at the theater takes place. Special music is provided by a large choir, and a holiday story is read by a well-known entertainer. Live entertainment and a fireworks show on **New Year's Eve** (no special ticket required) provide the grand finale for this festive and fun holiday season.

For more information about seasonal happenings in the park, see the *Getting Ready to Go* chapter; for specifics on upcoming special events, call the Guest Relations office (714-781-7290).

Where to Find the Characters

Look for the Disney characters in Town Square and in front of The Walt Disney Story, both on Main Street, U.S.A., as well as in Mickey's Toontown, where they live. The Little Mermaid greets guests at Ariel's Grotto, just north of Triton Garden. Pooh and his pals congregate in Critter Country. Belle, Cinderella, and Snow White drop by Tinker Bell Toy Shoppe in Fantasyland. In Adventureland, Jane and Terk hang out at Tarzan's Treehouse, while Aladdin and Jasmine stop to chat outside Aladdin's Oasis.

Cast Members at the Information Board can help locate characters. Also refer to *Good Meals, Great Times* chapter of this book, and your Disneyland guidemap.

Imagination Runs Wild in Fantasmic!

BIRNBAUM'S ★BEST★ This 22 minutes of magic, music, live performances, and special effects light up the Rivers of America nightly on weekends, holidays, and throughout the summer season. More than 50 performers put on an unforgettable show in a dazzling display of pyrotechnics, lasers, fiber optics, and giant props.

In this tale of good versus evil, it's up to Mickey to overcome an array of villains. He first appears in cartoon form at the tip of Tom Sawyer Island and uses his imagination to make comets shoot across the sky while the river waters dance. A live Mickey materializes in a cone of specially programmed lighting and a shower of sparks seems to shoot from his fingers.

Spectacular technology makes Fantasmic! all the more fantastic. Mickey works his magic, and a special film sequence appears, seemingly in midair above the river. This effect is achieved by projecting 70mm film

villains attempt to disrupt Mickey's fantasy. Fearsome creatures all have an opportunity, including an animated Chernabog demon and the evil Maleficent, who morphs into the 45-foot-tall, fire-breathing dragon from *Sleeping Beauty*.

The villains turn Mickey's dreams into nightmares, and he must overcome them with his own powers of goodness, plus a little help from his friends. The *Columbia* sailing ship glides through the show with the swashbuckling cast of *Peter Pan* on board, and the *Mark Twain* riverboat brings along a host of favorite Disney characters.

Where to Watch: The best spots are in front of Pirates of the Caribbean (be sure you can see the water and a clear view of Tom Sawyer Island, and get there at least one hour early) and on the balcony of The Disney Gallery, where a reservations-only dessert buffet costs $47 (if you decide to splurge, book a seat early at the Guest Services win-

onto three giant mist screens, each one 30 feet tall by 50 feet wide. The screens are transparent, so that the live performers behind and in front of them appear to be interacting with the filmed images.

In one scene, Monstro the Whale from *Pinocchio* makes waves in the real water of the Rivers of America. In the "Pink Elephants on Parade" scene, the animated pachyderms from *Dumbo* interact with live performers in flexible, glow-in-the-dark elephant costumes. The illusions build toward a breathtaking confrontation of good and evil, in which Disney

dow at the park entrance or call 714-781-4400). Late arrivals can usually find a decent place to watch below the Haunted Mansion, near the river's edge.

Note: Fantasmic! is shown twice nightly during busy seasons, and there can be a crush of people trying to leave after the show. Try exiting via the Big Thunder Trail, or hang out in New Orleans Square until the crunch eases. The later show is always less crowded. Parents, be aware that some of the effects are quite realistic and may be too intense for very young viewers.

Hot Tips

- Tuesday, Wednesday, and Thursday are the least crowded days to visit year-round. If you should come on a weekend, choose Sunday over Saturday.

- Measure your child's height before your visit so you'll know ahead of time which attractions he or she may be too short to ride. This can prevent intense disappointment later.

- Wear your most comfortable shoes. Blisters are the most common malady reported to First Aid.

- Main Street, U.S.A., often opens half an hour before the rest of the park. Take advantage of this to grab a quick snack, shop, or mingle with Disney characters.

- Check the daily entertainment schedule in your Disneyland guidemap and plan your day accordingly.

- Wait times posted at the attractions and on the Information Board at the north end of Main Street, U.S.A., are updated every hour.

- Break up your time in the park (unless you have only one day). Arrive early, see the major attractions until things get busy, return to your hotel for a swim or a nap, then go back to the park. Remember, you must have your hand stamped and your ticket to re-enter Disneyland.

- An attraction may reach its Fastpass limit before the end of the day, especially if the park is packed. Be sure to get yours early if you don't want to wait in the standby line.

- Try to have lunch before 11 A.M. or after 2 P.M., and dinner before 5 P.M. or after 8 P.M. to avoid lines (which tend to be shorter on the left side of the fast-food counters).

- For a change of pace foodwise, head to Downtown Disney or one of the three hotels on property. They have something for every budget and taste—from simple to sublime, sandwiches to sushi—as well as buffet meals with some of the more popular Disney characters.

- Avoid rides such as Star Tours, Splash Mountain, the Matterhorn Bobsleds, and the Mad Tea Party immediately after meals.

- On crowded days, you can make your way between the east and west sides of the park most quickly via the Big Thunder Trail.

- Lines for the Disneyland Railroad move more quickly at the Main Street station.

- Try to visit the major attractions—Honey, I Shrunk the Audience, Star Tours, the Indiana Jones Adventure, Big Thunder Mountain Railroad, Jungle Cruise, the Haunted Mansion, the Matterhorn Bobsleds, and Splash Mountain—early in the day or during parades. The lines move faster then.

- During the busy afternoon hours, go to the smaller attractions where the wait times are comparatively shorter; the *Mark Twain* riverboat is always a good choice. The afternoon is also prime time for shopping, enjoying outdoor musical performances, or taking in a show at the Golden Horseshoe Stage.

- Shops are a good place to escape the midday heat, but steer clear of them in late afternoon and at the end of the park's operating hours, when they tend to be crowded.

- For most rides, if you're in line even one minute before the park closes, you'll be allowed on. This is a great tactic for Splash Mountain and the Indiana Jones Adventure.

- Avoid the crowds by returning your stroller *before* the evening's fireworks presentation comes to an end.

Disney's California Adventure

Fame, fortune, and fun in the sun have lured adventurous spirits to California for centuries. But now visitors have a whole new way to enjoy the glories of the Golden State: through Disney's eyes. In February 2001, the company officially unveiled Disney's California Adventure theme park, the largest addition to the Disneyland Resort since Disneyland Park itself opened in 1955 (and premiering with just about as much anticipation and hoopla).

California Adventure sits snugly in the heart of the Disneyland Resort, sharing an entrance esplanade with Disneyland and neighboring Downtown Disney and the three Disney hotels. But once you set foot inside the park, you're in a world all its own—a kaleidoscope view of California. Unlike Disneyland, where each land's theming is kept separate from the next, the lines here are blurred. Districts blend into each other, and no matter where you stand inside the park, you're sure to see (or hear whoops and hollers coming from) one of the park's towering icons—the Golden State's sierra-inspired Grizzly Peak mountain, or Paradise Pier's gleaming white roller coaster, California Screamin'.

With a working vineyard and winery, educational micro-factories, upscale restaurants, and scream-inducing thrill rides, the 55-acre theme park is clearly geared toward grown-ups. But there's bound to be something here for everyone to enjoy. California, here we come.

HOLLYWOOD PICTURES BACKLOT

1. Disney Animation
2. The Twight Zone Tower of Terror
3. Hyperion Theater
4. Jim Henson's Muppet*Vision 3-D
5. Who Wants to Be a Millionaire—Play it!
6. The Hollywood Backlot Stage

GOLDEN STATE

7. Bountiful Valley Farm
8. Golden Dreams
9. Golden Vine Winery
10. Grizzly River Run
11. It's Tough to be a Bug!
12. Mission Tortilla Factory
13. Redwood Creek Challenge Trail
14. Soarin' Over California
15. The Boudin Bakery

PARADISE PIER

16. California Screamin'
17. Golden Zephyr
18. Jumpin' Jellyfish
19. King Triton's Carousel
20. Maliboomer
21. Mulholland Madness
22. Orange Stinger
23. S.S. Rustworthy
24. Sun Wheel

Getting Oriented

Disney's California Adventure is smaller in area than Disneyland, its sister park next door. So guests should have no trouble covering all of the theme park on foot, as long as they wear comfortable walking shoes.

In the esplanade directly outside the park, guests find themselves facing a giant three-dimensional picture postcard of California, where huge letters spell California and a stylized Golden Gate Bridge soars overhead, a conduit for monorails instead of automobiles. Guests are quickly enveloped in the postcard mural of landscapes and seascapes.

In the hub of the park's Sunshine Plaza gleams a huge sun icon. A high-tech mirror system bounces rays from the real sun onto the reflective surfaces of the icon to create a welcome for park guests. It may also conjure up a romantic image of the sun setting over the Pacific Ocean, while a fountain at the base celebrates the dynamic energy of that body of water.

Three vastly different districts compose Disney's California Adventure park. East of the Sunshine Plaza lies the Hollywood Pictures Backlot, a mock studio backlot where guests can, among other things, learn about movie-making and take in a Broadway-style show based on Disney's *Aladdin*. Southwest of the Gateway Plaza is the Golden State, a district dedicated to the cultures, industries, and natural beauty that have shaped California over the years, complete with a winery and micro-factories.

Paradise Pier, the third California Adventure district, is located southwest of the Golden State and can be accessed through the Bay Area. A tribute to early 1900s amusement parks, Paradise Pier features nostalgic thrill rides with a modern twist, located around a lagoon.

PARKING

Guests park in the six-level parking structure on Disneyland Drive, which can be accessed from the I-5 freeway. There are also some ground lots that guests may be guided to park in if the parking structure is full or overly congested.

Parking Fees: Guests arriving in passenger vehicles generally pay $8 to park. (The fee for vans and RVs is $10; for buses, $15.) You may leave the lot during the day and return later the same day at no extra fee. Just hold on to your parking stub as proof of earlier payment.

Hot Tip!

When you enter Disney's California Adventure through the Entry Plaza, east is to your left and west is to your right.

Lost Cars: Even if you take careful note of where you parked your car, you might have trouble remembering or recognizing the exact spot when you return hours later. Hundreds more vehicles will likely be parked around yours. If this happens, contact a cast member and tell him or her approximately when you arrived. With that little bit of information, parking lot personnel can usually figure out the car's general location, and someone will then comb the lanes for it on a scooter.

GETTING AROUND

You'll have to depend on your own two feet. There's no transportation within this easily traversed park. However, wheelchairs and Electric Convenience Vehicles are available.

Guests staying at Disney's Grand Californian and Paradise Pier hotels have their own private entries into the park (Grand Californian guests enter through the Golden State; Paradise Pier guests through the Paradise Pier area). All other visitors enter and exit the park through the main entrance, just across the esplanade from Disneyland's front gate. From here, trams transport guests to the Mickey & Friends tram station and the Timon parking lot. Since the area is pedestrian-friendly, guests may also opt to walk from the park along the esplanade to the hotel and Downtown Disney part of the property.

Park Primer

BABY FACILITIES

Changing tables, baby-care products, and facilities for nursing can be found at the Baby Care Center by Cocina Cucamonga.

DISABILITY INFORMATION

Many park attractions and nearly all shops and restaurants are accessible to guests using wheelchairs. Services are also available for those with visual or hearing disabilities.

FIRST AID

Minor medical problems can be handled at the First Aid Center, located by the Pacific Wharf's Mission Tortilla Factory.

HOURS

Disney's California Adventure is generally open from 10 A.M. to 6 P.M. Monday through Thursday and 10 A.M. to 8 P.M. Friday, Saturday, and Sunday. For the exact times, visit *www.disneyland.com* or call 714-781-4565.

INFORMATION

Guest Relations, located on the east side of the Entry Plaza, is equipped with guidemaps and a helpful staff. Free guidemaps are also available at most shops throughout the park. Information Boards: Updated hourly, these important resources for attraction wait times and show schedules are located in the Entry Plaza and on the bridge to Paradise Pier.

PHOTO BY JILL SAFRO

LOST & FOUND

The theme park's Lost & Found department is located next to Guest Relations on the far side of the entry esplanade.

LOCKERS

Various-size lockers are located just inside the main entrance and at Golden Gateway near the Golden Gate Bridge. Rental fees range from $4 to $6 per day, depending on size.

LOST CHILDREN

Report lost children at Child Services near Mission Tortilla Factory in Golden State, or alert the closest employee to the problem.

MONEY MATTERS

There are several ATMs in the park: near Guest Relations, Disney Animation, Golden Dreams, Cocina Cucamonga, at Paradise Pier. Currency exchange and Disney Dollar sales are handled at Guest Relations. Cash, credit cards, traveler's checks, and Disneyland Resort Hotel IDs are accepted for most purchases.

SAME-DAY RE-ENTRY

Be sure to have your hand stamped as you exit the park and hold on to your ticket if you plan to return later the same day.

STROLLERS & WHEELCHAIRS

Strollers, wheelchairs, and Electric Convenience Vehicles (ECVs) can be rented across from Guest Relations near the the Entry Plaza and in Condor Flats at Fly 'n' Buy. If you need a replacement, just present your receipt.

Ticket Prices

Although ticket prices are subject to change, the following will give you an idea of what you can expect to pay. Note that prices are likely to increase in 2005. For updates, call 714-781-4565 or visit *www.disneyland.com*. Refer to page 17 for complete details on ticket options and benefits, including annual passports and Resort Park Hopper Tickets.

	Adults	Children*
One-Day Ticket	$49.75	$39.75
Three-Day Ticket	$129	$99
Four-Day Ticket	$159	$129
Five-Day Ticket	$184	$149

*3 through 9 years of age; children under 3 free

Hollywood Pictures Backlot

Lights! Camera! Action! The spotlight is on you in the glitzy Hollywood district of Disney's California Adventure, where the action unfolds all around you. Motion picture soundstages and backlot scenery provide the setting for the numerous movie-making antics and entertaining demonstrations that reveal the secrets behind a few tricks of the trade. No movies are actually filmed here, so you'll have to keep waiting for your big break. But you can think of this area as the "Hollywood that never was and always will be."

Classic Los Angeles architecture was the inspiration for the buildings that line Disney's Hollywood Boulevard and Backlot area. The entertainment here comes in many surprising forms, and everyone gets in on the act—from actor Robin Williams as one of *Peter Pan*'s Lost Boys to Miss Piggy as a singing Statue of Liberty. Hooray for Hollywood!

Hollywood Boulevard

Pass through the studio gates and you enter into Disney's version of the legendary Hollywood Boulevard. And it all fits neatly into a two-block strip.

BIRNBAUM'S BEST **JIM HENSON'S MUPPET*VISION 3-D: FP** One of the most entertaining shows at the Disneyland Resort, much of the appeal of this 3-D movie is in the details. A funny song-and-dance pre-show, hosted by Gonzo and viewed on TV monitors, gives clues about what's to come. The theater (set inside a soundstage) looks just like the one from the classic television series *The Muppet Show*, and comes complete with an orchestra of penguins. Even the two curmudgeonly fellows, Statler and Waldorf, are sitting in the balcony, bantering with each other and flinging barbs at the performers and the audience.

Hot Tip!

Spend some time admiring the props displayed in the pre-show of Jim Henson's Muppet*Vision 3-D. They were all inspired by Muppet television and movie moments.

The production comes directly from Muppet Labs, presided over by Dr. Bunsen

Honeydew and his long-suffering assistant, Beaker, and introduces a new character, Waldo, the "spirit of 3-D." Among the highlights is Miss Piggy's solo, which Bean Bunny turns into quite a fiasco. Sam Eagle's patriotic grand finale leads to trouble as a veritable war breaks out, culminating with a cannon blast to the screen from the rear of the balcony, courtesy of everybody's favorite Swedish Chef.

The 3-D effects, spectacular as they may be, are only part of the show: There are appearances by live Muppet characters, fireworks, and lots of funny details built into the walls of the huge theater. Including the pre-show, expect to spend about 25 minutes with Kermit and company. Shows run continuously.

PLAYHOUSE DISNEY—LIVE ON STAGE!

Put on your dancing shoes! Bear, Tutter, Pip, Pop, and the rest of the gang will be disappointed if you don't join in the fun as they perform playful ditties from their Disney Channel show.

This show is presented at Playhouse Disney in the Animation Courtyard area of the theme park. Expect to see characters from *Rolie Polie Olie, Stanley,* and other Disney Channel favorites. Times guides list performance times. This show is a big hit with the toddler set.

WHO WANTS TO BE A MILLIONAIRE—
PLAY IT!: Ready for your turn in the "hot seat"? Then you'll be glad to hear that a version of the ABC game show *Who Wants to Be a Millionaire* is one of the latest additions to the list of Disney's California Adventure attractions. A fairly faithful recreation, Who Wants to Be a Millionaire—Play It! features the popular TV show's high-tech set and lighting, distinctive music, 50/50, Ask the Audience,

and Phone-a-Friend (or in this case, Phone-a-Complete-Stranger) lifelines. Players chosen from the audience answer trivia questions to win points that can be redeemed for T-shirts, hats, and other prizes. The attraction runs throughout the day. Check a park map for the schedule.

BIRNBAUM'S BEST **DISNEY ANIMATION:** When you look around at all the thrilling attractions, themed hotels, and dozens of familiar animated faces that Disney has become famous for, it's almost impossible to believe it all started with a simple sketch of a mouse. This fascinating behind-the-scenes exploration invites guests to step into Disney's wonderful world of animation. Here visitors are given a true insider's look at the entire process, the heritage, and, above all, the artistry of this world-renowned art form, along with a sneak preview of a few Disney animation feature works that are currently in progress.

Animation Courtyard: This central area makes visitors feel as if they are stepping into an animated film. Larger-than-life backgrounds from Disney film classics surround the area, as full-scale sketches of famous characters are projected onto the scene. Within moments, the sketches are transformed before guests' eyes into full-color animation. It's just one example of the Disney animation magic that awaits at the attractions inside.

Drawn to Animation: Mushu, the lovable wisecracking dragon from Mulan, doesn't quite get the idea that he's a product of an animator's imagination. This presentation, performed in a 230-seat theater, proves it to him by revealing the secrets of animated character development, from concept through constant change all the way to finished personality. The presentation is illustrated on an oversized television screen at a mammoth animator's desk.

Sorcerer's Workshop: Budding animators and artists particularly get a kick out of these three rooms. They are built around interactive exhibits featuring animation special effects. At Ursula's Grotto, for example, you can supply the voice of a favorite character from The Little Mermaid, and then see and hear the completed scene containing your own vocals. At Enchanted Books, you can take a personality survey (hosted by Beauty and the Beast's Lumiere and Cogsworth) to determine which Disney character or villain you most resemble.

Back to Never Land: A short, funny film starring Walter Cronkite and Robin Williams, *Back to Never Land* takes viewers through the entire animation process, from first sketch to finished product. The comedic spin makes this fun and educational film a Disney Animation highlight. Shows run continuously.

DISNEY'S ALADDIN—A MUSICAL SPECTACULAR: Disney brings Broadway to its backyard with this 40-minute show, presented on the grand stage of the 2,000-seat Hyperion Theater. Inspired by the animated feature, this production tells the story of Aladdin, the magic lamp, and his trusty blue sidekick, Genie. The engaging staging even includes a magic carpet ride or two. Don't forget to look up!

You'll recognize all your favorite ditties from the classic Disney film, and be introduced to a new one penned by renowned composer Alan Menken.

Note: The show is quite popular and schedules vary. Check a park map for performance schedule, and plan to arrive at least 15 minutes before showtime

The Backlot

In contrast to star-struck Hollywood Boulevard, the Backlot peels away the facade and takes a backstage look at Hollywood without its makeup. Alongside soundstage buildings, behind-the-scenes support departments do their unseen, essential work: props are put into position (even the trees here are on wheels), Klieg lights are set to shine on the scene, and the crew is busy making sure every performer is on his or her mark before the director yells "Action!"

BIRNBAUM'S BEST TWILIGHT ZONE TOWER OF TERROR: **FP**

The Hollywood Tower Hotel is the creepy home of a new thrill ride. On the facade of the 199-foot-tall building hangs a sparking electric sign. As the legend goes, lightning struck the building on Halloween night in 1939. An entire guest wing disappeared, along with an elevator carrying five people.

The line for the popular ride runs through the hotel lobby, where dusty furniture, cobwebs, and old newspapers add to the eerie

atmosphere. As guests enter the library, they see a dark TV set suddenly brought to life by a bolt of lightning. Rod Serling invites them to enter The Twilight Zone.

Guests are led toward the boiler room to enter the ride elevator. (This is your chance to change your mind about riding. Simply ask the attendant to direct you toward the "chicken exit.") Once you take a seat in the elevator, the doors close and the room begins its ascent. At the first stop, the doors open and guests have a view down a corridor. Among the many effects is a ghostly visit by the hotel guests who vanished. The doors close again and you continue your trip skyward.

At the next stop, you enter another dimension, a combination of sights and sounds reminiscent of *The Twilight Zone* TV series. In fact, Disney Imagineers watched each of the 156 original *Twilight Zone* episodes at least twice for inspiration. This part of the ride is a disorienting experience, in part because the elevator moves horizontally.

What happens next depends upon the whim of Disney Imagineers, who have programmed the ride so that the drop sequence can change. At press time, the elevator was taking an immediate plunge (of about eight stories) before shooting up to the 13th floor. At the top (about 157 feet up), passengers can look out at the Studios below. Once the doors shut, you plummet 13 stories. The drop lasts about two seconds, but it seems a whole lot longer.

Just when you think it's over, the elevator launches skyward, barely stopping before it plunges again. And again. From the time you are seated, the trip takes about five minutes.

Note: You must be at least 40 inches tall to ride. It is not recommended for pregnant women, those with a heart condition, or people with back and neck problems. Though thrilling (and rather scary), the drops are surprisingly smooth.

Did You Know?

The "Hyperion" name has a special Disney heritage. The Walt Disney Studios moved to 2719 Hyperion Street, Los Angeles, in 1926. It was there that Mickey Mouse was born. In 1940 Walt moved his studios to a bigger lot in Burbank, but he took some of the original Hyperion buildings with him.

FP = Fastpass attraction (see page 64)

Golden State

From pristine forests to fertile farmlands, the colorful valleys of wine country to the cultural hills of San Francisco, this district celebrates California's diverse geography, culture, and lifestyles. Whether it's through a bird's-eye view of the state or a bug's-eye view of the world, the Golden State's attractions offer guests a whole new perspective.

Condor Flats

Inspired by California's Vandenburg Air Force Base, home to some of aviation's most prominent pioneers, this airfield and its display area pay tribute to famous flyers and their aircraft. A huge aircraft hangar, the focus of this site, houses the Soarin' Over California attraction.

BIRNBAUM'S BEST **SOARIN' OVER CALIFORNIA:** 🅵🅿 It's no wonder California has an ongoing romance with aviation—how better to experience its breathtaking landscapes than soaring through the skies above them. On this high-flying attraction, you're suspended up to 45 feet in the air, above a giant Omnimax projection dome that showcases some of the state's most glorious sights. With the wind in your hair and your legs dangling in the breeze, the hang glider feels so convincingly real that you may even be tempted to pull up your feet for fear of tripping over a treetop as you dip down toward the ground. During the journey, flyers glide toward the Upper Yosemite Falls of Yosemite Valley, past an

active naval aircraft carrier in San Diego Bay, by San Francisco's Golden Gate Bridge, and then down over the vast deserts in Death Valley and the lush wine country of Napa Valley, and up past

> ## Hot Tip!
> For a really soaring experience, sit in the first row—it flies the highest, while the third row stays closest to the ground.

skiers swooshing down the slopes in Lake Tahoe. In all, the airborne trip takes about four minutes and employs synchronized wind currents, scent machines, and a moving musical score set to a film that wraps 180 degrees around you, making this a thoroughly enveloping experience.

Note: You must be 42 inches tall and free of back problems, heart conditions, motion sickness, and other physical limitations to ride. If you're afraid of heights, skip this one.

Grizzly Peak Recreation Area

Just north of Condor Flats lies Grizzly Peak Recreation Area. Its centerpiece is the unmistakable grizzly-bear-shaped mountain peak that juts 110 feet into the California Adventure skyline. The eight-acre mini-wilderness surrounding Grizzly Peak pays tribute to California's spectacular rural areas.

GRIZZLY RIVER RUN:

BIRNBAUM'S **★BEST★** Disney legend says that Grizzly Peak was once chock-full of gold—which made it a magnet for miners in search of riches, as is evidenced by the mining relics scattered about the mountain. But the gold rush has come and gone, and the peak has since been taken over by another enterprising group—the Grizzly Peak Rafting Company. They converted the area into a rafting expedition known as Grizzly River Run.

Each circular raft whisks six passengers on a drenching tour of Grizzly Peak. The trip begins with a 45-foot climb, and it's all gloriously downhill from there. Fast-moving currents send adventurers spinning and splashing along the river, bumping off boulders and through an erupting geyser field. Because the raft is constantly spinning as it moves through the water, each rider's experience is slightly different, but one thing's for sure—everyone gets wet. During the expedition, rafters encounter two major drops. It's the 21-foot drop that earns Grizzly River the distinction of being the world's tallest, fastest raft ride.

Hot Tip!

Don't bring cameras or other valuables that must stay dry onto Grizzly River Run. They will get drenched!

Note: Passengers must be free of back problems, heart conditions, motion sickness, and other physical limitations to ride. Pregnant women, guests not meeting the 42-inch height requirement, and children under 3 will not be permitted to board.

REDWOOD CREEK CHALLENGE TRAIL:

Lace up your sneakers and test your skills on this simple obstacle course set adjacent to the eastern slope of Grizzly Peak. The campsite features cable slides, rocks to scale, bouncy rope bridges, "floating" logs, and climbable cargo netting connecting treetops, to keep young mountaineers on their toes. Need a hand to assist you through the course? Just whistle for one of the workers outfitted in ranger gear. He or she will be happy to help.

The ranger's station has towers to climb (perfect for burning off excess energy) and an adjoining stage, the Ahwahnee Camp Fire Circle Story Theater (for when a rest is needed). Here, performers share animal folklore and tales of the land through storytelling and song. Keep an eye out for creature tracks; they lead to information on each type of species. There is also an amphitheater, which presents shows with a *Brother Bear* theme five times a day.

A Bug's Land

BOUNTIFUL VALLEY FARM: The Farmer's Expo hosts its own farmer's market here each day; it resembles a cluster of rural roadside stands. Some of California's culinary staples are integrated into healthy snacks and meals.

While fruit smoothies and shaded picnic benches appeal to the grown-ups in the group, small children enjoy the area's interactive water course. Kids of all ages can splash through a simple maze made up of sprinklers and water gates that open and close when triggered. Budding horticulturalists are treated to an up-close view of gardens teeming with avocados, artichokes, citrus fruits, and other crops native to California, all grown and harvested on-site.

FLIK'S FUN FAIR: Guests of all ages are invited, but this area caters to the little ones. Who better to enjoy the experience of seeing the world from the vantage point of a bug?

Among the many diversions in this neck of the woods are a simulated hot-air balloon ride called Flik's Flyers, a mini railroad known as Heimlich's Chew Chew Train, and a drive-it-yourself bug-themed car ride called Tuck and Roll's Drive 'Em Buggies. Princess Dot's Puddle Park, a playground themed around a giant lawn sprinkler, is especially appealing to youngsters eager to make a big splash. Afterward they can spin themselves silly at Francis's Ladybug Boogie.

IT'S TOUGH TO BE A BUG!: FP

BIRNBAUM'S **★BEST★** The underground Bug's Life Theater, by the entrance to the Bountiful Valley Farm, features an eight-minute, animated 3-D movie augmented by some surprising "4-D" effects. The stars of the show are the world's most abundant inhabitants—insects. They creep, crawl, and demonstrate why, someday, they just might inherit the earth. It's a bug's-eye view of the trials and tribulations of their multi-legged world.

As guests enter the dark auditorium, the orchestra can be heard warming up amid the chirps of crickets. When Flik, the emcee (and star of *A Bug's Life*), makes his first appearance, he dubs audience members honorary bugs and instructs them to don their "bug eyes" (or 3-D glasses). Then our oh-so-mild-mannered hero introduces some of his not-so-mild-mannered pals, including the black widow spider, a duo of dung beetles, and "the silent but deadly member of the bug world"— the stinkbug. Hopper, Flik's nemesis and the leader of the evil grasshopper pack, crashes the show and adds to the antics. What follows is a manic, often hilarious, not-to-be-missed revue.

Note: The combination of intense special effects and frequent darkness tends to frighten toddlers and young children. In addition, anyone leery of spiders, roaches, and their ilk is advised to skip the performance, or risk being seriously bugged.

Pacific Wharf

Inspired by Monterey, California's Cannery Row, this industrial waterfront salutes the diverse cultures, products, and industries that make California so international in nature. Guests can tour working micro-factories and watch local products, such as San Francisco sourdough bread and Mission tortillas, being prepared. There are also many tables scattered about, making this a good place to stop to enjoy a rest or a snack.

THE BOUDIN BAKERY: Soft sourdough bread is featured at this working bakery. While baking tips are shared in the walk-through corridor tour (courtesy of a short

Hot Tip!

Drivers, take note: In order to prove that you are 21 years old, you must present an official photo ID. So if your mug is not emblazoned on your license, be sure to bring it and a photo ID. Otherwise, you won't be allowed to imbibe—even though your driver's license is indeed the real McCoy.

video starring Rosie O'Donnell and *Whose Line Is It Anyway*'s Colin Mochrie), the famous Boudin-family recipe remains a well-kept secret.

MISSION TORTILLA FACTORY: Flour and corn tortillas are rolled flat and baked at Mission's display factory. Sample (at no charge) a warm tortilla once you're in the open kitchen, where chefs demonstrate simple ways to cook with the versatile wrap.

Golden Vine Winery

Northern California's fruitful Napa Valley provides inspiration for the Golden Vine Winery. Both an active micro-vineyard and a wine-tasting facility, the courtyard complex, nestled against the base of Grizzly Peak, is designed as a contemporary version of a classic Mission-style estate.

SEASONS OF THE VINE: Set in a 50-seat wine-aging room, this show provides a window on the world of wine-making. As the smell of aged wine fills the air, the show's host reveals the scientific nature of wine production by narrating a seven-minute presentation on the vineyard's seasonal cycles.

The Bay Area

A rotunda suggesting San Francisco's Palace of Fine Arts defines this section of the Golden State, which re-creates the "City by the Bay." The palace's grand rotunda is the entrance to Golden Dreams, a cinematic look at the people and events that have shaped California.

GOLDEN DREAMS: Many tourists (and a few locals!) don't know that the name *California* was inspired by a 16th-century Portuguese myth. In it, a sun-kissed paradise is presided over by the Goddess Califia. This 20-minute movie about the history of the Golden State is hosted by an irreverent Califia, the spirit of California (embodied by Whoopi Goldberg).

Califa takes the audience on an educational journey through time to find out why so many generations of immigrants have been drawn to this land of plenty. But, as Califia discovers, the Midas touch is more elusive than it seems.

Paradise Pier

Just south of the Bay Area, it's all about fun in the sun at Paradise Pier, a throwback to California seaside boardwalks of yesteryear. Like most classic amusement zones, the rides here offer simple thrills of speed and weightlessness—but don't let the nostalgic look fool you: The technology is quite current.

At night, the district undergoes a dazzling transformation. Thousands of tiny lights illuminate the rides and building facades, creating a magical display especially as you soar past them on one of the thrilling attractions.

 CALIFORNIA SCREAMIN': FP
Like many classic boardwalks, the centerpiece of Paradise Pier is a gleaming white roller coaster. A steel coaster, California Screamin' is designed to look (and sound) like an old-fashioned wooden roller coaster, but the thrills are as modern as they get. The ride starts at lagoon level, where the long car bursts up the track, as if catapulted up by a crashing wave. The car goes from zero to 55 mph in 4.7 seconds—before reaching the first hill. Several long drops are combined with an upside-down loop around the giant Mickey head that adorns the coaster, as well as a blasting sound track. The result is the longest and fastest roller coaster in the Disneyland Resort.

Along the way, vehicles travel through blue "scream" tubes that trap guests' yells as they test their vocal cords on the big drops, magnifying the hoots and hollers, and adding to the excitement. Every time you approach a tube, you know you're in for a big thrill, so brace yourself and prepare to scream!

Daredevils should save this ride for after the sun goes down, when the night sky is speckled with the pier's glowing lights, and the topsy-turvy twists and turns on the roller coaster will prove even more disorientingly thrilling.

Note: Passengers must be at least 48 inches tall and free of back problems, neck problems, heart conditions, motion sickness, and other physical limitations to ride.

SUN WHEEL: A modern loop-de-loop, this beaming Ferris wheel, centered by a huge sunburst, takes guests on a head-spinning trip. If you think this is a run-of-the-mill Ferris wheel, you're in for quite a surprise: while the wheel

Did You Know?

The origin of the roller coaster can be traced back to the 1400s in Russia, where thrill seekers took turns riding chairs down a series of icy wooden slides.

turns, most of its cabins rotate in and out along the interior edges of the wheel's giant frame—which creates a dizzying effect. At 150 feet, this is one of California Adventure's tallest attractions, and while it may wreak havoc on sensitive stomachs, thrill seekers rave over its ride within a ride.

Note: Passengers must be free of back problems, heart conditions, motion sickness, and other physical limitations to ride. Afraid of heights? Better skip this one!

Hot Tip!

A few Sun Wheel cars remain fixed on the edge as the wheel spins. Request to sit in one of these if you'd prefer to take a more tranquil trip.

ORANGE STINGER: This ride, set inside the giant swirl of a California orange peel, is sure to leave your brain buzzing. Riders take flight in swings resembling yellow-and-black-striped bumblebees. As the attraction's momentum picks up, buzzing sounds fill the air, and the bees swarm into a frenzy inside the peel.

Note: Riders must meet the Orange Stinger's height requirement of 48 inches, plus be free of back problems, heart conditions, motion sickness, and other physical limitations to follow this flight of the bumblebee.

MULHOLLAND MADNESS: FP No license? No problem. This compact (though jarring) coaster, inspired by the famous road that winds

its way from Hollywood to the Malibu coast, invites "drivers" of all ages to jump into a vehicle and experience the hectic and harrowing nature of California's congested freeways. Small police cars, red fire engines, and old vans follow a winding freeway map while careening over a maze of roundabout roadways and interchanges. Unlike the real thing, riders of this attraction won't be stuck in the infamous Southern California traffic—unless, of course, you count the line for the ride.

Note: Although it's small as roller coasters go, the ride's sudden stops and herky-jerky motion during turns may prove too scary for riders not used to more strenuous coasters. Riders must be at least 42 inches tall and free of back problems, neck problems, heart conditions, motion sickness, and any other physical limitations to take this jolting ride. This attraction may not be operating during your visit.

JUMPIN' JELLYFISH: A dense kelp bed tops this sea-themed attraction, from which riders sitting in brightly colored jellyfish seats are lifted straight up in the air. When you reach the top, hang on to your tentacles! A parachute unfolds, and fish and friend float safely back down to the ground. While the trip is a gentle one with special appeal to younger

PHOTO BY JILL SAFRO

riders, it might take a few minutes for guests with the most sensitive of stomachs to get their land legs back.

Note: Guests must be at least 40 inches tall and be free of back problems, heart conditions, motion sickness, and other physical limitations to ride.

SS RUSTWORTHY: A cleverly themed McDonald's playground, the SS *Rustworthy* is a nice place for young children to cool down and burn off some excess energy. Don't forget to pack kids' bathing suits or a change of clothes (and a supply of waterproof diapers for toddlers), and remember to reapply kids' sunscreen after they're finished romping around the soggy vessel.

MALIBOOMER: Along the boardwalks of yesteryear, strollers were sure to hear the resounding ring of the high bell on a slam machine, followed by uproarious cheers for the sledgehammer-wielding contestant, who had just won the game of strength. This ride represents Disney's twist on that old game. Only this updated version is more a test of endurance than strength. Here, guests challenge their nerves as they become the high-flying projectiles on this extra large, ultramodern slam machine.

Riders are strapped into the vehicle, enveloped by a plastic shield, where they wait for the gong to sound. That's the cue to launch them skyward toward the target, 180 feet into the air, in two seconds. A string of bells and flashing lights erupt when the goal is hit, sending the vehicle dropping to the ground.

Note: Guests must be at least 52 inches tall and be free of back problems, heart conditions, claustrophobia, motion sickness, and other physical limitations to ride.

KING TRITON'S CARROUSEL: Take a spin under the sea on this majestic merry-go-round inspired by *The Little Mermaid*, and presided over by Ariel's father, King Triton. The deep-sea theme is carried out in aquatic detail right down to the ride vehicles themselves. The only horses you'll find here are golden sea horses. They're joined by dolphins, sea otters, seals, and fish, which rise up and down to classic organ tunes as the elegant carousel revolves. Be sure to notice all of the marine mammals as they float by—each one was hand-carved, and no two creatures are exactly alike.

Hot Tip!

Even the hardiest stomachs may start to suffer if the thrilling Paradise Pier rides are tackled back to back. Spend time at the Midway when you need to take a short break.

GOLDEN ZEPHYR: Disney Imagineers took the rocket ride to new heights with the launch of Astro Orbitor in Disneyland. But long before those space-age ships took off, riders were taking flights in rocket-shaped swings on boardwalks and amusement piers across America. Disney pays homage to these old-fashioned attractions with rocket ships that take guests for a spin beneath the Golden Zephyr tower. As speed picks up, the rockets lift into the air and fly over the lagoon several times before touching down for a landing.

Note: Passengers must be free of back problems, neck problems, heart conditions, motion sickness, and other physical limitations to ride. This attraction may not be operating during your visit. (It doesn't run when it's windy.)

MIDWAY: The games of skill and chance that make up Paradise Pier's Midway are themed to Southern California locales and sea creatures. Guests can try their hand at amusements like Rebound Beach (a basketball toss) and Dolphin Derby (a wooden-ball–propelled porpoise race).

Note: The games here are pay per play (usually about $2), but winners may be rewarded with a prize, possibly in the form of a small plush toy.

Shopping

While Mickey Mouse and his cartoon cohorts adorn much of the merchandise sold at Disneyland, the wares here are somewhat less recognizably Disney. When characters do crop up on merchandise, they appear in a much more subtle form. That said, a Disney theme park would not be complete without at least a few shelves of plush toys.

Hot Tip!

Looking for more traditional (i.e., character-adorned) Disney souvenirs? Greetings from California and Engine-Ears Toys are your best bets.

Entry Plaza

ENGINE-EARS TOYS: Located in an oversized model train, this store sells innovative interactive toys, mini train sets and related railroad items, small versions of theme park rides, plush toys, and character merchandise. This store is a package pick-up location (if you purchase items elsewhere in the park, you may have them sent here for pick-up).

PHOTO BY JILL SAFRO

GREETINGS FROM CALIFORNIA: The counterpart to the sprawling Emporium in Disneyland, this well-stocked shop is the place to head for nearly everything under the sun at Disney's California Adventure—souvenirs, books, toys, clothing, and Disney character plush toys. Merchandise themed to all the major attractions in the park can be found here, along with a selection of items specific to each district. Also, if you need film or other camera supplies, or assistance with your camera, head here.

Hollywood Pictures Backlot

GONE HOLLYWOOD: "Kitsch" is the key word in this larger-than-life boutique, which parodies the shopping styles of Hollywood's rich and famous. Here you'll find what is hot and current in Hollywood merchandise: at-home spa and sleepover kits, costumes, and over-the-top cosmetics and accessories.

OFF THE PAGE: The magic of Disney animation leaps off the page at this special shop that showcases collectible Disneyana pieces. Cels, limited-edition prints, and figurines are sold here, as well as attraction-inspired items. A selection of books about Disney history, art, and animation is also available.

RIZZO'S PROP & PAWN SHOP: The wares at this wacky gift shop reflect the Muppets' irreverent sense of humor. Clothes, toys, and souvenirs featuring Kermit, Miss Piggy, Gonzo, Fozzie, and other familiar Muppet faces are for sale here. The stand is worth a browse for the clever Prop Shop theming, which feels like an extension of the nearby Muppet*Vision 3-D attraction.

Golden State

FLY 'N' BUY: When you see the large selection here, you know this is no fly-by-night operation. The aviation-inspired merchandise includes model airplanes, pilot patches, decals, and other accessories. To enhance the wardrobe of aspiring pilots, there are also authentic flight jackets, T-shirts, hats, ties, designer sunglasses, and watches. Merchandise from Soarin' Over California—postcards, music, videos, books, and T-shirts—is showcased here as well.

GOLDEN VINE WINERY: Bottles of California wine line the shelves of this spot catering to wine connoisseurs. Different vintages are available, as well as corkscrews, bottle stoppers, souvenir wine glasses, and wine-inspired books, art, and clothing.

PT FLEA MARKET: Named after the infamous circus owner from *A Bug's Life*, this retail outlet celebrates the wonders of bugs and the natural world.

RUSHIN' RIVER OUTFITTERS: This outpost is the perfect place to gear up for an adventure in the wilderness. Expect to find hiking wear, gear, and supplies—items such as backpacks, sport bottles, polar fleece pullovers, multi-pocket jackets, and compass watches. California wildlife is represented in animal

wood carvings, patches, plush hats, and jackets. And don't overlook the great Grizzly Bear icon of Disney's California Adventure, represented in an assortment of goods themed to the great outdoors.

Paradise Pier

DINOSAUR JACK'S SUNGLASS SHACK: The California look is not complete without a pair of shades. Head here for the ultimate selection in eyewear—sun specs in both classic and wacky styles.

MAN, HAT 'N' BEACH: Beach towels, swimwear, flip-flops, surfboards, and headgear line the shelves and vie for space with beach-themed souvenirs, such as key chains, magnets, and decals at this lakeside shop.

POINT MUGU: Fashion accessories are the stock in trade at this shop. Point Mugu has watches, earrings, necklaces, bracelets, and a large selection of hair accessories (barrettes, combs, headbands, and hair twisters), along with sunglasses, purses, and bags. To add sparkle, there's also a selection of lip gloss, glitter, nail polish, and tattoos (the temporary kind, of course).

Hot Tip!

Can't find the particular Pooh you're looking for? Head to the World of Disney shop in nearby Downtown Disney. It's teeming with character merchandise and Disney souvenirs. (This is also one of the many spots to offer a discount to Premium Annual Pass-holders.)

SIDESHOW SHIRTS: The spotlight here is on shirts of all sorts—tanks, tees, and sweatshirts representing Paradise Pier attractions, as well as other surf-inspired gear. To complete the look, hats with similar logos are also available.

SOUVENIR 66: The well-traveled road, Route 66, provides the inspiration for this roadside souvenir shop. The mementos here come in the form of Paradise Pier–themed key chains, magnets, pins, iron-on patches, and postcards. Many items, such as mugs, beaded necklaces, and T-shirts, can be personalized.

TREASURES IN PARADISE: Here you'll find a vast assortment of Paradise Pier–themed merchandise, such as plush sea creatures and candy containers inspired by King Triton's Carrousel. There's also California Screamin' memorabilia—toys, earrings, necklaces, wristwatches, and the like.

Pin Trading

It's the latest collectibles craze to sweep through Disney's land—pin trading. These small enamel pins (there are hundreds of different styles) can be purchased all over the property, but buying them is only half the fun. The real joy comes when you encounter another pin trader with a worthy swap. To get a head start, bring pins from home (the Disney Store carries its own line). Once on-property, keep an eye out for cast members sporting a good selection of pins—they tend to be agreeable to almost any trade. And when negotiating with a cast member, always remember these rules: (1) only Disney pins may be traded, and (2) every trade must be an even pin-for-pin exchange.

Entertainment

ARTSVENTURES: There are interactive areas in the Bountiful Valley Farm, Condor Flats, and Pacific Wharf sections of the park. These crafty corners invite kids to create an artistic masterpiece—not to mention conversation piece.

BLOCK PARTY BASH: Impromptu parties, celebrating Disneyland's fiftieth anniversary, erupt throughout the day. For more information, refer to page 40.

CHANCE TO SHINE: Get that autograph pen ready. This show gives guests a taste of what life is like as a lowly Hollywood movie extra. (On second thought, forget about the autographs.) Performances take place in the Hollywood Pictures Backlot area.

DISNEY'S ELECTRICAL PARADE: A sequel of sorts to the Main Street Electrical Parade, the classic processional first performed at Disneyland Park in 1972, this updated version made its California Adventure debut in the summer of 2001. It features 30 floats aglow with more than half a million twinkling lights, as well as a cast of 100 performers and a score of electronically synthesized Disney favorites. Performed select nights; check a park guidemap for schedules, and grab a spot along the route at least 30 minutes before it starts. *Note that the Electrical Parade may not be presented during your visit.*

GOLDEN STATE: At the Ahwahnee Camp Fire Circle, located along the Redwood Creek Challenge Trail, camp leaders host sing-alongs, share animal folklore, and tell tales inspired by the great outdoors. Refer to a park guidemap for performance times.

MICKEY'S GARDEN: Stop by Mickey Mouse's Garden for a corn-poppin', carrot-flyin' hoedown. Kids can join Chip and Dale to help with the harvest at the Bountiful Valley Farm. Check a park map for showtimes.

TRASH CAN TRIO: Are these entertainers custodians or musicians? They're both! This surprising group of percussionists has the wonderful ability to turn trash cans into musical instruments. Four days a week. (They used to play across the street, at Disneyland park.)

UGLY BUG BALL: Just as A Bug's Land was built with little critters, er, guests, in mind, so was this nearby child-friendly show. It is presented several times a day at the Bountiful Valley Farm stage. For showtimes, check a park map or inquire at Guest Relations.

Hot Tips

- Disney characters (including Mickey Mouse) make scheduled appearances throughout the day. Check a park map for specifics.

- Check the Information Boards often to get an idea of showtimes and crowds.

- It's sometimes possible to get a free sample at the Mission Tortilla Factory.

- The line for Soarin' Over California tends to dwindle a bit by midday. Ride it then if you choose to forgo the Fastpass option (the experience is enjoyable any time of day).

- Shops in the Entry Plaza stay open a half hour after the park closes.

- On a sweltering day, head to Grizzly River Run, the SS *Rustworthy*, or Princess Dot's Puddle Park in A Bug's Land, splashy spots that provide relief from the heat.

- Need a break from the park? Head to neighboring Downtown Disney for a shopping spree or to grab a bite to eat. There are several (relatively) cost-efficient snacking spots to choose from (i.e., Wetzels Pretzels, Häagen Daz, and La Brea Bakery).

- Some of the park's entertainment may take you by surprise—be on the lookout for performers such as starlets in the Hollywood Backlot area.

- Don't risk water-logging your valuables while riding Grizzly River Rapids. Take advantage of the complimentary lockers (located near the ride's exit). Each locker is free for up to one hour.

Good Meals, Great Times

Dining at the Disneyland Resort is definitely an adventure—and not just in Adventureland. There's more to any meal in a theme park, Downtown Disney, or Disneyland Resort hotel than just food. Goofy, Tigger and Pooh, Merlin and Minnie, or Chip and Dale might drop by your table to say hello. A colorful parade or a romantic paddle wheeler could drift by. Or you might find yourself surrounded by twinkling stars and fireflies (in the middle of the day!) as you savor Cajun cooking in a bayou setting.

In this chapter, the Disneyland Resort restaurant section is divided by location (Disneyland Park, Disney's California Adventure, the three Disney hotels, and Downtown Disney), within the theme parks arranged by area, and then by category—table service or fast-food and snack facilities, including food courts; individual eateries are alphabetized within each category.

If you're hankering for something to do after dinner, or you just need to take a break from the theme parks, you'll find plenty of suggestions at the end of the chapter. Downtown Disney, the property's new dining and entertainment district, is party central. For a more relaxed atmosphere, select a lounge at one of the Disneyland Resort hotels. If it's a particular concert or dinner show in Orange County that interests you, spend the evening at that locale or venue.

Dining
In Disneyland Park

GOOD MEALS, GREAT TIMES

Restaurant Primer

Eateries in this chapter have been designated inexpensive (lunch or dinner under $10), moderate ($11 to $20), expensive ($21 to $45), and very expensive ($46 and up). Prices are for an entrée, a soft drink, and either soup, salad, or dessert for one person, excluding tax and tip.

The letters at the end of each entry refer to the meals offered: breakfast (B), lunch (L), dinner (D), and snacks (S). An asterisk (*) after a letter means that the meal is served only during the park's busy seasons.

Cash, credit cards, traveler's checks, or personal checks with proper ID can be used as payment at all of the following full-service restaurants and fast-food spots. Disneyland Resort hotel guests can charge meals from most theme park eateries to their rooms. Only cash is accepted at snack carts.

While only a few theme park restaurants (Blue Bayou, in Disneyland; and Ariel's Grotto and the Vineyard Room, both in California Adventure) take reservations, you can book a table at most dining spots in Downtown Disney and at the Disney hotels. Unless otherwise noted, make arrangements by calling 714-781-3463.

The most popular food in Disneyland is the hamburger, followed closely by ice cream and *churros* (sticks of deep-fried dough rolled in cinnamon and sugar). But health-conscious eaters will also find salads, grilled chicken, and vegetable stew, plus fresh fruit and juices. Disneyland's two popular table-service

Hot Tip!

For a jolt of java, head to the Blue Ribbon Bakery on Main Street, Bengal Barbecue in Adventureland, or Royal Street Veranda in New Orleans Square. Their iced and hot specialty coffees are sure to please.

restaurants, the Blue Bayou and the Carnation Cafe, provide full-course meals and lighter fare, respectively, plus a welcome break from long lines and the California sun.

Main Street, U.S.A.
Table Service

CARNATION CAFE: On the west side of Main Street, near Town Square, this outdoor cafe is exceptionally pleasant, especially in springtime, when its planters are bursting with seasonal flowers. Stroll through a gazebo to enter the courtyard dining area, filled with umbrella-shaded tables and surrounded by a cast-iron fence; from your table you'll get glimpses of any passing parade. Breakfast choices include Mickey Mouse waffles, cinnamon-roll french toast, sticky buns, "croissantwiches" (egg, cheese, and ham grilled in a croissant), cereal, or continental breakfast, along with coffee or tea and fresh-squeezed orange juice.

For lunch and dinner, deli-style sandwich plates are the big draw, with thick potato chips and either potato salad, pasta salad, or coleslaw. The sandwiches include smoked ham and cheddar cheese, peppered turkey, tuna salad, and a veggie medley. Beef Stroganoff, chicken puff pastry, Caesar salad (with or without chicken), soup, and kids' specials are also on the menu, along with dessert items such as pecan torte, caramel nougat cheesecake, strawberry shortcake, fruit pies, and coffees. This cafe is one of only two restaurants at Disneyland that offers table service for lunch and dinner (Blue Bayou, in New Orleans Square, is the other). **B L D** $-$$

Fast Food & Snacks

BLUE RIBBON BAKERY: Enticing aromas emanate from the espresso machines; fresh cinnamon rolls, muffins, scones, chocolate croissants, giant sticky buns, mini-Bundt cakes, biscotti, jumbo cookies, and demi-baguettes beckon from the display counter; and a chef adds finishing touches to freshly baked cakes and pastries in an open preparation area. Among the less caloric choices: yogurt;

B breakfast **L** lunch **D** dinner **S** snacks   **$** under $10 **$$** $10–$20 **$$$** $21–$45 **$$$$** $46 and up

PHOTO BY JILL SAFRO

vegetables, tuna fish, peppered turkey, or smoked-ham sandwiches in bread pouches; and hot chocolate, soft drinks, orange juice, lemonade, fresh-brewed coffee, cappuccino, caffè latte, and café mocha (the coffees are served iced or hot). It's hosted by Nestlé Toll House. **B L D $**

GIBSON GIRL ICE CREAM PARLOR: Next door to the Blue Ribbon Bakery, this perennially popular place, with a polished wood soda fountain, marble countertop, and black-and-white-checkered floor, serves up a delightful array of scoops and toppings in cups, sugar cones, or handmade waffle cones, plain or

dipped in chocolate. Fantasia is the most interesting flavor on the menu. There is also frozen yogurt, including low-fat, nonfat, and no-sugar-added selections. Don't be daunted by the long line; it moves fast. The ice cream parlor is hosted by Nestlé Ice Cream. **S $**

LITTLE RED WAGON: Between the Main Street Photo Supply Co. and the Plaza Inn, it's a throwback to the delivery trucks of the early 1900s, with ornate beveled and gilded glass panels. Step right up and get your hand-dipped corn dogs, the specialty of the wagon. Lemonade and soft drinks are also served. **L D S $**

MAIN STREET CONE SHOP: Located between Disney Clothiers Ltd. and Market House, behind the fruit cart, this busy window dispenses single or double cones with vanilla, strawberry, chocolate, mocha almond fudge, chocolate chip, and chocolate mint ice cream, and orange sherbet. Two-scoop sundaes are smothered in hot fudge or caramel and topped

GOOD MEALS, GREAT TIMES

Where to Dine with the Characters

Character breakfasts take place at Disneyland's Plaza Inn and at Storytellers Cafe in Disney's Grand Californian Hotel. You can share breakfast, lunch, or dinner with the characters at Goofy's Kitchen in the Disneyland Hotel. Or go next door to Disney's Paradise Pier Hotel for breakfast with Minnie & Friends.

B breakfast **L** lunch **D** dinner **S** snacks   **$** under $10 **$$** $10–$20 **$$$** $21–$45 **$$$$** $46 and up

with whipped cream and a cherry. Mickey Mouse Ice Cream Bars, Nestlé ice cream bars, apple slices covered with caramel, and soft drinks are also available. Tables with umbrellas provide a pleasant resting spot. It's hosted by Nestlé Ice Cream. **S S**

MAIN STREET FRUIT CART: Parked between Disney Clothiers Ltd. and Market House, this old-fashioned cart is stocked with fresh fruit and chilled juices, bottled water, and soft drinks. It's the perfect pit stop for a healthy snack. **S S**

MARKET HOUSE: This quaint Victorian-style market offers a generous selection of cookies in tins, tangy dill pickles plucked right from a barrel, dried fruit, and various candies. Hot coffee and ice-cold apple cider are also available. The market is hosted by Hills Bros. **S S**

PLAZA INN: On the east side of Central Plaza, this fast food restaurant (though it certainly doesn't look like one) is the one Walt Disney was most proud of, and with good reason. Tufted velvet upholstery, gleaming mirrors, and a fine, ornate floral carpet elevate this cafeteria well above similar eateries. Two ceilings are stained glass, framed by elaborate painted moldings. Sconces of Parisian bronze and Baccarat crystal are mounted on the walls, and two dozen basket chandeliers hang from the ceiling.

This setting, including front-porch and terrace dining (with heat lamps at night), creates a lovely backdrop for the food—roast chicken; choice of pasta with marinara, Bolognese, or Alfredo-pesto sauce with chicken; puff pastry topped with vegetable stew, pot roast, or turkey; Cobb salad; and specialty desserts.

An extremely popular character breakfast is held here daily, from park opening until 11 A.M. Pooh, Tigger, Eeyore, and Piglet make the rounds,

PHOTO BY JILL SAFRO

signing autographs and posing for pictures with guests. A fixed-price buffet ($19.99 for adults, $10.99 for children 4 through 12) features made-to-order omelettes, scrambled eggs, french toast, Mickey waffles, cheese blintzes, sausage, bacon, fresh fruit, pastries, and more. **B L D S** **S-$$**

REFRESHMENT CORNER: Better known as Coke Corner, this lively eatery at the northern end of Main Street opposite Main Street Photo Supply Co. is presided over by a talented ragtime pianist who tickles the ivories periodically throughout the day while visitors nibble foot-long beef hot dogs, Mickey Mouse pretzels (cheese optional), and cookies. Soft drinks, lemonade, and coffee are sold. It's hosted by the Coca-Cola Company. **L D S** **S**

Adventureland
Fast Food & Snacks

BENGAL BARBECUE: Opposite the entrance to the Jungle Cruise, this is a great place to listen to the rhythms of Alturas while munching on a skewered snack of bacon-wrapped asparagus (a local favorite), chicken, beef, or veggies. Other menu items include fresh fruit with yogurt dressing, Mickey Mouse pretzels, leopard tails (bread sticks), and cinnamon snake twists (pastries). A variety of specialty coffees is also available. **L D S** **S**

PHOTO BY JILL SAFRO

THE BENGAL BARBECUE

TIKI JUICE BAR: Located at the entrance to the Enchanted Tiki Room, this thatch-roofed kiosk sells fresh Hawaiian pineapple spears and pineapple juice, but the biggest draw here is the Dole Whip soft serve—an extremely refreshing pineapple sorbet (it's nondairy). Coffee is also offered. It's presented by Dole Pineapple. **S S**

Critter Country
Fast Food & Snacks

CRITTER COUNTRY FRUIT CART: This peddler's cart is filled with healthy selections, including fresh fruit, muffins, dill pickles, chilled bottled water, and soft drinks. It's perfect if you need some fortification after taking the big plunge. **S** **$**

HARBOUR GALLEY: If you're looking for McDonald's french fries and soft drinks, stop here. If not, keep moving. **S** **$**

New Orleans Square
Table Service

BLUE BAYOU: The lure of this popular dining spot is as much the atmosphere as it is the menu. Occupying a terrace alongside the bayou in the Pirates of the Caribbean attraction, the restaurant appears perpetually moonlit. Fireflies twinkle above bayou grasses, and stars shine through Spanish moss draped languidly over the big, old live oaks. Off in the distance, an old settler rocks away on the porch of a tumbledown shack.

This enchanting restaurant, located on Royal Street, is the only eatery in Disneyland that accepts reservations (many of the tables are set aside for walk-ins, however); these arrangements must be made the day of dining, so head to the restaurant and schedule a dining time as soon as the park opens.

For lunch, choose from New Orleans-style chowder, Creole gumbo, colorful Mardi Gras salad, jambalaya, and the decadent Monte Cristo sandwiches. Shrimp cocktail, calamari rings with Creole sauce, mushrooms stuffed with andouille sausage, bayou roast pork loin, Caribbean crab cakes, prime rib, and bronze chicken are served at lunch and dinner.

Hot Tip!
A gratuity is automatically added to the bill at some Disney restaurants. Examine the bill, and tip accordingly.

The dinner menu also features grilled salmon, shrimp, and steak Diane. All dinner entrées come with sautéed vegetables and a choice of salad, clam chowder, or gumbo. Be sure to save room for pecan pie or crème brûlée. Children's selections include Mickey chicken nuggets, mini-corn dogs, and Mickey pasta, served with a beverage and dessert.

The busiest periods are from about noon to around 2 P.M. and again from about 5 P.M. until 9 P.M. **L D** **$$-$$$**

Fast Food & Snacks

CAFE ORLEANS: Guests dine inside on small, oak-topped tables, or outside under umbrellas on a terrace overlooking a gristmill on Tom Sawyer Island, and the *Columbia* and the *Mark Twain* plying the Rivers of America.

The menu offers roast beef po'boys, muffaletta sandwiches (turkey, ham, salami, and provolone cheese with an olive relish), turkey and ham croissants, chowder and salad combos, Cajun chicken Caesar salad, and beef bourguignon. There's also *poulet de la maison*, chicken sautéed in Creole sauce and served over rice. Kids like the Mickey-shaped peanut butter and jelly sandwiches. **L D S** **$-$$**

FRENCH MARKET: Beside the old-time train depot in New Orleans Square, this eatery is a destination in its own right.

On a pleasant day, nothing beats sitting on the open-air terrace, munching on fried chicken, beef stew, fettuccine, clam chowder served in a bowl made from a scooped-out loaf of bread, pasta salad, or jambalaya, the house specialty. Roast chicken sandwiches are available at lunch only. Cakes and cheesecakes are the featured desserts. Children's portions

---

Happy Birthday, Disney Style

Goofy's Kitchen, at the Disneyland Hotel, hosts birthday parties with characters on hand to help celebrate the occasion. Cost is $5 a person, plus the price of the meal.

If you prefer a character-filled party at Disneyland, order a cake at the Plaza Inn five days in advance; the servers will bring it out, sing "Happy Birthday," and slice it for the guest of honor and friends. (Characters are available for breakfast only.) Cost is $10 per person.

Another park party option is Redd Rocket's Pizza Port. The cost is $29 per adult, and $20 per child. It may be booked up to 30 days ahead and includes a meal.

Finally, the Paradise Pier Hotels' PCH Grille has birthday celebrations, too. Cost is $5 per person (plus the price of the meal) and includes party favors.

---

of fried chicken and fettuccine are available. Dixieland music is played onstage periodically throughout the evening; in summer, the Royal Street Bachelors hold forth with such spirit that you could listen for hours. It's hosted by Stouffer's. **L D S** **$-$$**

LA PETITE PATISSERIE: Located behind Café Orléans, this snack shop serves funnel cakes covered with powdered sugar, chocolate, raspberry sauce, strawberries, or nuts. Wash them down with specialty coffees, frozen nonalcoholic drinks, and cold beverages. There's limited seating. **S** **$**

MINT JULEP BAR: Beside the New Orleans Square train station, this window-service bar serves fritters (doughy concoctions), croissants, bagels and cream cheese, biscotti, cookies, ice cream, hot chocolate, coffee, cappuccino, and espresso.

The mint juleps taste a bit like lemonade spiked with mint syrup (definitely an acquired taste); happily, real lemonade is also on tap. A variety of sweets and frozen novelties, including Mickey's ice cream sandwiches, round out the selections. Head to one of the tables on the French Market's terrace. **B S** **$**

ROYAL STREET VERANDA: Situated opposite Café Orléans, this little snack stand has bread bowls overflowing with creamy clam chowder or vegetable or steak gumbo; fritters that come with a fruit dipping sauce; and a

variety of beverages. Check out the wrought-iron balustrade above the Royal Street Veranda's small patio. The initials at the center are those of Roy and Walt Disney (this balcony belonged to an apartment that was being constructed for Walt before he died; it now houses the Disney Gallery). **B L D S** **$**

Frontierland
Fast Food & Snacks

CONESTOGA FRIES: The smell coming from this little chuck wagon is awfully familiar. Yup, McDonald's fries. **S** **$**

RANCHO DEL ZOCALO: Casa Mexicana and Big Thunder BBQ fans need not shed a tear over the apparent absence of those two distinct dining spots. They've simply combined forces and reopened as a festive food court designed to resemble a grand Spanish manor.

Situated by the entrance to Big Thunder Mountain Railroad, this latest addition to the Frontierland food scene features south-of-the-border specialties as well as western barbecued favorites. Classic Mexican dishes such as tacos, quesadillas, nachos, and burritos are sure to hit the spot, while beef and pork ribs and barbecued chicken, served with substantial side dishes, are perfect for sharing. Chicken, barbecue, and Texas-style steak sandwiches are on the menu for lunch, while prime rib is featured for dinner. The food is a cut above usual theme park fare. **L D S** **$**

PHOTO BY JILL SAFRO

GOOD MEALS, GREAT TIMES

RIVER BELLE TERRACE: The terrace, between the Golden Horseshoe Stage and the Pirates of the Caribbean, offers one of the best views of the Rivers of America and of the passing throng, and the food is wholesome and hearty. Walt Disney himself used to have breakfast here most Sunday mornings. The menu features scrambled eggs, country-style potatoes, a fresh-fruit plate, and cinnamon rolls. Of the breakfast fare, the popularity prize goes to the Mickey Mouse pancakes—a large flapjack for the face, two small pancakes for the ears, a curve of pineapple for the mouth, a cherry for the nose, and berries for the eyes.

For lunch or dinner, the restaurant offers vegetable stew in a carved-out loaf of bread, steak, catfish, and salmon, ham and turkey sandwiches, a fruit plate, and kid's meals (miniature hot dogs or Mickey-shaped peanut-butter-and-jelly sandwiches served with fresh fruit)—enough to quell even the most serious of hunger pangs prior to viewing Fantasmic! With its lovely interior, it's almost as pleasant to dine inside as it is to eat outside. **B L D** **$-$$**

Sweet Treats

The biggest treat in the park is the dessert buffet served on the Disney Gallery balcony whenever Fantasmic! is performed. Guests enjoy unlimited servings of pastries, fruit, and coffee, tea, and other beverages, plus they see Fantasmic! from the best possible vantage point. At $47 per person, this constitutes a super splurge. The 20 or so seats sell out quickly, call 714-781-4000 up to 30 days in advance or sprint to the Guest Relations window at the entrance to the park (it's to the right of the turnstiles) and make your reservation first thing.

Another option involves viewing Fantasmic! from the water's edge, near The Haunted Mansion. This "Premium Viewing" presentation has 50 seats and costs $47 for adults and $37 for kids. The view is a bit different, but the treat selection's the same.

Or make a beeline for Main Street, U.S.A., and the Blue Ribbon Bakery, the Gibson Girl Ice Cream Parlor, and the Candy Palace, which has tasty saltwater taffy. And by all means, sample a *churro* (fried dough rolled in cinnamon and sugar) from a food cart—it's quite popular.

STAGE DOOR CAFE: This small fast-food stand adjoins the Golden Horseshoe Stage and serves hot dogs, burgers, french fries, side salads, cookies, and beverages. A children's meal is available. Grab a seat at a cafe table outside. **L D S** **$**

Fantasyland
Fast Food & Snacks

FANTASIA GARDENS: Next door to the Matterhorn, this cluster of carts can supply a quick post-ride pick-me-up in the form of a hot dog, choice of soft drinks, or bottled water. **S** **$**

TROUBADOUR TREATS: Located within the Fantasyland Theatre, this spot is open only during the theater's operating hours, dispensing cheese or pepperoni pizza, hot dogs, potato chips, pretzels, nachos, and ice cream. **L S** **$**

VILLAGE HAUS: Near Pinocchio's Daring Journey, this house with its gables, pointy roof, and wavy-glass windows could easily have been relocated to Fantasyland from an alpine village. Inside, murals recount the story of Pinocchio. The menu features personal pizzas, burgers and fries, chef's salad, and cookies. A children's meal is available. **L D S** **$**

Mickey's Toontown
Fast Food & Snacks

CLARABELLE'S FROZEN YOGURT: On Toon Square, adjacent to Pluto's Dog House, Clarabelle's specializes in "udderly" tasty chocolate and frozen vanilla yogurt swirled together, along with toppings, cookies, and Mickey Mouse rice crispy treats. Wet your whistle with lemonade, root beer, milk, or other soft drinks. **L D S** **$**

DAISY'S DINER: Daisy's Diner serves up individual cheese and pepperoni pizzas, along with garden salads. Cookies, milk, juice, soft drinks, root beer, and lemonade round out the menu. **L D S** **$**

GOOFY'S FREE-Z-TIME: The vacation trailer parked by Goofy's House is a dispenser of large frozen slurpy drinks. **S*** **$** (*Seasonal)

PLUTO'S DOG HOUSE: Nestled between Clarabelle's Frozen Yogurt and Daisy's Diner, this is the place to get Pluto's Hot Dog Combo, a foot-long hot dog served with chips and a large soft drink. Extras include cookies, potato chips, Pluto's crispie treats, soft drinks, lemonade, and root beer. The kid's meal comes with a small hot dog, chips, and small soft drink. **L D S** **$**

Tomorrowland
Fast Food & Snacks

CLUB BUZZ: Near the Premiere Shop, this is one of the largest dining facilities in Disneyland. Breakfast choices include scrambled eggs with bacon (or egg substitute with turkey sausage), potatoes, muffin, and beverage; a fruit plate with yogurt dressing, muffin, and beverage; or french toast sticks with powdered sugar, syrup, and fresh fruit.

At lunch and dinner, guests bear trays piled high with fried chicken, corn-on-the-cob, a biscuit, and wedge-cut fries; over-

sized deli sandwiches; smoked chicken and pepper jack cheese in a wrap with avocado, lettuce, and tomato; Caesar salad with optional grilled chicken; or charbroiled burgers. At full capacity, the eatery can—and often does—handle about 3,000 people an hour. **B L D** **$**

MOONLINER: Near the entrance to Redd Rockett's Pizza Port, this refreshment stand set in the base of the Moonliner rocket "launches" bottled beverages right into the server's hands (on request). **S** **$**

REDD ROCKETT'S PIZZA PORT: Situated directly across from Innoventions, this food court overlooks the Moonliner and Cosmic Waves. Three food stations serve fresh pasta, pizza, and large salads, all prepared in an open display kitchen.

Menu choices include pizzas (cheese, pepperoni, and a daily special, all sold by the slice or pie), Celestial Caesar Salad, Planetary Pizza Salad, Mars-inara (spaghetti with tomato sauce), Terra Nova Tomato Basil Pasta, Count-Down Chicken Fusilli, the Mother Chip, and Midnight Oreo Cluster. A beverage counter and cooler supply drinks. The pasta dishes here are large enough to share. **L D S** **$-$$**

Hot Tip!

Children's meals, including a small entrée, side dish, and beverage, come in kid-pleasing shapes and sizes. They're reasonably priced and available at most Disney dining spots.

A+ for Atmosphere

Disney's talent for creating a unique and memorable setting extends to the eateries throughout the park. For atmosphere, we pick:

New Orleans Square
The Blue Bayou restaurant, for its perpetual moon glow and grown-up atmosphere, and the French Market when the Royal Street Bachelors croon.

Main Street, U.S.A.
The Plaza Inn, for its antiques, charm, and front-porch seating.

Critter Country
Harbour Galley restaurant, for a wooded setting that lets you feel in the heart of things, yet curiously removed.

Frontierland
River Belle Terrace, for its pleasant Rivers of America views.

B breakfast **L** lunch **D** dinner **S** snacks   **$** under $10 **$$** $10–$20 **$$$** $21–$45 **$$$$** $46 and up

In Disney's California Adventure

PHOTO BY JILL SAFRO

With both a winery and an elegant lagoonside eatery, the tastes at Disney's California Adventure are clearly grown-up. But several fast-food spots and snack stands supply theme park fare with an entertaining flair—retro Hollywood decor or a laid-back surfer setting. Guests can picnic by the Golden State's Bountiful Valley Farmer's Market, or enjoy a juicy burger at Taste Pilots' Grill. Just remember: it's best not to gorge just before riding any of the attractions along Paradise Pier.

Both of the full-service restaurants here—Ariel's Grotto and the Vineyard Room—accept reservations. Call 714-781-3463 to book a table.

Entry Plaza

BAKER'S FIELD BAKERY: Follow the enticing aroma that wafts out over California Adventure's entrance area, and you'll end up at this bustling bakery. Shelves are filled each morning with freshly baked muffins, croissants, and pastries—each, along with a fresh-brewed cup of coffee, is a sweet way to start the day. Brownies, large cookies, and slices of cake round out the tasty options. A variety of refreshing iced specialty coffees and steaming hot brews (including espresso drinks) makes the perfect pairing with your pastry of choice. **S $**

BUR-R-R BANK ICE CREAM: Cones, shakes, and sundaes are the chilly treats served here. A chocolate-dipped, candy-coated waffle cone piled high with ice cream is a favorite. Expect the line to be longest at midday, when the energy-sapping sun is at its peak. **S $**

Hollywood Pictures Backlot

Fast Food & Snacks

AWARD WIENERS: Hot and heaping cheese and chili dogs—with the occasional autograph request or two—are the specialties here. **S $**

FAIRFAX MARKET: A healthy selection of fresh fruit, vegetables, and soft drinks are provided here, for guests who want a guilt-free snack. **S $**

SCHMOOZIES: Yogurt-and-fruit smoothies are the specialty. For some, these chilly drinks are a meal unto themselves. Lattes, cappuccinos, and other coffees are also available. `S` `$`

PHOTO BY JILL SAFRO

Golden State
Table Service

THE VINEYARD ROOM: This second-story restaurant, divided between an indoor dining area and a covered balcony at this mission-style villa, offers some of the finest (and most expensive) American cuisine on Disneyland property. A three-course, fixed-price meal is matched by some of the winery's best pressed wines (grape juice is served to teetotalers and guests under 21). Chefs prepare a selection of appetizers and entrées in serving skillets; the menu constantly evolves to incorporate the season's freshest ingredients. A limited *à la carte* menu is available on the balcony. Reservations are suggested. `L D` `$$$-$$$$`

Fast Food & Snacks

BOUNTIFUL VALLEY FARMERS' MARKET: A good number of California's indigenous products are incorporated into the items available at this market's stands, from ice cream blended with dates to healthy California sandwich wraps. The local turkey and chicken leg cart provides a quick—and popular—snack, but can attract long lines at mealtimes. A bounty of picnic tables can be found nearby. `B L D S` `$`

COCINA CUCAMONGA MEXICAN GRILL: Tasty corn and flour tortillas are the house specialties and serve as the foundation for most menu items. This cocina cooks steak, pork, and grilled chicken or fish tacos. A creamy, sweet rice pudding makes the perfect finale to the meal. Plan to tour the adjoining tortilla factory before dining at this fast food spot; the educational trip will make the meal all the more enjoyable. You may even snag a free sample. `L D` `$-$$`

PACIFIC WHARF CAFE: An extension of Boudin's display bakery, guests here have the opportunity to sample some of the country's finest sourdough bread (a secret family recipe dating back to 1850). Hearty soups and salads are served up in thick bread bowls for lunch and dinner. Croissants and muffins are offered in the morning hours. `B L D S` `$-$$`

TASTE PILOTS' GRILL: The juicy patties grilled at this Condor Flats establishment just may leave flame-broiled burger lovers on cloud nine. (These vittles are best enjoyed *after* taking a high-flying voyage at Soarin' Over California next door.) Hot stuff is the name of the game here, so expect items such as ribs, chicken wings, and onion rings to round out the menu. `B L D S` `$`

THE LUCKY FORTUNE COOKERY: Foods found in the Pacific Rim are featured on the menu here. Select from egg rolls, California rolls, dumplings, rice bowls, and chicken and beef noodle bowls. `L D S` `$-$$`

RITA'S BAJA BLENDERS: This colorful kiosk next to Cocina Cucamonga serves up slushy fruit drinks and cocktails in your

B breakfast **L** lunch **D** dinner **S** snacks   **$** *under $10* **$$** *$10–$20* **$$$** *$21–$45* **$$$$** *$46 and*

choice of lemon-lime, strawberry, peach, banana, and other favorite flavors. **S** **$**

WINE COUNTRY MARKET: Located on the lower level of the mission house, this deli provides the perfect complement to a glass of wine—cheese, soups, salads, fruit, and finger sandwiches. Dine at one of the shaded tables beside the vineyard. **L S** **$-$$**

Paradise Pier
Table Service

ARIEL'S GROTTO: This dining spot offers enchanting views of Paradise Pier's amusements and the water below (dinner is especially festive, when the boardwalk is aglow with twinkling lights). What's more, Disney characters have been known to mingle with diners. Guests pay one price and select one item for each course. (Soup and dessert cost extra at lunch.) Fish, salads, and pastas fill the menu. Reservations are suggested. **L D** **$$$**

Fast Food & Snacks

BURGER INVASION: An "out-of-this-world" burger stand, it's memorable more for the cheeseburger spaceship that hovers above it than for the McDonald's food it serves. **L D** **$**

CATCH A FLAVE: Swirl's up at this beachy ice cream stand. A selection of refreshing soft-serve flavors helps guests cool off after a long day of fun in the sun. **S** **$**

CORN DOG CASTLE: Hot dogs, links, and cheese, fried to a golden brown and served on a stick, reign supreme. **L D S** **$**

MALIBU-RITOS: The steaming, stuffed burritos offered here make for some of the healthier Paradise Pier meals, for vegetarians and meat eaters alike. **B L D S** **$**

PIZZA OOM MOW MOW: Surf's up, dude! California's Venice Beach and its colorful culture is inspiration for this pizza place's decor. Surfing memorabilia provide the backdrop for the cheesy entrées of choice—available plain or with a combination of toppings. **L D** **$**

STRIPS, DIPS, 'N' CHIPS: The fried chicken, fish sticks, zucchini strips and fab fries (with choice of dipping sauces) are no paltry snack-on-the-go. Though you may be tempted, do resist the urge to indulge before heading over to ride California Screamin', the topsy-turvy roller coaster nearby. **L D S** **$**

In the Disneyland Resort Hotels

Disneyland Hotel

The diverse dining possibilities here range from grand to Goofy. For reservations or information, call 714-781-3463.

CAPTAIN'S GALLEY: Specialty coffees, muffins, bagels, cereal, fruit, kid's meals, and boxed lunches (salads and sandwiches) are sold in this tucked-away shop. Perfect for a poolside meal or a healthy snack on the go. Alcohol, including bottles of California wine, is available. **B L S $**

THE COFFEE HOUSE: Order biscotti, bagels, muffins, pastries, fruit, yogurt, cookies, and coffee in this small coffee shop. Outside seating only. Expect long lines in the morning. **B S $**

CROC'S BITS 'N' BITES: Part of the Never Land pool area, it's perfect for a quick burger, grilled chicken sandwich, or ice cream. There's outdoor seating nearby. **S $**

PHOTO BY KEITH GROSHANS

GOOFY'S KITCHEN: This whimsical dining room features perennially popular meals and personal encounters with Goofy, Donald Duck, and other Disney friends. Service here is buffet style, so fill your plate as high and as often as you please.

Highlights at breakfast include Mickey Mouse–shaped waffles and breakfast lasagna. Lunch and dinner offer carved ham, prime rib, pasta, chicken dishes, macaroni and cheese, pizzas (including tasty peanut-butter-and-jelly pizza, a favorite with the youngsters and Birnbaum editors), salads, breads, fruit, and a selection of desserts. Don't forget your camera—Disney characters provide prime photo opportunities. Reservations suggested (same-day reservations are not accepted, but you can put your name on the standby list). **B L* D $$-$$$** (*Open seasonally for lunch)

> ## Hot Tip!
> Expect a long line at The Coffee House in the morning, and head to Captain's Galley for a quick breakfast or cup of coffee.

GRANVILLE'S STEAK HOUSE: An upscale dining establishment, Granville's is decorated with oak paneling, etched glass, and paintings that depict the American Southwest. Soft music plays as servers deliver a "3-D" menu of cuts of fresh meats, cooked to your specifications. All the entrées—such as juicy prime rib, fresh Maine lobster, and rack of lamb, among others—come with a baked potato, wild rice, or french fries. The wine list touts fine California vintages, and the desserts are delectable. Reservations suggested. Menu selections are subject to change. **D $$$$**

HOOK'S POINTE & WINE CELLAR: This sophisticated, contemporary dining room overlooks the Never Land pool. Mesquite-grilled specialties include chicken breast with sweet-pea risotto and roasted garlic sauce, sea bass with a citrus-flavored glaze, and cognac-marinated rib-eye steak. Pastas, sandwiches, pizzas, salads, and spring rolls are also featured on the menu, along with children's selections. Reservations suggested. **L D $$$**

Disney's Paradise Pier Hotel

It has all the bases covered—from sushi to wood-fired pizza. And wait till you see what Minnie's cooked up for breakfast! For reservations, call 714-781-3463.

DISNEY'S PCH GRILL: Besides hosting a character breakfast with Minnie & Friends that offers both table service and a buffet, Disney's PCH Grill—the initials stand for Pacific Coast Highway—reflects classic California tastes. The focal point is the open kitchen, which features a large pizza oven. The decor incorporates primary colors and Mickey silhouettes, while the menu, designed like a road map, features tasty

American dishes. For lunch or dinner, consider sampling the burgers, sandwiches, fried calamari, fish tacos, pasta, or wood-fired specialty pizzas. Kids can "design" their own pizzas. Reservations suggested. **B L D** $$

YAMABUKI: This restaurant is named after a flower known as the Japanese rose. Authentic traditional and contemporary Japanese dishes, described clearly and concisely on the menu, are served *à la carte* or as part of a set menu, almost always with miso soup, salad, and

> ## Hot Tip!
> PCH Grill's fresh, hearty fare and peaceful setting make it the perfect place to take a lunch break when the parks are packed and the midday sun seems inescapable.

steamed rice or a California roll. Japanese beers and sake are served, along with wine and other beverages. The *à la carte* menu items include tiger prawns, shrimp and vegetable tempura, sushi, and sashimi, as well as New York steak cooked to order, a daily grilled fish special, and children's portions of chicken or beef teriyaki. Some dishes are cooked at your table. The sushi bar offers a fine selection of fresh fish and it rarely has a wait. Reservations suggested for the dining room. **L* D** $$$ (*Lunch weekdays only)

> ## Hot Tip!
> For Japanese dining in the most traditional setting, ask to sit in the Tatami Room at Yamabuki.

Disney's Grand Californian Hotel

The restaurants at Disney's newest hotel offer a taste of (and a twist on) California cuisine. For reservations, call 714-781-3463.

NAPA ROSE: This popular, elegant restaurant features a creative menu of market-fresh, wine

country–inspired dishes flavored by fruits of the sea and vine (the eatery is named after California's most famous valley of vineyards). A striking 20-foot stained-glass window offers sweeping views of Disney's California Adventure, while the open kitchen gives insight into California cooking. The offerings evolve as new items are introduced each season. Consider grapevine-smoked salmon with lemon, capers, and goat cheese panini, or grilled free-range veal with truffled white

> ## Hot Tip!
> Napa Rose's adjoining lounge offers several of the restaurant's appetizers as well as an impressive wine list.

beans and a cabernet vinaigrette. The dessert tray offers a trio of citrus temptations: Key lime custard, orange napoleon, and a lemon cream nut tart. The California wine list is one of the most extensive on property. Reservations suggested. **L D** $$$-$$$$

HEARTHSTONE LOUNGE: Though primarily a drinking spot, this lounge is open in the morning for early risers in search of hot coffee and the day's paper. Continental breakfast items are also available. **B S** $

> ## Hot Tip!
> Any full-service dining location at a Disneyland Resort hotel will validate your parking at that hotel; remember to get your parking pass stamped before you leave.

STORYTELLERS CAFE: It's hard to imagine a time before computers and television (especially for the youngest members of the group), when children were exposed to new cultures

and histories only through the stories of others. This restaurant salutes tales set in California, like "The Jumping Frogs of Calaveras County" and "Island of the Blue Dolphin," through seven-foot murals that act as backdrops to the chefs at work in the exhibition kitchen. In the morning, the stage is set

> ## Hot Tip!
> If you don't have a reservation, expect a *long* wait at mealtimes. It is next to impossible to snag a table at a Disneyland Resort hotel or Downtown Disney eatery with any spontaneity. Don't get caught with your stomach growling—plan ahead!

for a festive character-hosted buffet. Chip, Dale, and other Disney characters entertain guests, while the buffet offers a bounty of breakfast options, from pancakes and waffles to eggs, sausage, and a selection of fresh fruit. Lunch and dinner offer such pleasers as wood-fired pizzas, homemade pastas, and burgers, plus salads, grilled fish, and spit-roasted chicken, all prepared and served by chefs from their cooking islands. Reservations suggested for breakfast. **B L D** $$-$$$

WHITE WATER SNACKS: The splish-splash of the waterfall and kids soaring down the slide at the Redwood pool set the mood for this ultra-casual dining spot. Open for breakfast, lunch, and dinner (though hours vary), the snack bar serves coffee, muffins, bagels, sweet rolls, and breakfast burritos in the morning. Large salads, deli sandwiches, pizzas, burgers, hot dogs, and grilled chicken are lunch and dinner options. **B L D S** $

In Downtown Disney

The settings and menus of the restaurants at Downtown Disney may differ, but many serve meals with a side of entertainment.

CATAL RESTAURANT & UVA BAR: A sun-kissed balcony, outdoor tapas bar, and villa-style dining room set the Mediterranean mood at this casual but elegant restaurant. The menu focuses on grilled seafood, chicken, and vegetables, infused with olive oil and citrus accents. With several pastas and salads available, vegetarians have much to choose from here. The large courtyard bar serves appetizers as well as cocktails. Reservations are suggested; 714-774-4442. **B L D** $$$

ESPN ZONE: This sporty spot serves up baskets of ballpark fare, plus items like Cajun fettuccine, grilled chops, and New York strip steaks. If you want to get close to the action, you'll need to get a table (and be prepared to place an order). Sports fans may want to see ask about the "Zone Thrones" — leather easy chairs complete with sound systems and serving tables. Call 714-300-3776. **B* L D S** $$ (*Breakfast served on weekends only)

HAAGEN-DAZS: The dessert specialist offers ice cream, frozen yogurt, sorbet, and gelato— as well as baked goods and coffee. **S** $

HOUSE OF BLUES: Diners with a craving for Southern cookin' will find bliss at this Delta dive (all part of the theme). With a menu set deep in the South, the eatery offers items such as Memphis-style ribs, voodoo shrimp, jambalaya, and tasty thin-crust pizzas. On Sundays guests sing hallelujah for the all-you-can-eat Southern-style Gospel Brunch (gospel touring groups provide the stirring entertainment). Reservations suggested; 714-778-2583. **B L D** $$$

JAMBA JUICE: In the mood for a paradise smoothie? Perhaps one with protein or a berry bent? They've got all that and more. **S** $

LA BREA BAKERY: The offerings at this casual Downtown Disney spot—breakfast treats, grilled panini sandwiches, and crostini (small, open-face sandwiches)—are built on their legendary bread. A juice and coffee bar blends up healthy concoctions and smoothies, plus coffees. Wine by the glass and micro-brewed beers are available. **B L D S** $-$$$

NAPLES RISTORANTE E PIZZERIA: Dine indoors or alfresco at this contemporary Italian trattoria. A large outdoor terrace provides perfect views of the Disney landscape, plus a peaceful and romantic setting for lunch or dinner. Pizzas are served in individual portions or *al metro* (one meter long and perfect for a hungry family to share). The menu also includes *piccoli piatti* (small salads served tapas-style), fresh pasta dishes, and seafood entrées. Reservations suggested; 714-776-6200. **L D** $$$

NAPOLINI: Adjacent to the popular Naples Ristorante e Pizzeria, this spot also offers Italian fare, but on the lighter side than that served by its neighbor.

RAINFOREST CAFE: It's a jungle inside this tropical paradise of a restaurant. Greenery, misty waterfalls, tropical storms, Audio-Animatronic animals, and several real-life creatures create a sometimes hectic, always colorful atmosphere. The menu features sizable, environmentally conscious appetizers and entrées, including pastas, burgers, and sandwiches. Reservations suggested; 714-772-0413. **B L D S** $$-$$$

RALPH BRENNAN'S JAZZ KITCHEN: Sample some home-style New Orleans specialties at this comfy cafe while listening to the soothing sounds of jazz. Gumbo, jambalaya, Cajun chicken, and fresh pasta dishes are house favorites. Reservations suggested; 714-776-5200. **L D S** $$-$$$

WETZEL'S PRETZELS: Whether you prefer pretzels on the salty or sweet side, Wetzel's has something to satisfy. Ambitious snackers enjoy the Mexicali, the Sinful Cinnamon, and the Three Cheese varieties. **S** $

> ## Hot Tip!
> Many Downtown Disney dining spots serve simple breakfasts. Grab a bite to eat before heading to Disney's California Adventure or Disneyland.

Restaurant Roundup

There are more dining choices than ever before at the Disneyland Resort. We've picked our favorites, based on food quality, restaurant atmosphere, and overall value. Use these Birnbaum's Bests to help you decide where to grab a quick bite or have a hearty meal.

BEST RESTAURANTS FOR FAMILIES

TABLE SERVICE

Goofy's Kitchen . . . . .Disneyland Hotel (p. 126)
Blue Bayou . . . . .Disneyland Park (p. 119)
Storytellers Cafe . . . . .Grand Californian Hotel (p. 127)
Rainforest Cafe . . . . .Downtown Disney (p. 129)

FAST FOOD

Royal Street Veranda . . . . .Disneyland Park (p. 120)
Rancho del Zocalo . . . . .Disneyland Park (p. 120)
Refreshment Corner . . . . .Disneyland Park (p. 118)
Pacific Wharf Cafe . . . . .California Adventure (p. 124)
Award Wieners . . . . .California Adventure (p. 123)

BEST PIZZA

Naples Ristorante e Pizzeria
Downtown Disney (p. 129)

BEST SUSHI

Yamabuki
Paradise Pier Hotel (p. 127)

BEST BARBECUE

Rancho del Zocalo
Disneyland Park (p. 120)

BEST CHARACTER MEAL

Goofy's Kitchen . . . . .Disneyland Hotel (p. 126)

RUNNERS-UP

Plaza Inn . . . . .Disneyland Park (p. 118)
Storytellers Cafe . . . . .Grand Californian Hotel (p. 128)

BEST RESTAURANTS FOR ADULTS

Napa Rose . . . . .Grand Californian Hotel (p. 127)
Ralph Brennan's Jazz Kitchen . . . . .Downtown Disney (p. 129)

RUNNERS-UP

Hook's Pointe & Wine Cellar . . . . .Disneyland Hotel (p. 126)
Catal Restaurant & Uva Bar . . . . .Downtown Disney (p. 129)
House of Blues . . . . .Downtown Disney (p. 129)

BEST SNACKS

Blue Ribbon Bakery . . . . .Disneyland Park (p. 116)
Bur-r-r Bank Ice Cream . . . . .California Adventure (p. 123)

GOOD MEALS, GREAT TIMES

130

Entertainment
Disney Hotels

There's more to Disney than thrill rides and characters. Whether you're looking for a break from the parks or a place to party the night away, the following options are sure to please. There's plenty to do at Disney's three hotels and in Downtown Disney. We've also included some Anaheim-area options for those interested in venturing beyond Disney borders.

Note: For additional information on evening theme park happenings, refer to the *Disneyland Park* and *Disney's California Adventure* chapters of this book.

Lounges

DISNEYLAND HOTEL: The cozy **Wine Cellar** (pictured below) is located on the lower level of Hook's Pointe & Wine Cellar and serves California wines by the bottle, glass, or taste. **Top Brass** bar, with its leaded-glass door, brass rails, and striking watercolor of the Anaheim orange groves circa 1962, provides an intimate meeting place.

An open-air lounge, offering a menu long enough that the place could almost be called a restaurant (burgers, sandwiches, and such are served), the **Lost Bar** is this hotel's most happening hot spot, especially when the resident musicians are performing. Outdoor tables are kept toasty warm by the heat lamps that are lit each evening. The Lost Bar tends to stay open as late or later than other Disneyland lounges.

DISNEY'S PARADISE PIER HOTEL: The small lobby Coffee Bar & Lounge has perhaps the only cappuccino maker and "Henri Rousseau" print with Mickey ears in existence.

Hot Tip!
Pinocchio's Workshop at Disney's Grand Californian keeps kids entertained when parents want to share a night out *sans* children. Call 714-781-4560 for details.

The small lounge inside the Yamabuki restaurant is a quiet retreat and the perfect place to join friends for a nightcap.

DISNEY'S GRAND CALIFORNIAN HOTEL: The lounge adjoining the elegant Napa Rose restaurant offers an extensive selection of wines by the glass and a soothing atmosphere.

At the handsome Hearthstone Lounge, you can sip a cocktail or after-dinner cordial opposite a roaring fireplace.

Live Entertainment

DISNEYLAND HOTEL: At the free Fantasy Waters, fountains and lights dance in rhythm to Disney tunes; it occurs twice nightly (seasonally). Hear music most nights in summer and on weekends the rest of the year at The Lost Bar; other performers croon at various locations.

DISNEY'S GRAND CALIFORNIAN HOTEL: As a tribute to the early 1900s storytelling tradition, entertainers tell tall tales in the hotel's main lobby throughout the day. A piano player adds to the ambience.

Fun & Games

DISNEYLAND HOTEL: Kids can steer small, remote-control Jungle Cruise Boats by the hotel's lagoon. The beach's volleyball court is a hit, especially in the afternoon; the Game Arcade in the shopping enclave scores high points on evenings when the parks close early. And, of course, Fantasy Waters is always fun.

DISNEY'S GRAND CALIFORNIAN HOTEL: The Grizzly Game Arcade features all the latest whistles and bells.

DISNEY'S PARADISE PIER HOTEL: Youngsters have a blast at this hotel's arcade, located off the main lobby.

Downtown Disney

Easily accessed by foot (from the Disneyland Resort hotels or theme parks) or monorail (from Disneyland Park's Tomorrowland), this entertainment district offers escape from the hustle and bustle during the day, and a place to mix and mingle in the evening hours. Many Downtown Disney venues serve double (or triple) duty—as dining and dancing (and sometimes shopping) spots.

Shops open early and don't close until late in the evening. Club performers generally hit the stage post dinner and wrap past midnight.

GOOD MEALS, GREAT TIMES

Clubs & Concerts

HOUSE OF BLUES: Don't let the name of this jumping joint fool you—the lineup features a rousing mix of rock, R&B, hip-hop, reggae, and Latin music, along with a touch of the blues. Big-name bands and local acts are slotted to perform throughout the week. Call 714-778-2583 to learn the House's schedule during your visit. Ticket prices range from about $5 to $30, depending on the performer. Call TicketMaster or visit *www.ticketmaster.com* to purchase tickets in advance, or stop by the club's box office the day of the performance.

RALPH BRENNAN'S JAZZ KITCHEN: The sounds of jazz set the tone for the relaxed atmosphere at this restaurant's lounge. Bands and singers entertain on select days of the week. A smooth sound track provides music when the stage is dark. Special tickets may be required for certain performances. Call 714-776-5200 to inquire about ticket reservations.

Lounges

CATAL RESTAURANT AND UVA BAR: Designed to resemble the Art Nouveau–style of a Paris metro station, this large wine and tapas bar tempts guests with the fruits of the vine and sea. Guests can drink under the stars at the outdoor bar or mingle indoors, and can select from the extensive wine list.

ESPN ZONE: Stop by the bar area of the Zone's Studio Grill for a tall one before heading upstairs to play arcade games at the Sports Arena. With large-screen TVs blaring from each section of the room, expect the joint to be jumping on big-game nights.

MAGIC MUSHROOM BAR: Part of the lush Rainforest Cafe, this circular drinking hole is capped by a giant mushroom, and serves up aptly named blended beverages, such as the Margarilla and the Tropical Toucan (nonalcoholic versions are also available). Known as a family-friendly spot, don't be surprised if a tiny tot is sitting at the zebra-legged bar stool beside you, especially at lunch or dinnertime.

Shopping

BASIN: Indulge in the lavish bath and body products available at this inviting boutique.

BUILD-A-BEAR WORKSHOP: Create your own stuffed animal, as you "choose, stuff, stitch, fluff, name, and dress" your way through a series of bear-making stations. It's a "beary" special experience.

COMPASS BOOKS AND CAFE: This branch of the West's oldest (since 1851) independent bookstore is heavy on the travel tomes, and also features a coffee bar and outdoor newsstand.

DEPARTMENT 56: 'Tis always the season to be jolly at this shop featuring miniature houses and other holiday collectibles.

HOUSE OF BLUES COMPANY STORE: A slew of spicy sauces lets you take a bit of this House back to your house. Home accessories and House of Blues logo merchandise round out the options here.

HOYPOLOI: This gallery, which displays ceramics, sculptures, and other decorative items, provides the perfect retreat on a crowded day.

ILLUMINATIONS: Light up your life with an assortment of handcrafted candles, aromatherapy products, and accessories.

ISLAND CHARTERS: Ahoy! This shop offers one-of-a-kind nautical and aviation gifts for seafarers and landlubbers alike.

LEGO IMAGINATION CENTER: Four hundred of the world's most famous building brick sets and products are for sale, along with Lego shirts, hats, and other apparel (and, no, they're not made of Lego bricks).

LIQUID PLANET: Simple surfer wear and accessories help guests dress the part of the laid-back beachcomber.

MAINSPRING: Time never stands still at this watch shop, where more than 5,000 brands and styles are on display.

MARCELINE'S CONFECTIONERY: Named for Walt Disney's hometown, this sweet shop offers classic and contemporary candies.

PETALS: Leather is the look of choice at this cozy boutique. Jackets, handbags, and other accessories are for sale.

RAINFOREST SHOP: Large butterflies and vibrant parrots perched atop looping jungle vines define this tropical shop, adjacent to the Rainforest Cafe. Plush animals, environmentally themed toys, plus Rainforest Cafe logo items, candy, cookies, and coffee are for sale.

SEPHORA: A black-and-white motif provides a perfect backdrop for the colorful palette of products in this cosmetics mecca. Sephora's own line of makeup and bath products is complemented by a wide selection of popular and hard-to-find beauty products and perfumes. It's possible to mix and match to create personalized gift baskets.

SOMETHING SILVER: Perfect for celebrating a 25th anniversary, or just creating a look, the jewelry here is simple and stylish. Note that there are many lovely non-silver selections to choose from, too.

SPORTS CENTER STUDIO STORE: Sports fans and couch potatoes alike will cheer over the ESPN, SportsCenter, and Monday Night Football branded apparel and other merchandise at this shop inside the ESPN Zone.

STARABILIAS: Shoppers can walk down memory lane at this spot, which showcases TV, movie, music, and political memorabilia.

WORLD OF DISNEY: Shelves are stacked sky-high at this souvenir shopper's dream come true. Each overflowing room features a different theme and type of merchandise: the Lion King room is well suited to adult apparel, while Disney Villains add dastardly decor to the watch and accessory department. With an entire room dedicated to plush toys (the 20-foot wall of plush features more than 15,000 characters), and rooms for dolls, figurines, toys, videos, clothing, accessories, and collectibles, everyone is bound to find what they are looking for here. Classic Disney films play continuously on the big screen to occupy restless young (and old) shoppers. Expect the place to be packed most evenings and all day on the weekends.

Fun & Games

AMC MOVIE THEATRES: Moviegoers enjoy wall-to-wall movie screens and comfy stadium seating at each of the 12 cinemas located inside this megaplex. Current releases are shown throughout the day, with special matinee and late-night screenings. The first showing of the day usually comes at a discount.

ESPN ZONE: This sports shrine offers dining options (see page 129) and a lounge area, plus two distinct fun zones. In the Screening Room, sports fans can cheer their team to victory, as games from around the world are televised on one central 16-foot screen and a dozen additional 36-inch video monitors.

With multi-game viewing capabilities and direct audio control, picture-in-picture is taken to a whole new level. Even bathroom breaks won't mean a minute missed: the restrooms are equipped with TVs tuned to the main event.

The Sports Arena challenges guests with sports-themed games that put your skills, strength, and smarts to the test. Game cards (necessary to play the arena's games) can be purchased in $5 increments.

Beyond the Disneyland Resort

Clubs & Concerts

ARROWHEAD POND OF ANAHEIM: Besides being the home of the Mighty Ducks hockey team, "the Pond" accommodates 17,000 fans for major concerts, from rock to rap to country. 2695 E. Katella Ave.; Anaheim; 714-704-2500. Note that "tailgating" is not permitted in the parking lot of this venue.

CERRITOS CENTER FOR THE PERFORM-ING ARTS: This state-of-the-art theater presents popular artists, musicians, dance companies, and Broadway shows. Performers have included Isaac Stern, the Alvin Ailey American Dance Theater, Whitney Houston, Peabo Bryson, Trisha Yearwood, and Bernadette Peters. 12700 Center Court Dr.; Cerritos; 562-916-8500 or 800-300-4345.

HYATT NEWPORTER SUMMER JAZZ SERIES: On Friday nights from June through October, jazz artists perform in the hotel's amphitheater. Tickets cost $5 to $45. 1107 Jamboree Rd.; Newport Beach; 949-729-1234.

IMPROV COMEDY CLUBS: Two sister comedy venues present shows four or five nights a week; call or visit *www.improv.com* for current schedules and headliners. 4555 Mills Circle; Ontario; 909-484-5411; and 71 Fortune Dr.; Irvine; 949-854-5455.

ORANGE COUNTY PERFORMING ARTS CENTER: This 3,000-seat theater hosts symphony orchestras, opera and dance companies, and touring Broadway shows. Jazz, and cabaret shows are staged in the intimate 250-seat Founders Hall, where drinks are served. 600 Town Center Dr.; Costa Mesa; 714-556-2787.

Dinner Theater

MEDIEVAL TIMES: Guests feast on several-courses served by wenches and knaves while knights on horse-back twist and joust. 7662 Beach Blvd.; Buena Park; 714-521-4740.

PLAZA GARIBAL-DI: It's a Mexican fiesta with mariachis, singers, dancers, traditional food, margaritas, and more. 500 N. Brookhurst; Anaheim; 714-758-9014.

Lounges

In Anaheim, **J.T. Schmid's Brewhouse & Eatery**, across the road from the Pond, has home-brewed ales, with gleaming vats on view; 2610 E. Katella Ave.; 714-634-9200. In nearby Orange, the **Alcatraz Brewing Company** is ensconced in the lively Block at Orange; 20 City Blvd. West; Orange; 714-939-8686. On the coast, the **Huntington Beach Beer Company** mixes brews with free live jazz on Tuesday nights, rock and blues on Saturday nights, and its seating offers ocean views all the time; 201 Main St.; Huntington Beach; 714-960-5343.

The **National Sports Grill** has sports memorabilia, 4 big-screen TVs, 63 TV monitors, and 11 pool tables; 450 N. State College Blvd.; Anaheim; 714-935-0300.

Fun & Games

THE BLOCK AT ORANGE: This outdoor entertainment complex, only five miles from Disneyland, has a 30-screen **AMC Cinema**, **Dave & Buster's** billiards parlor, and **The Powerhouse**, a state-of-the-art arcade. Valet parking available. 20 City Blvd. West; Orange; 714-769-4001.

Sports

Southern California's appealing combination of warm, sunny weather and invigorating ocean breezes has created a population of outdoors and exercise enthusiasts. Well-toned athletes flex their muscles on golf courses and tennis courts; atop surfboards, bicycles, and in-line skates; on hiking and jogging trails; or 15 feet underwater, mingling with schools of fish.

In Orange County alone, there are more than 10,000 acres of parkland and several hundred miles of bike trails. Hiking paths and fishing streams crisscross 70,000 acres of mountain terrain in Cleveland National Forest. Just 15 miles south of Anaheim, prime Pacific Ocean beaches, perfect for basking in the sun or catching the ultimate wave, await the wayfarer. In fact, 42 miles of glistening sand and sleepy seaside communities lie within an hour's drive of Anaheim.

Those who delight in spying on Mother Nature can catch glimpses of California's gray whales as they migrate to Mexico for the winter, or ospreys, blue herons, and swallows returning to the area in the spring. A team of Orange County's most entertaining creatures, the Mighty Ducks, can be spotted on the ice at the Arrowhead Pond of Anaheim, September through April (and later, if they make another run for the Stanley Cup). Even Angels have been sighted, gracing the bases at Edison International Field, April through September.

To be sure, the sporting life in Orange County is bountiful.

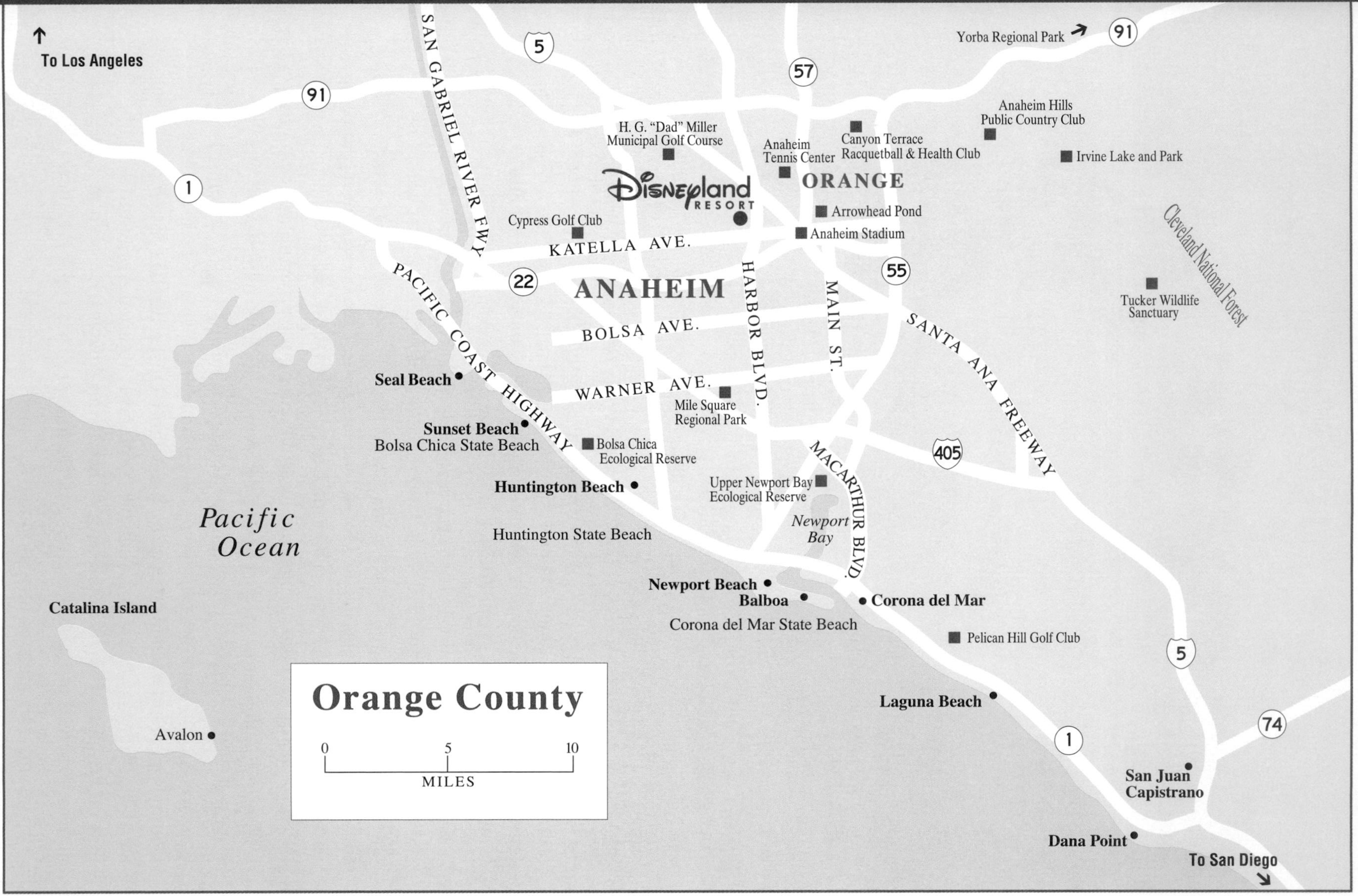

Orange County

To Los Angeles

To San Diego

Cleveland National Forest

Tucker Wildlife Sanctuary

Yorba Regional Park

Irvine Lake and Park

Anaheim Hills Public Country Club

Canyon Terrace Racquetball & Health Club

Anaheim Tennis Center

ORANGE

Arrowhead Pond

Anaheim Stadium

SANTA ANA FREEWAY

San Juan Capistrano

Dana Point

Pelican Hill Golf Club

Laguna Beach

MACARTHUR BLVD.

MAIN ST.

Upper Newport Bay Ecological Reserve

Newport Bay

Corona del Mar

Balboa

Newport Bay

Newport Beach

Corona del Mar State Beach

Disneyland RESORT

H. G. "Dad" Miller Municipal Golf Course

HARBOR BLVD.

ANAHEIM

BOLSA AVE.

WARNER AVE.

Mile Square Regional Park

KATELLA AVE.

Cypress Golf Club

Bolsa Chica Ecological Reserve

Huntington Beach

Huntington State Beach

PACIFIC COAST HIGHWAY

SAN GABRIEL RIVER FWY.

Seal Beach

Sunset Beach

Bolsa Chica State Beach

Pacific Ocean

Catalina Island

Avalon

Orange County

0   5   10

MILES

Eye on the Ball

Golf

ANAHEIM HILLS PUBLIC GOLF CLUB:
This challenging championship course is a hilly, par-71, 6,245-yard layout nestled in the valleys and slopes of the scenic Anaheim Hills. Greens fees are $42.50 Monday through Thursday, $52.50 on Friday, and $57.50 on weekends and holidays, cart included. Guests ages 62 and older can play standby Monday through Thursday for $28.50. Clubs can be rented for $15. The golf course is busiest on weekends; the least crowded days are Monday, Tuesday, and Wednesday, but even then reservations are recommended (call seven days ahead for both weekend and weekday play). 6501 Nohl Ranch Rd.; Anaheim; 714-998-3041.

CYPRESS GOLF CLUB: Lakes, streams, bunkers, trees, and scenic vistas decorate this serene par-71, 6,500-yard course, which is designed to harmonize with the environment by Perry O. Dye, son of the legendary Pete Dye. Fees are $55 to play Monday through Thursday, $65 Friday, and $75 weekends, cart included. Twilight rates ($45 to $65), and birthday specials ($40 to $50 with ID) are also available. Reservations are recommended and can be made up to ten days in advance. Collared shirts and soft spikes are required; no jeans or sneakers. It's a 15-minute drive from the Disneyland Resort. 4921 E. Katella Ave.; Los Alamitos; 714-527-1800 (pro shop and reservations).

H.G. "DAD" MILLER MUNICIPAL GOLF COURSE: "Dad" Miller made a hole in one on this course (on the 112-yard 11th hole) when he was 101 years old, and it's still a favorite with older guests, who appreciate the flat, walkable terrain. But if you're a tad on the younger side, don't let that keep you from playing here. This par-71, 6,025-yard golf course is one of the busiest in California—partly because of its convenient location in the middle of the city, but also because it's just right for the strictly recreational golfer. The cost to play here is $23 Monday through Thursday, $32 Friday, $35 on Saturday, Sunday and holidays. Guests 62 and older can play standby for only $12 Monday through Friday. Golf carts cost $24 for 18 holes, $15 for nine holes. Reservations are suggested, and may be made up to a week in advance. 430 N. Gilbert St.; Anaheim; 714-765-3481 (pro shop); 714-765-4653 (reservations).

PELICAN HILL GOLF CLUB:
Test your skills on two Tom Fazio–designed courses. The 6,634-yard, par-70 Ocean South course features two holes that play right along the water, while the 6,856-yard, par-71 Ocean North course, which is set above the ocean, provides panoramic views from every hole, especially the 12th. For reservations made 15 to 60 days in advance, the cost to play at either course is $195 Monday through Thursday, and $270 Friday through Sunday, golf cart included (these reservations can't be canceled). Arrangements made one to fourteen days in advance cost $20 less and can be canceled with 24-hours notice. Twilight rates (between noon and 4 P.M., depending on the time of year) are $99 Monday through Thursday, and $135 Friday through Sunday (reservations are

Practice Makes Perfect

Check out **The Greens at Park Place**, a PGA-approved, 18-hole championship putting course (a small golf course, really), for $10 a round Monday through Thursday, and $13 Friday through Sunday and holidays (near Newport Beach, at 3301 Michelson Dr.; Irvine; 949-250-7888).

Harbor Greens Golf Practice Center is a 60-tee driving range open long hours, with free shuttle and use of clubs for area hotel guests, grass and mat tees, a pro shop that lets you test out any of its clubs, night lighting, and one bucket of balls for $6 (behind the Hyatt Regency Orange County, at 12261 Chapman Ave.; Garden Grove; 714-663-8112).

taken up to 7 days in advance). The club has a pro shop with golf attire for the whole family. 22651 Pelican Hill Rd. South; Newport Coast; 949-760-0707 (pro shop and reservations).

Tennis & Racquetball

ANAHEIM TENNIS CENTER: This public facility has all the perks of a private tennis club—an inviting clubhouse, a well-stocked pro shop, computerized practice machines, lockers, and showers. The accommodating staff will even try to pair you with a suitable partner if you make a request in advance.

There are 12 fast, hard-surface courts, all lighted for night play. Singles and doubles rates range from $3.50 to $8 per person per hour, depending on time of day. Use of ball machines is $5; they are separated from the courts, but this area is still a good place to practice forehand and backhand strokes.

Playing hours begin at 8 A.M. and end at 10 P.M. Monday through Thursday, 9 P.M. Friday, and 6 P.M. weekends and holidays. Racquets rent for $3. Locker and shower facilities are free (you must supply towels). A half-hour private lesson with the resident pro costs $24; call for rates for semiprivate and group lessons.

Reservations (bookable up to four days in advance) are suggested, especially for court times after 5 P.M. It's about three miles from

the Disneyland Resort. 975 S. State College Blvd.; Anaheim; 714-991-9090.

CANYON TERRACE RACQUETBALL AND HEALTH CLUB: A real find for visitors, this facility has six air-conditioned racquetball courts and low court fees—$7 to $8 per person per hour for nonmembers ($7 per person for three players, and $7 per person for four players). The rates are lower on weekends and before 4 P.M. weekdays. The club rents racquets and offers its full-size weight room to nonmembers for $6. The hours are 5:30 A.M. to 10 P.M. Monday through Thursday, 5:30 A.M. to 9 P.M. Friday, 7 A.M. to 7 P.M. weekends. 100 N. Tustin Ave.; Anaheim; 714-974-0280.

Spectator Sports

BASEBALL
Anaheim Angels
(April–September): Edison International Field of Anaheim; 2000 Gene Autry Way; Anaheim; call 714-634-2000, or visit *www.angelsbaseball.com*
Los Angeles Dodgers
(April–September): Dodger Stadium; 1000 Elysian Park Ave.; Los Angeles; 323-224-1448; *www.dodgers.com*

BASKETBALL
Los Angeles Clippers
(October–April): Staples Center; 1111 S. Figueroa St.; Los Angeles; 213-742-7500; *www.clippers.com*

Los Angeles Lakers (October–April): Staples Center; 1111 S. Figueroa St.; Los Angeles; 310-419-3865; *www.nba.com/lakers*
Los Angeles Sparks (May–August): Staples Center; 1111 S. Figueroa St.; Los Angeles; 310-426-6033 (tickets); *www.wnba.com/sparks*

HOCKEY
Los Angeles Kings (September–April): Staples Center; 1111 S. Figueroa St.; Los Angeles; 888-546-4752 or 213-365-3600 (tickets); *www.lakings.com*
Mighty Ducks of Anaheim
(September–April): Arrowhead Pond of Anaheim; 2965 E. Katella Ave.; Anaheim; 714-740-2000; *www.mighty ducks.com*

SPORTS

Surf & Sun

Beaches

Orange County's public beaches cover 42 miles of coastline—some dramatic, with high cliffs and crashing waves; others tranquil, with sheltered coves and tide pools. In summer, the water temperature averages 65 degrees but can get as high as 75 or 80; in winter, it's a nippy 57 to 60 degrees.

Beaches are open from around 6 A.M. to 10 P.M., with lifeguards on duty in the summer. Bicycles, in-line skates, and roller skates are available for rent. Public access is free, but parking in beach lots costs about $6.

BALBOA/NEWPORT BEACH: The Balboa Peninsula juts into the Pacific ocean, creating beaches—Newport on the mainland, Balboa on the peninsula—that are long and horseshoe-shaped, pleasant and sandy, and popular with families, surfers, and sightseers alike.

The largest small-craft harbor in the world, Newport Harbor shelters almost 10,000 boats. For the best view, drive south along the peninsula on Newport Boulevard to Balboa Boulevard; turn right on Palm Street, and you'll find parking for the Balboa Pier.

Hot Tip!

For a scenic 45-minute walk, follow the harbor-hugging pathway around Balboa Island. For a mini-expedition, head to Little Balboa Island—it can be easily circumnavigated in about 20 minutes.

Throughout the fall and winter months, the 900-acre Upper Newport Bay Regional Park and Ecological Reserve teems with great blue herons, ospreys, and other glorious winged creatures. The park's partially subterranean Interpretive Center, at Irvine Avenue and University Drive, features several exhibits on bird life, the watershed, and the history of Newport Bay.

During the migratory season (October through March), Friends of Newport Bay leads free walking tours through the reserve on the second Saturday of the month, pointing out interesting birds, as well as fossils, marsh plants, and fish.

The reserve is generally open daily from 10 A.M. to 4 P.M. To get there from Anaheim, follow I-5 south to Highway 55 to the Pacific Coast Highway south; turn left onto Jamboree Road, take the first left onto Back Bay Drive, and follow it to the Ranger Station.

To obtain updated driving directions and information about guided tours and various special events year-round, contact Upper Newport Bay headquarters (information is accessible weekdays only); 949-640-6746; *www.newportbay.org.*

CORONA DEL MAR MAIN BEACH: Secluded Corona del Mar State Beach is a favorite for swimming and snorkeling; and the lookout point above the beach is a great place to watch the sun set. There are picnic tables, grills, fire rings, a snack bar, and showers. For information, call 800-942-6278.

HUNTINGTON BEACH: The self-proclaimed "Surfing City" hosts annual competitions, and on any summer day, enthusiasts make a beeline for the water; only diehards in wet suits venture out in winter. Concessions on the beach rent and sell surfboards and wet suits.

The long stretch of sand fronting the town is a popular place for jogging and beach volleyball. The pier provides an ideal spot for fishing and a good vantage point for observing the passing scene. For surf information, call 714-536-9303.

Bolsa Chica Ecological Reserve, 1,200 acres of Pacific Ocean marshland a mile north of Huntington Beach pier on Pacific Coast Highway, harbors fish, sea hares, and wetland birds. To get there, cross the bridge from the beach parking lot and follow a trail through the marsh; 714-846-1114; *www.bolsachica.org.*

LAGUNA BEACH: Thirty different beaches and coves line this six-mile coastline, popular with surfers, kayakers, body boarders, and snorkelers. Laguna is the best spot in Orange County to scuba dive, though you'll need a wet suit no matter what time of year you visit.

Laguna Sea Sports (925 N. Coast Hwy.; 949-494-6965; *www.lagunaseasports.com*) offers full rentals, guided beach dives, classes, general information, and more; there's a pool on the premises, and it's only about one block from the beach. Beach (the central strip of sand) offers basketball and volleyball courts as well as a playground.

A short walk from here, Heisler Park has picnic areas, beaches for swimming and sunning, cliff-top lookout points, lawn bowling, and shuffleboard; stairs lead to tide pools. Serious hikers like to head for Crystal Cove State Park, Aliso and Wood Canyons Wilderness Park, or Laguna Coast Wilderness Park. Watch the sun set from the gazebo near the art museum or from Laguna Village.

Fishing

In Orange County, you can cast for bass, catfish, and trout in tranquil lakes; troll the Pacific for bonitos, barracuda, halibut, and more; and scoop grunions off the beach.

SPORTFISHING: Boats set out from Davey's Locker, at the Balboa Pavilion in Balboa (call 949-673-1434), and from Dana Wharf Sportfishing, at Dana Point Harbor (named for Richard Henry Dana, who wrote *Two Years Before the Mast*); call 949-496-5794. Reservations are suggested. Licenses, necessary for deep-sea sportfishing, are available at either location and cost about $8 per day.

FRESHWATER ANGLING: At Irvine Lake, no fishing license is required and there is no charge for fish caught, unless you visit the "pay-per-pound" pond. Daily gate fees are $17 for adults ($14 for guests 62 and older) and $9 for children 4 through 12; under 4 free.

Fishing poles, motorboats, rowboats, and pontoons may be rented, or you can launch your own craft for an $8 fee. A tackle shop and cafe are on-site. No pets allowed. 4621 Santiago Canyon Rd.; Silverado; 714-649-2168 (for recorded information) or 714-649-9111.

GRUNION ALERT: You can try your hand—literally—at catching grunion at Bolsa Chica State Beach in March, June, July, and August, when the tiny fish come ashore to lay eggs in the sand and then head back out to sea on outgoing waves. They're slippery, and you have to catch them with your bare hands; fortunately, they also shimmer in the moonlight so they're fairly easy to spot. The best time to

go: about an hour or two after high tide on the second and third nights of each four-night period. Visit *www.dfg.ca.gov* for additional information. If you unable to access the Internet, call 714-536-5281. (Please call only if absolutely necessary.)

Note: Catching grunions is illegal in April and May; any other time of year, feel free to help yourself. A fishing license is required for anyone older than 16. No parking after 10 P.M. at Bolsa Chica State Beach.

Parks

IRVINE PARK: Located in Santiago Canyon, near Irvine Lake, this peaceful place has hiking and equestrian trails that wind through 477 hilly acres and 800-year-old sycamores and oaks. The oldest county park in California, it offers miles of bike trails, plus a petting zoo, playground, small waterfall, lake, and picnic facilities. There is a $2 to $5 parking fee per vehicle year-round. 1 Irvine Park Rd.; Orange; 714-973-6835.

MILE SQUARE REGIONAL PARK: It's one square mile in area—thus the name. Besides 15 miles of winding bike trails, the park features a fitness course with 20 stations, a nature area with bulletin boards detailing the park's plant and animal life, and picnic areas and shelters. Bicycles may be rented here on weekends and holidays. 16801 Euclid Ave.; Fountain Valley; 714-973-6600.

TUCKER WILDLIFE SANCTUARY: This 12-acre sanctuary in the Santa Ana Mountains' Modjeska Canyon is an oasis of flowers, plants, and wildlife. Naturalists are on duty to answer questions, and there are two short nature trails. A donation is suggested. 29322 Modjeska Canyon Rd.; Silverado; 714-649-2760.

YORBA REGIONAL PARK: These 175 acres in the Anaheim Hills cradle four lakes, picnic areas, playgrounds, and trails for hiking, equestrian activities, and biking (bike rentals are available in summer). Five miles of pleasant trails link up with the Santa Ana River Trail, a bike route through Orange County to Huntington Beach. Visitors can walk or bike into the park without charge; there is a $2 to $5 parking fee for vehicles. 7600 E. La Palma Ave.; Anaheim; 714-973-6615.

Orange County & Beyond

Walt Disney considered several spots in Southern California for his pioneering amusement park before finally settling on Anaheim, a quiet, rural community dominated by orange groves. In the decades since "The Happiest Place on Earth" welcomed its first guests, Anaheim has blossomed into the second-largest city in Orange County, with a population of more than 300,000, home to a Major League Baseball team, a National Hockey League team, and the largest convention center on the West Coast.

Like Anaheim, Buena Park is filled with family-oriented attractions; Santa Ana, the county's largest city, is developing an impressive museum mile; and Orange emanates small-town charm, with cafes, one-of-a-kind shops, and even an old-fashioned soda fountain. The beach communities of Newport and Laguna mix seaside culture with a vibrant arts scene, while nearby San Juan Capistrano bears witness to the area's mission heritage.

An hour's drive north from Anaheim, and a fun excursion, Los Angeles is a dynamic mix of culture, glamour, museums, shops, restaurants, and entertainment venues, interspersed with parks, palm trees, and traffic. Due west of L.A., legendary beaches attract beauty and brawn like a magnet. A 90-minute drive south from Anaheim, along coast-hugging I-5, leads to Legoland California, in Carlsbad, and to San Diego, with its world-famous zoo. There's no doubt about it: Southern California has something for everyone.

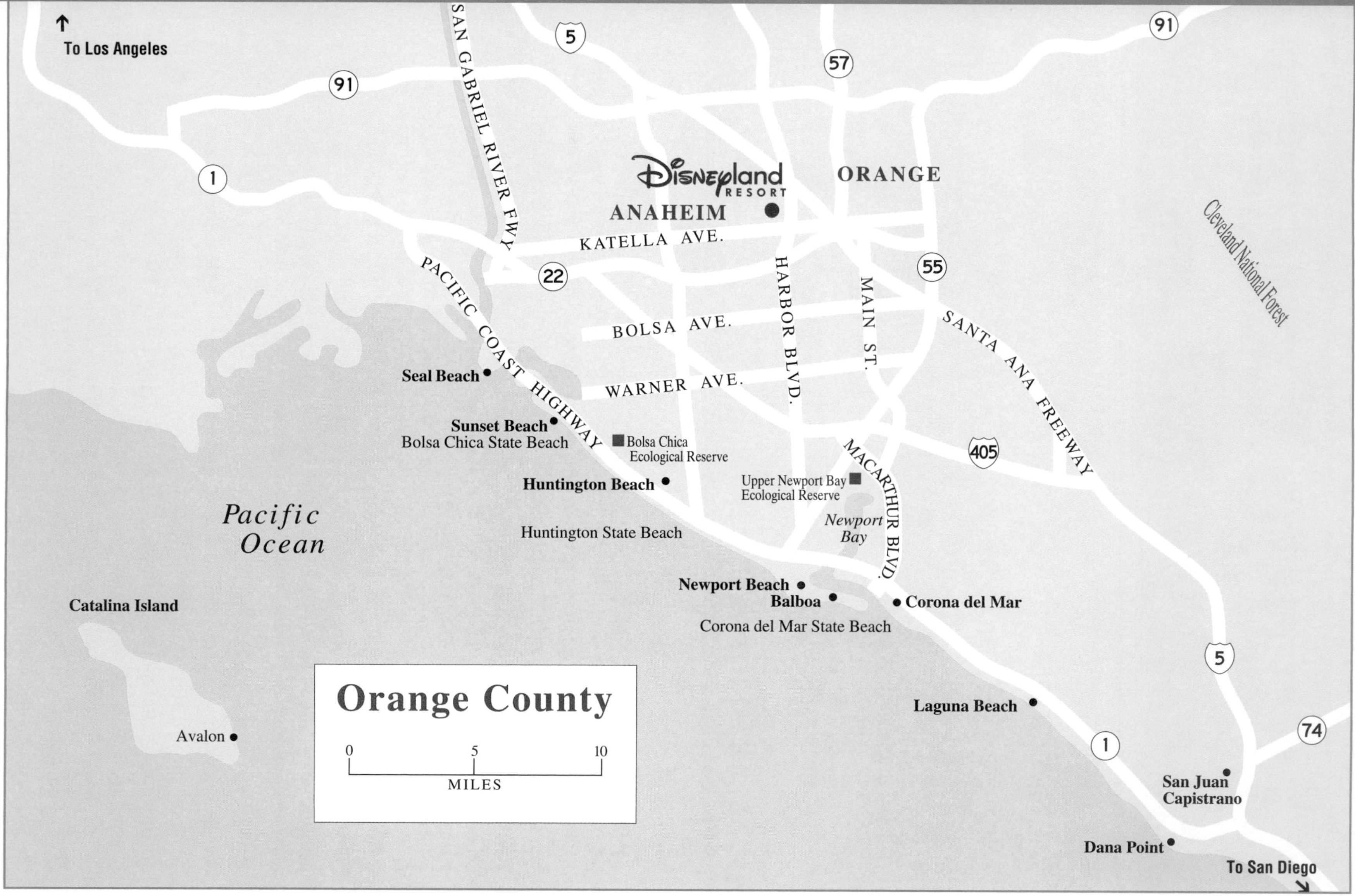

To Los Angeles

91

5

57

91

1

SAN GABRIEL RIVER FWY.

Cleveland National Forest

91

ORANGE

55

57

5

74

SANTA ANA FREEWAY

405

5

San Juan Capistrano

Dana Point

To San Diego

1

MAIN ST.

MACARTHUR BLVD.

Laguna Beach

Corona del Mar

Newport Bay

HARBOR BLVD.

Upper Newport Bay Ecological Reserve

Balboa

Newport Beach

Corona del Mar State Beach

Disneyland RESORT

ANAHEIM

KATELLA AVE.

BOLSA AVE.

WARNER AVE.

Bolsa Chica Ecological Reserve

Huntington Beach

Huntington State Beach

PACIFIC COAST HIGHWAY

22

Sunset Beach

Bolsa Chica State Beach

Seal Beach

Pacific Ocean

Catalina Island

Avalon

Orange County

0   5   10

MILES

Orange County
Anaheim

ADVENTURE CITY: This sweet little theme park was created for children ages 2 through 12, but parents are welcome to go on every ride except one, the kid-powered Crank 'n' Roll. There are 17 attractions and activities in all, including two roller coasters, puppet shows, children's theater, a petting farm, and a 25-foot rock-climbing wall for kids ages 5 and older.

Adventure City is within walking distance of Hobby City (see the Doll and Toy Museum, on this page). Days and hours vary; admission charge. It's located four miles from the Disneyland Resort and two miles from Knott's Berry Farm. 1238 S. Beach Blvd.; 714-236-9300.

ANAHEIM MUSEUM: Housed in the only remaining Carnegie library building in Orange County (there used to be five), the museum depicts Anaheim's history from its beginnings as a rural society to the opening of Disneyland in 1955. It also pays tribute to the area's original German settlers. Changing exhibits focus on different aspects of Southern California's history.

Open Wednesday through Friday 10 A.M. to 4 P.M. and Saturday from 12 P.M. to 4 P.M. Museum admission is free, but a small donation is suggested. About a mile from the Disneyland Resort. 241 S. Anaheim Blvd.; 714-778-3301.

DISNEY ICE: Forget mild-weather outdoor pursuits for a moment to consider gliding over the ice in a building that resembles an escapee from Mickey's Toontown. Designed by noted architect and hockey fan Frank Gehry, Disney ICE houses an Olympic-size rink for public skating for all ages and skill levels, plus an adjacent NHL regulation rink where the Mighty Ducks train. There's also drop-in hockey for men and women 18 and older, a pro shop, snack bar, and lockers. Day and evening skating sessions are available; birthday parties can be held here. Admission charge for skating. It's two miles north of the Disneyland Resort. 300 West Lincoln Ave.; 714-535-7465; *www.disneyice.com.*

DOLL AND TOY MUSEUM: Collector Bea DeArmond has been gathering dolls and toys for more than 70 years, and the results are displayed in a building that is a half-scale replica of the White House. Inside are more than 5,000 dolls and other toys, including teddy bears dating from 1907 and 500 Barbies that fill an entire wall. Old and new dolls are for sale in the gift shop.

The museum is part of Hobby City, a group of 20 hobby, crafts, and collector shops. Open daily; admission charge. Four miles from the Disneyland Resort and two miles from Knott's Berry Farm. 1238 S. Beach Blvd.; 714-527-2323.

Inland Orange County

BOWERS MUSEUM: The original Mission-style Bowers building dates back to 1936, and with two major expansions since that time, the museum has become the largest in Orange County. It celebrates the fine arts of indigenous peoples—notably pre-Columbian, Native American, Oceanic, and African—and reflects the multicultural population of California.

The Bowers is also a repository for early California artifacts. Tangata, far more sophisticated than most museum eateries, features creative ethnic dishes, while the outstanding museum shop sells artwork, jewelry, clothing, and other gift items from around the world.

Kidseum, part of the Bowers Museum but a short walk away (at 1802 N. Main St.), is a large, airy space where children get to learn in a hands-on way about the cultures of other places and people. Supervised activities here focus on art and music, and costumes are plentiful, colorful, and fun.

The Bowers Museum is open Tuesday through Sunday; Kidseum, Tuesday through Sunday in summer and weekends in winter (limited hours). There is a separate admission for each museum. The museums are approximately five miles from the Disneyland Resort. 2002 N. Main St.; Santa Ana; 714-567-3600; 714-480-1520 (Kidseum information line); *www.bowers.org*.

CRYSTAL CATHEDRAL: More than 10,000 panes of glass cover a weblike steel skeleton and tower in this startling structure created by the architect Philip Johnson. Established in 1980 by the Reverend Robert H. Schuller and affiliated with the Reform Church of America, the Crystal Cathedral houses a 16,000-pipe organ, 52-bell carillon, Steuben glass cross, 33 marble columns, and 3,000 seats.

Schuller began his ministry in a drive-in theater, and those attending services today still have the option to sit in their cars and watch on a giant television screen. Worship here has definite theatrical elements. A shop sells music, books, cards, and assorted gifts.

The visitors center is open from 9 A.M. to 3:30 P.M. Monday through Saturday. Free tours are available. Sunday services are in the main cathedral at 9:30 A.M., 11 A.M., 1 P.M. (in Spanish), and 6 P.M. It's three miles from the Disneyland Resort. 12141 Lewis St.; Garden Grove; 714-971-4000; 714-971-4013 (tour info).

DISCOVERY SCIENCE CENTER: This place gives new meaning to the term "hands-on." In seven themed areas with 120 exhibits, guests get to experience an earthquake, lie on a bed of nails, climb a rock wall, create clouds, walk through a tornado, tread on a musical floor, fingerpaint electronically, pilot a plane, play virtual volleyball, and make an impression in a pin wall. There is a shop on the premises.

Open daily, except major holidays. There is an admission charge (3-D laser theater is extra). It's located five miles from the Disneyland Resort. 2500 N. Main St.; Santa Ana; 714-542-2823; *www.discoverycube.org*.

KNOTT'S BERRY FARM: This is not a farm at all, but a themed amusement park depicting much of the history and culture of California. It began in 1920 as the Knott family's boysenberry patch (hence the name). During the Great Depression, Walter Knott's wife, Cordelia, started a tearoom to help make ends meet, and her chicken dinners were such a success that Walter built a wander-through ghost town to keep hungry patrons from getting impatient. Things progressed from there.

Owned by the Knott family until 1997, the 160-acre park now offers 165 rides (including nine roller coasters), shows, attractions, restaurants, and shops in six themed areas.

Ghost Town (what remains of the original park) is home to GhostRider, a massive wooden roller coaster created from 2.5 million feet of yellow pine and 310 tons of steel. Fiesta Village is a re-creation of colonial Spanish America. The Boardwalk is a combination California beach enclave and seaside amusement park. It features the Supreme Scream tower, the world's tallest descending thrill ride (with a 30-story, three-second drop), and Perilous Plunge, the world's tallest, deepest water drop ride (with a 115-foot drop at a 75-degree angle).

Recent additions to the thrill-ride family include Xcelerator, a high-octane launch roller coaster that sends riders from 0 to 80 mph in 2.3 seconds, and Silver Bullet, a coaster which climbs to a dizzying height of 146 feet.

Wild Water Wilderness is a turn-of-the-century river wilderness park with California flora. The Indian Trails area celebrates the arts, crafts, and rich traditions of Native Americans.

Camp Snoopy, a six-acre play area themed around the world's most beloved beagle, features Woodstock's Airmail (a mini-Supreme Scream), the Red Baron biplane ride. Children also get to meet Snoopy and his *Peanuts* pals here.

Across Beach Boulevard from the park's main gate stands Independence Hall West, Knott's replica of Independence Hall in Philadelphia, completely renovated in late 1998. (Guests enter through a tunnel in the main parking area near the shops. There's never a charge to visit it.) Chandeliers, furniture, and the shape and size of the rooms are precisely reproduced, and there is a replica of the Liberty Bell, crack and all.

Also adjacent to the park, you'll find Knott's Soak City U.S.A. This 13-acre water park boasts 21 rides, including tube and body slides, vertical chutes, wave pool, and children's wading pool, all designed in the style of the 1950s California coast.

Knott's California MarketPlace is filled with shops and eateries. There is no admission charge for this area. Chicken dinners and boysenberry pies are still on the menu here, but try to dine early to avoid the crowds.

Knott's Berry Farm is open daily all year long (with Christmas day as the lone exception); Soak City U.S.A. is open daily from mid-June through early September and weekends through late September.

It costs extra to park a vehicle. However, if you come exclusively to shop, dine, or pay a visit to Independence Hall, you're entitled to three hours of free parking (four hours during holidays). Call for current admission charges for adults and kids. Admission prices exclude Pan for Gold and Games and Arcades. Group rates (with a minimum of 15) are available. Children under age 3 get in free. Prices, operating hours, and attraction availability are subject to change without notice. 8039 Beach Blvd.; Buena Park; 714-220-5200; *www.knotts.com*.

OLD TOWNE ORANGE: For an idea of what Southern California was like before the advent of the freeway (or of Disneyland, for that matter), visit the historic area of Orange. Highlights include a pharmacy (complete with an old-fashioned soda fountain) that's been in business since 1900, art galleries, antiques shops, two teahouses that serve afternoon tea, a church that's now a restaurant (P.J.'s Abbey), a bridal museum where you can order a vintage-style gown, and Victorian and Craftsman houses galore.

Old Towne Orange is approximately 15 minutes due east of Anaheim via Chapman Avenue. The Visitor Bureau is located at 439 E. Chapman Ave.; 714-538-3581 or 800-938-0073; *www.orangechamber.com*.

MOVIELAND WAX MUSEUM: Silver-screen star Mary Pickford was on hand to dedicate Movieland when it opened here in 1962. Today more than 300 film and television performers are depicted in scenes from their better-known roles: Leonardo DiCaprio and Kate Winslet in *Titanic*, Mike Myers in *Austin Powers*, Judy Garland in *The Wizard of Oz*, Robert Redford and Paul Newman in *Butch Cassidy and the Sundance Kid*, and Marilyn Monroe in *Some Like It Hot.* Some of the more recent additions to the star-studded lineup include Julia Roberts, Robin Williams, Britney Spears, Ricky Martin, Jennifer Lopez, and John Lennon.

Many of the costumes and props on display were donated by the stars themselves. During a visit, you'll walk under marquees and lights, along a yellow brick road, and through watery wreckage from *The Poseidon Adventure.*

Open daily. Admission charge; combination tickets with Ripley's Believe It or Not (across the street) are available. The museum is located about seven miles from the Disneyland Resort. 7711 Beach Blvd.; Buena Park; 714-522-1154; *www.movielandwaxmuseum.com*.

RICHARD NIXON PRESIDENTIAL LIBRARY AND BIRTHPLACE: In a restored house built by his father, this 22-room library chronicles the life of the 37th president of the United States. There are changing exhibits, and a Lincoln Continental used by four American presidents is on permanent display. Both Richard Nixon and former First Lady Pat Nixon are buried here.

Open daily; admission charge. It's about a 15-minute drive from the Disneyland Resort. 18001 Yorba Linda Blvd.; Yorba Linda; 714-993-3393; *www.nixonlibrary.org*.

RAGING WATERS: Raging Waters is a water park with acres of rides, slides, chutes, and lagoons. Highlights include Dragon's Den, the 109-foot High Extreme II, and Volcano Fanta-Sea. Open weekends May and in September; daily from June through Labor Day.

Guests age 10 and older pay full admission. Kids under 10 pay less. Discounts are available after 4 P.M. Parking is extra. Raging Waters is about a half-hour drive from Disneyland (it's actually next door to Orange County). 111 Raging Waters Dr.; San Dimas; 909-802-2200.

RIPLEY'S BELIEVE IT OR NOT!: Here you'll discover 10,000 square feet of curiosities amassed by cartoonist, world traveler, and collector of oddities Robert Ripley. The Riddler Room is an interactive area for kids. Open daily. Admission charge; combination tickets with the Movieland Wax Museum (across the street) are available. Seven miles from the Disneyland Resort. 7850 Beach Blvd.; Buena Park; 714-522-7045.

WILD RIVERS WATER-PARK: More than 40 attractions include wave pools, a seven-story "mountain" with sheer-drop and high-speed slides, and small-scale rides and pools for young visitors. Open weekends from mid-May through early June and in late September; daily from early June through early September. Admission charge. It's about 20 minutes from Disneyland. 8770 Irvine Center Dr.; Irvine; 949-788-0808.

On the Coast

Corona del Mar

ROGER'S GARDENS: This public nursery fills 7½ acres of landscaped grounds with splendid flowers, plants, shrubs, and trees; and from mid-October through December 30, themed holiday trees draw enthusiastic crowds. Free lectures and demonstrations are given in the amphitheater on Saturday and Sunday year-round (subjects and times vary; call for specifics). The gift shop sells items for the home, as well as holiday decorations year-round, including hand-painted glass ornaments designed by the world-famous Christopher Radko.

Open daily 9 A.M. to 7 P.M. in the spring and summer; 9 A.M. to 5 P.M. in fall until November and December, when the hours are 9 A.M. to 9 P.M.; 9 A.M. to 5 P.M. in January and February. It is approximately a 35-minute drive from the Disneyland Resort. 2301 San Joaquin Hills Rd.; Corona del Mar; 949-640-5800; *www.rogersgardens.com*.

SHERMAN LIBRARY & GARDENS: The gardens are a veritable museum of plants and flowers ranging from desert flora to exotic tropical vegetation, displayed amid fountains and sculptures, brick walkways, and manicured lawns. They surround the library, which is a major research center devoted to the history of the Pacific Southwest, particularly the past century. A shop and cafe are on the premises.

The gardens are open daily from 10:30 A.M. to 4 P.M.; the library, from 9 A.M. to 4:30 P.M. Tuesday, Wednesday, and Thursday. Admission is $3 for adults, $1 for kids 12 through 16; free for kids under 12; free to all on Monday. It's a 35-minute drive southeast of the Disneyland Resort. 2647 E. Pacific Coast Hwy.; Corona del Mar; 949-673-2261; *www.slgardens.org*.

Dana Point Area

OCEAN INSTITUTE: There's a lab to visit at this institute, and a whale skeleton to admire; plus the tall ship *Pilgrim* may be toured, but only on Sunday, from 10 A.M. to 2:30 P.M. Educational cruises take place on weekends aboard the historic schooner *Spirit of Dana Point* and the *RV Sea Explorer*. Prices, times, and themes vary. The institute is open to the public from 10 A.M. to 3 P.M. on weekends; the gift shop is open daily. Admission is $5 for adults, and $3 for kids 3 through 12. It's about a 45-minute drive from the Disneyland Resort. 24200 Dana Point Harbor Dr.; Dana Point; 949-496-2274; *www.ocean-institute.org*.

LOS RIOS HISTORIC DISTRICT: Situated beside the Capistrano train depot (1894), just three miles from the coast, this small enclave captures the flavor of Southern California at the turn of the century. The district encompasses three adobe homes built between 1794 and the 1880s. Among them is the O'Neill Museum, a Victorian house built in the 1870s, filled with period furniture, and open to the public. Hours vary. For information, call 714-493-8444.

The district is within walking distance of Mission San Juan Capistrano. Take I-5 south (or the train) to the mission; about 50 minutes from Anaheim. For more information, contact the San Juan Capistrano Chamber of Commerce; 949-493-4700.

MISSION SAN JUAN CAPISTRANO: The famous mission at the southern tip of Orange County retains a wistful air of grandeur, even though these five buildings on 10 acres are all that remain of the original 225,000-acre tract. Highlights of the self-guided walking tour

include a 350-year-old gilt altar, a Moorish fountain, ancient pepper trees, a mission cemetery, the quarters of the early padres, and the Spanish soldiers' barracks. Once the most remarkable in the entire mission chain, the church was shattered by a powerful earthquake in 1812. The four bells of the tower and a small sanctuary called the Serra Chapel were miraculously spared; the chapel still holds services daily in English at 7 A.M. and in Latin on Saturdays (call for schedules).

The other local miracle is the return of the swallows to Capistrano every year on March 19 (Saint Joseph's Day). Christians take this as a sign of the holiness of this place, while ornithologists explain it as no more than a predictable natural phenomenon. The Mission hosts a summer concert series, arts and crafts expositions, the Swallows Day parade, and other events.

Open from 8:30 A.M. to 5 P.M. daily. Admission is $6 for adults, $5 for seniors 60 and older, and $4 for children 4 through 11. Take I-5 (or the train) south to the mission, which is about 50 minutes from Anaheim. Corner of Ortega Hwy. and Camino Capistrano; San Juan Capistrano; 949-234-1300; *www.missionsjc.com.*

Huntington Beach

Life at Huntington Beach revolves around the surf—it's the perfect spot for catching a wave, or watching others do so. The Huntington Beach Visitor and Information Center is at 301 Main Street, Suite 208; 714-969-3492 or 800-729-6232; *www.hbvisit.com.*

HUNTINGTON BEACH ART CENTER:
Founded in 1995, this is an excellent place to see avant-garde and cutting-edge work: art installations, videos, sculpture, and group and solo exhibitions of emerging American artists. The center has three galleries and a theater that seats 100 people.

Open Wednesday through Sunday, in the afternoon. There is no charge for admission. It's about a 40-minute drive south of the Disneyland Resort. 538 Main St.; Huntington Beach; 714-374-1650.

INTERNATIONAL SURFING MUSEUM:
Expect to find all that's surfing-related here—artwork, jewelry, vintage surfboards and

paddleboards, even skateboards. Chances are, you'll hear a bit of surfer music, too. Open afternoons daily in the summer; Thursday through Monday the remainder of the year. Small admission charge. 411 Olive St.; Huntington Beach; *www.surfingmuseum.org.* For museum opening times, call 714-536-3266.

PIER PLAZA: In the heart of town, this sweeping oceanfront plaza has a palm tree grove with benches, bike and pedestrian paths, and an amphitheater for weekend entertainment (call 714-374-1657 to get the performance schedule). It's about a half hour from the Disneyland Resort.

Laguna Beach

A professional artists' colony since 1917, Laguna Beach continues to thrive as Orange County's artistic hot spot, with more than 90 galleries, antique shops, and boutiques displaying local artists' masterpieces. Painters find inspiration in the dramatic cliffs, carved-out coves, and pearl-white sand that define the beach's setting.

LAGUNA ART MUSEUM: Founded in 1918 (a year after the town itself), California's oldest museum focuses its energies on and devotes its gallery space to work produced by the state's artists, past and present. Permanent exhibitions highlight California Impressionism, while several changing exhibits feature contemporary artists. A visit here can easily be combined with browsing in some of the local art galleries, most within walking distance of the museum.

It is open daily from 11 A.M. until 5 P.M. There is an admission charge. It's about a 40-minute drive from the Disneyland Resort. 307 Cliff Dr.; Laguna Beach; 949-494-8971; *www.lagunaartmuseum.org.*

LAGUNA PLAYHOUSE: Now in its 82nd season, this is the oldest continuously operating theater company on the West Coast. Since 1969, the Laguna Playhouse has called the 420-seat Moulton Theater home. Screen star Harrison Ford was discovered in a Laguna Playhouse production in 1965. Actress Julie Harris has also appeared here, as has Bette Davis. The theater stages dramas, musicals, and comedies, often to rave reviews.

It's about a 40-minute drive from Disneyland. 606 Laguna Canyon Rd.; Laguna Beach; 949-497-2787; *www.lagunaplayhouse.com*.

Newport/Balboa

Pastimes here extend beyond beaches to celebrate the worlds of sports, history, and the arts.

BALBOA FUN ZONE: Established in 1936, this area looks like an old-fashioned boardwalk, complete with amusements, shops, and sweet treats. But most people come to admire the historic pavilion, take a harbor cruise, or board the car ferry to tiny Balboa Island to shop or dine. Ferry service is continuous. It's about a half-hour drive from the Disneyland Resort. 600 E. Bay Ave.; Balboa Peninsula; for harbor tour information, call 949-673-0408; *www.thebalboafunzone.com*.

BALBOA PAVILION: This landmark building is the departure point in Orange County for Catalina Island, via Catalina Passenger Service; 400 Main St.; 949-673-5245. The company also offers harbor cruises, supplying views of ritzy shorefront houses. It's about a half-hour drive from Disneyland.

NEWPORT HARBOR NAUTICAL MUSEUM: The *Pride of Newport* riverboat has housed this museum since 1995 as a tribute to Newport Harbor, Southern California, and the Pacific. There are more than 58,000 photos on display. The Newport Gallery details the history of the harbor, the extensive The Model Gallery is home to world-class models and features a 3-foot-long destroyer made of gold and silver. There are approximately 35 major models and 200 smaller models in the gallery. The Riverboat restaurant serves lunch and dinner onboard, as well as brunch with music on weekends. The museum is closed Monday. It's 20 minutes from the Disneyland Resort. 151 East Coast Hwy., at Bayside, Newport Beach; 949-673-7863; *www.nhnm.org*.

NEWPORT SPORTS MUSEUM: View Muhammed Ali's gloves; jerseys worn by the likes of Michael Jordan, Shaquille O'Neal, Norris Trophy recipients, and all Cy Young Award winners; footballs signed by all Heisman Trophy winners; Dwight Eisenhower's golf clubs; seats from every major baseball stadium built in the 20th century, including Ebbets Field, Fenway Park, and Yankee Stadium.

Closed Sunday. Free admission. About a half-hour drive south from Disneyland. Located in Fashion Island; 100 Newport Center Drive; Newport Beach; 949-721-9333.

ORANGE COUNTY MUSEUM OF ART: Founded in 1961, this is the county's premier contemporary and modern-art museum. It focuses primarily on post-World War II California art and sculpture. California artists were isolated from the East Coast and European centers of art for the first half of the 20th century, and the influences of the Mexican and Pacific Rim cultures are notable.

There is a charge for those age 12 and older, but Tuesday are free. Closed Monday. It's about a 20-minute drive from Disneyland. 850 San Clemente Dr.; Newport Beach; 949-759-1122; *www.ocma.net*.

Catalina Island

A delightful day trip from Anaheim, this large island off the coast of Southern California resembles an unspoiled Mediterranean isle. Snorkeling, scuba diving, kayaking, whale watching, sportfishing, golf, hiking, and horseback riding keep the more athletically inclined guests on their toes. Less active folks will enjoy a tour of the local "casino," an entertainment complex built in Avalon, the island's center, by William Wrigley, Jr. in 1929 (dancing, not gambling, was the preferred form of entertainment here). Other island exploring possibilities include a marine tour in a glass-bottom boat, a voyage on a semi-submersible vessel for a fish's perspective of underwater life, and an island "safari" in a jeep for glimpses of buffalo (300 roam the island), bald eagles, wild goats, and deer.

From the Balboa Peninsula, Catalina Passenger Service makes the 26-mile trip on the *Catalina Flyer* in about 75 minutes; 949-673-5245. The *Catalina Express* offers round-trip service to the island from Dana Point, Long Beach, and San Pedro; 800-618-5533. The ride over can be choppy, so those prone to seasickness should take precautions.

For more information, call the Catalina Island Chamber of Commerce and Visitors Bureau; 310-510-1520.

Shopping in Orange County

There is no question that the Disneyland Resort is chock-full of fanciful shopping opportunities. But for those guests who crave even more retail fantasy, Southern California is bound to deliver. Malls may not have been invented in these parts, but some say they were perfected here to appeal to a discerning, largely suburban, population. Most are open from 10 A.M. to 9 P.M. weekdays, from 10 A.M. to 7 P.M. Saturdays, and from 11 A.M. to 6 P.M. Sundays. Call for exact hours. At press time sales tax was 7.75 percent in Orange County.

FASHION ISLAND: This outdoor mall has more than 200 stores and restaurants in a Mediterranean-themed setting of potted flowers, towering palms, and plazas with fountains, fish pools, and umbrella-topped tables. The four major department stores here are Bloomingdale's, Neiman Marcus, Robinsons-May, and Macy's (women's merchandise only); the enclosed Atrium Court houses many small shops. The mall also features seven cinemas, Hard Rock Cafe, California Pizza Kitchen, and The Cheesecake Factory, in addition to a selection of other dining spots.

The mall is on Newport Center Drive, in Newport Beach, about a half-hour drive south of the Disneyland Resort; 949-721-2000.

TRIANGLE SQUARE: This boldly modern shopping complex is home to Niketown (a super-sized sneaker store) in California. It also has, among other things, Barnes & Noble, Virgin Megastore, Gap, eight cinemas, and a Yard House restaurant (with 250 beers on tap).

The Costa Mesa Freeway (55) dead-ends into Triangle Square, at Newport and Harbor boulevards in Costa Mesa, a 45-minute drive from the Disneyland Resort; 949-722-1600.

WESTFIELD SHOPPINGTOWN MAINPLACE: Formerly known as Mainplace Mall, this place is home to a Disney Store, with its character-conscious toys, videos, books, gift items, collectibles, and clothing for adults and children. Here you'll find Macy's, Nordstrom, Robinsons-May, Barnes & Noble, and Crate & Barrel, along with many other shops and restaurants, one-hour photo development, shoe repair, cinema complex, concierge desk, and American Express Travel Service. A shuttle, which operates during mall hours, runs often between many of the Anaheim hotels and the mall. 2800 N. Main St. (at the intersection of I-5 and Hwy. 22); Santa Ana, about four miles from the Disneyland Resort; 714-547-7000.

SOUTH COAST PLAZA: Festive, airy, upscale, and downright enormous, it's home to more than 260 restaurants and shops, including the Disney Store, Macy's, Nordstrom, Saks Fifth Avenue, Coach, Chanel, Christian Dior, the Rainforest Cafe, and Wolfgang Puck Cafe. A bridge connects the two sides of South Coast Plaza. Shuttles operate to and from Anaheim hotels. At the intersection of the San Diego Freeway and Bristol Street in Costa Mesa, approximately ten miles from the Disneyland Resort; 714-435-2000 or 800-782-8888.

"MALL-TERNATIVES": If you've had your fill of the local shopping mall scene, check out The LAB, a self-proclaimed "anti-mall" with indoor/outdoor shops, cafes, and free entertainment for teens and families; 2930 Bristol St.; Costa Mesa (714-966-6660). Or try the fine Gallery Store at the Bowers Museum of Cultural Art; 2002 N. Main St.; Santa Ana (714-567-3600); and all the shops at the Disneyland Resort, with special emphasis on those at Downtown Disney. (For more information on this shopping enclave, refer to pages 132–133.)

Los Angeles

From the rugged ridges of the Santa Monica Mountains to the vast San Fernando Valley to downtown L.A. itself, Los Angeles County spreads close to 5,000 square miles (including 81 miles of shoreline), knit together by 500 miles of freeways. To get to L.A. from Anaheim, take I-5 north and Route 101 or 10 west. All of the places described below can be reached in about 45 minutes to 2 hours. For information or maps, contact the Visitor Information Center, 685 S. Figueroa St., Los Angeles, CA 90017; 213-689-8822; *www.visitlanow.com*.

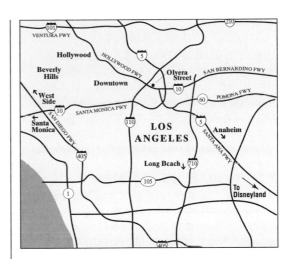

Attractions

Downtown

EXPOSITION PARK MUSEUMS: Here you get three museums for the price of one. At the California Science Center, hands-on exhibits probe the inner workings of everything from a single-cell bacterium to a 100-trillion-celled human being. Take a ride on the high-wire bicycle ($2 charge); Gertie's Gut; or Tess, the 50-foot marvel. Call 323-724-3623.

There's also an IMAX theater; 213-744-7400. Open daily. The California African American Museum highlights the art and achievements of African Americans; 213-744-7432 (free; closed Monday). The Natural History Museum features dueling dinosaurs and an insect zoo; 213-763-7432 (admission charge; open daily). Closed on major holidays. Parking costs between $6 and $10.

FARMERS MARKET: An L.A. fixture since 1934 and popular with locals for Sunday brunch (among other meals), it's filled with stands piled high with fresh produce, plus all manner of

prepared foods. The French Crepe Company's sweet and savory crepes are not to be missed. Tables allow for casual outdoor dining. Shops offer a variety of souvenirs and cooking items. Open Monday through Friday 9 A.M. to 9 P.M.; Saturdays 9 A.M. to 8 P.M.; and Sundays from 10 A.M. to 7 P.M.; 6333 W. Third St. and Fairfax Ave.; 323-933-9211.

LA BREA TAR PITS: If you have ever wondered what Los Angeles looked like before the studios and skyscrapers, visit the 40,000-year-old pools of *brea* (Spanish for "tar"), in Hancock Park, where a replica depicts one unlucky mastodon perpetually trapped in the mire. There is an admission charge. Inside the tar pits sits the George C. Page Museum (open daily; admission charge) displaying bones excavated from the area and (living) paleontologists doing research in a "fishbowl" lab. Open daily. 5801 Wilshire Blvd.; Park La Brea; 323-934-7243; *www.tarpits.org*.

LOS ANGELES COUNTY MUSEUM OF ART: Expect to be dazzled by the permanent collection of pre-Columbian, Islamic, and African art; costumes and textiles; and a distinguished collection of 19th- and 20th-century art and photography. Admission charge. Closed Wednesday. 5905 Wilshire Blvd.; 323-857-6000; *www.lacma.org*.

OLVERA STREET: The name of this small pedestrian street refers to the area where the city began in 1781. Today it's home to strolling mariachis, colorful Mexican shops, and food stalls selling tacos, burritos, and enchiladas. Free walking tours are offered Tuesday through Saturday. Union Station is across the street. 125 Paseo de la Plaza; 213-628-1274.

Hollywood

DISNEY'S EL CAPITAN THEATRE: The Walt Disney Company and Buena Vista Pictures Distribution restored this Hollywood Boulevard landmark, formerly the Paramount, and reopened it in 1991. Built in 1926 (the classic film *Citizen Kane* premiered at the El Capitan in 1941); 6838 Hollywood Blvd.; 800-347-6396.

GRIFFITH PARK ATTRACTIONS: The largest park in the U.S. that is surrounded by a city, 4,063-acre Griffith Park is home to the Los Angeles Zoo and its more than 1,200 inhabitants; the Autry Museum of Western Heritage, which salutes the American West; an equestrian center; and many walking trails. Ranger Station; 4730 Crystal Springs Dr.; 323-913-4688.

HOLLYWOOD ENTERTAINMENT MUSEUM: The sets from such shows as *Star Trek* and *Cheers* are highlights at this starstruck museum. In the Main Hall, you can listen to a recording of Walt Disney talking about animation. There is an admission charge. The museum is open daily from Memorial Day through Labor Day. It's closed Wednesdays the rest of the year. 7021 Hollywood Blvd.; 323-465-7900; *www.hollywoodmuseum.com.*

HOLLYWOOD HISTORY MUSEUM: Ensconced in the restored Art Deco Max Factor Building, nostalgic spot salutes Tinseltown, from the silent era of movies to the present, with costumes, props, posters, and more. Admission charge. Open Thursday through Sunday 10 A.M. to 5 P.M. 1660 N. Highland; 323-464-7776; *www.hollywoodhistorymuseum.org.*

MANN'S CHINESE THEATRE: Catercorner to the Hollywood Roosevelt Hotel and better known to movie fans around the world as Grauman's Chinese Theatre, this is probably the most visited site in Old Hollywood. (Ted Mann took it over in 1973.) The theater's forecourt contains the world-famous celebrity handprints and footprints—some surprisingly small—immortalized in cement. Inside is one of the world's most impressive and elaborate movie palaces. Tours of the stars' homes depart from here. 6925 Hollywood Blvd. (for tours, 800-959-3131; for movies, 323-464-8111).

UNIVERSAL STUDIOS HOLLYWOOD: First-timers to this theme park might start with the 45-minute Studio Tour, which passes sets from *Jurassic Park*, *Gladiator*, *Jaws*, and *The Mummy*, and Van Helsing: Fortress Dracula, based on the movie, not to mention King Kong's impressive flight-simulator experience, and Jurassic Park—The Ride, complete with life-like dinosaurs and a steep drop into a pool of water. Tamer by comparison is Nickelodeon's Blast Zone, where kids can let loose with flying foam balls and water spritzers, and Animal Planet Live, which brings the cable animal show to life.

There is an admission charge for the park. Open daily, except for Thanksgiving and Christmas; hours vary.

You can eat, shop, and be entertained at just outside the park's gate at Universal CityWalk, an outdoor promenade lined with shops, restaurants, an 18-screen cinema complex, three-dimensional facades, and neon galore; there is no admission charge, but parking is $8. Universal Studios CityWalk is open daily. For information, call 818-622-4455.

Universal Studios is located off the Hollywood Freeway (aka Route 101) at Lankershim Boulevard. It is served by Metro Rails's Red Line (Universal City Station). 100 Universal City Plaza; Universal City; 818-622-3801; *www.universalstudioshollywood.com.*

Tours & Tapings

See the posh homes of movie stars in L.A. and Beverly Hills with **Starline Tours**; 1-800-959-3131. Explore after-dark hot spots with the **L.A. NightHawks**; 310-392-1500.

The **Warner Bros**. studio tour costs $32 per person. It's located at Hollywood and Olive; Gate 4; Burbank. It's closed weekends. Children under the age of 8 will not be admitted. Prices are subject to change. For information and reservations, call 818-954-1744.

The **Sony Pictures** tour costs $20 per person (only guests 12 and older will be admitted). It runs Monday through Friday, 9 A.M. to 3 P.M. The lot is located at 10202 W. Washington Blvd., in Culver City. For information or to make a reservation, call 818-520-TOUR.

NBC Studios tours cost $7.50 for adults, $4 for kids. For information, call 818-840-3537.

Tapings: Nab a free ticket to *The Tonight Show* by calling NBC; 818-840-3537 (long before your visit). For tickets to other programs, call Audiences Unlimited; 818-753-3470 or 818-506-0067; *www.tvtickets.com.*

Index

INDEX